BEYOND THE BLACK POWER SALUTE

SPORT AND SOCIETY

A list of books in the series appears at the end of this book.

BEYOND THE BLACK POWER SALUTE

Athlete Activism in an Era of Change

GREGORY J. KALISS

UNIVERSITY OF ILLINOIS PRESS
Urbana, Chicago, and Springfield

Manufactured in the United States of America
1 2 3 4 5 C P 5 4 3 2 1
This book is printed on acid-free paper.

Publication supported by a grant from the Winton U. Solberg U.S. History Subvention Fund.

Library of Congress Cataloging-in-Publication Data
Names: Kaliss, Gregory J., author.
Title: Beyond the Black Power salute : athlete activism in an era of change / Gregory J. Kaliss.
Description: Urbana : University of Illinois Press, [2023] | Series: Sport and society | Includes bibliographical references and index.
Identifiers: LCCN 2022040997 (print) | LCCN 2022040998 (ebook) | ISBN 9780252044915 (cloth) | ISBN 9780252087066 (paperback) | ISBN 9780252054075 (ebook)
Subjects: LCSH: Discrimination in sports—United States—History—20th century. | Racism in sports—United States—History—20th century. | African American athletes—History—20th century. | Women athletes—United States—History—20th century. | College athletes—United States—History—20th century. | United States—Race relations—History—20th century.
Classification: LCC GV706.32 .K35 2023 (print) | LCC GV706.32 (ebook) | DDC 796.089/960730904—dc23/eng/20221013
LC record available at https://lccn.loc.gov/2022040997
LC ebook record available at https://lccn.loc.gov/2022040998

For my parents, Bud and Millie Kaliss,
who have always provided love and support.

CONTENTS

ACKNOWLEDGMENTS

Writing a book like this takes lots of help and encouragement. Many dedicated and smart people helped with the research. I am especially grateful to the librarians at Franklin & Marshall College, Towson University, and Dickinson College, who provided needed resources and support. Anna Boutin-Copper and Christopher Raab at F&M deserve special mention for their aid in tracking down useful images for this text. A number of other individuals and institutions enabled me to provide the photos used in this book: Stacy Davis with the Gerald R. Ford Presidential Library; Margaret Dunlap with the Richland Library in Columbia, South Carolina; Josue Hurtado at Temple University; Cymonne New, communications manager for the Minnesota Lynx; Zachary Palitzsch at the State Historical Society of Missouri; Ryan Pettigrew with the Richard M. Nixon Presidential Library; Doug Remley with the Smithsonian Museum of African-American History and Culture; Carolyn Sautter at Gettysburg College; and Li-Anne Wright of *The Yackety Yack* at the University of North Carolina. I thank them all for their help in making this book come alive.

A substantial group of scholars made this book better through their comments and suggestions. The anonymous book proposal reviewers and book manuscript reviewers for the University of Illinois Press helped tighten the book's focus and push its claims more forcefully. For their suggestions, I am grateful. My co-panelists at various events over the years offered critical feedback and modeled excellent scholarship, especially Tom Aiello, Dexter

Blackman, Amira Rose Davis, Louis Moore, and Johnny Smith. Commentators and other scholars asked helpful and perceptive questions at national conferences for the North American Society for Sport History, the Association for the Study of African American Life and History, and the Popular Culture Association / American Culture Association. Dave Wiggins provided excellent suggestions throughout; he has also been one of my biggest cheerleaders as a scholar and job seeker, and I am especially grateful for all of his support. At the University of Illinois Press, Aram Goudsouzian, Daniel Nasset, Mariah Mendes Schaefer, and Jaime Schultz have helped in a variety of ways to make this book become a reality. To all, I give my heartfelt thanks.

All of my colleagues in American Studies and History at Franklin & Marshall, Dickinson, and Towson were instrumental to this project. There are too many to name here, but I thank you all for making me feel at home, for boosting my spirits, and for offering kind words of support and guidance. My colleagues at Franklin & Marshall, especially Alison Kibler and Cristina Pérez, have been stalwart in their guidance and help, especially in pandemic times. Ann Wagoner provided all kinds of assistance, ranging from research help and advice to pep talks. Dennis Deslippe read earlier versions of chapters and provided much-needed guidance on black capitalism, organized labor, and ongoing wealth disparities. Blake Slonecker read drafts and provided especially useful suggestions regarding 1960s campus activism and critiques of labor policies. Patrick O'Neil, as always, homed in on the key issues of the text, reading drafts of nearly every chapter. His suggestions for writing style and content have been invaluable. This book would not exist without his keen editorial eye.

Of course, writing a book requires inspiration. For the athletes who have inspired me with their craft and their activism, thank you for using your public prominence to try to make positive change. My family and friends make the journey worthwhile every day. I am especially grateful to my in-laws, Paul and Patti Butler, wonderful people who have helped out (and provided a refuge) so many times over the years. And I give special thanks to my parents, Bud and Millie Kaliss, who inspired a love of learning and teaching and who have always been there to help in all kinds of ways—and always with love. To them, I dedicate this book. Finally, I am grateful every day for Leigh and Holly (and, while I'm at it, Skinny Minnie, Lando, and Artemis), who make home a great place to be. Love is not a big enough word to express how I feel.

TIMELINE OF KEY EVENTS

February 26, 1964	Cassius Clay (later, Muhammad Ali) defiantly challenges media following upset victory over Sonny Liston for heavyweight boxing championship
January 13, 1966	Formation of Main Bout Inc. with Jim Brown as one of five shareholders
February 1966	Los Angeles offices of Negro Industrial and Economic Union (later, Black Economic Union) open
April 19, 1966	Bobbi Gibb runs in the Boston Marathon without a race bib
April 19, 1967	Gibb runs Boston Marathon for a second time; Kathrine Switzer runs the race with an official number and eludes Jock Semple's efforts to remove her from the course
April 28, 1967	Muhammad Ali refuses induction into Vietnam War
June 20, 1967	Ali arrested for draft evasion
October 13, 1967	First game of the American Basketball Association
November 24, 1967	Harry Edwards announces plans for boycott of 1968 Olympic Games by black athletes
April 1, 1968	Billie Jean King announces decision to turn professional
October 16, 1968	Tommie Smith and John Carlos protest on the medal stand of the 200-meter dash at the Olympic Games in Mexico City

October 20, 1968	Wyomia Tyus wears black shorts in women's 4 x 100-meter relay, and dedicates gold medal victory to Smith and Carlos
February 18, 1969	Charlie Scott and Bill Chamberlain participate in meeting with BSM members and UNC chancellor J. Carlyle Sitterson
October 17, 1969	"Wyoming 14" meet with Coach Lloyd Eaton and are dismissed from the team
December 24, 1969	Curt Flood sends letter to MLB commissioner Bowie Kuhn asking to be granted right to sign with club of his choosing
February 1970	BEU launches "Food First" program in Holly Springs, Mississippi
September 24, 1970	Billie Jean King and other members of the "Original Nine" sign contracts to play on the Virginia Slims Tour in defiance of United States Lawn Tennis Association
December 30, 1970	Muhammad Ali and Joe Frazier announce fight plans, including shared $5 million purse
March 8, 1971	Ali and Frazier fight in the "Bout of the Century"
October 18, 1971	Judge Kerr denies lawsuit by Wyoming 14 for the second time
June 23, 1972	Title IX of the Education Amendments of 1972 passes
September 8, 1972	Brown endorses Richard Nixon for president
September 30, 1972	Black football players at Troy State University leave game at halftime in protest of various policies
October 24, 1972	Jackie Robinson dies from a heart attack at age fifty-three
January 1973	NCAA changes scholarships from four-year commitments to one-year, renewable offers
August 11, 1973	DJ Cool Herc hosts house party in the South Bronx, introducing hip-hop music to the local community
September 20, 1973	Billie Jean King defeats Bobby Riggs in the "Battle of the Sexes"
May 1974	First issue of *womenSports* magazine, with Billie Jean King on the cover
April 8, 1975	Frank Robinson debuts as manager for the Cleveland Indians, the first African American manager in MLB history
December 23, 1975	Arbitrator Peter Seitz grants free agent status to two MLB players

January 27, 1976	ABA holds the first-ever slam dunk contest, won by Julius Erving
August 5, 1976	ABA and NBA announce merger plans
August 14, 1976	Renée Richards denied entry in U.S. Open Women's Tennis Tournament

BEYOND THE BLACK POWER SALUTE

PROLOGUE

Cassius Clay Declares Independence

The date was February 26, 1964. It was nearly seventeen years after baseball pioneer Jackie Robinson took the field for the first time for the Brooklyn Dodgers. Almost ten years since the U.S. Supreme Court decided by a 9–0 vote that segregated schooling was unconstitutional. Just over one year since Betty Friedan had stirred up a new women's rights movement in the United States with her classic text *The Feminine Mystique*. Only five months since Martin Luther King Jr. had captivated hundreds of thousands with his "I have a dream" speech.

But on that February day in the convention hall in Miami, the man at the front of the room wasn't dreaming, and he wasn't trying to uplift the assembled masses before him. He was just a boxer facing the media, trying to explain something that, to many, seemed impossible. Just one day earlier, he had shocked the sporting establishment by defeating the heavily favored Sonny Liston via technical knockout. Weary from the fight and the after parties of the night before, Cassius Clay, the new heavyweight champion of the world, did not seem in the mood to entertain. The champ wore a dark suit and answered questions in an uncharacteristically subdued manner, dismissing Liston's punching power, celebrating his own agility, and chiding the assembled media for doubting his ability to win. He also defended the Nation of Islam, a sect of the Muslim faith that centered on black lives and promoted racial separatism. Although he had not yet officially joined the group, photographs of him with Malcolm X and reports of his attendance at meetings had circulated for weeks. Reactions in the press had been nearly unanimously negative, painting the fighter as a dupe of a religious cult and a pawn of radicals dead-set on destroying America. But Clay was defiant: "I know where I'm going and I know the truth and I don't have to be what you want me to be. I'm free to be what I want."[1] It was a remarkable statement. In two sentences, Clay—even before his official conversion and name change to Muhammad Ali—declared his independence from the media and their expectations of compliant black athletes. It marked his emergence as an outspoken critic of white America and the powers that be inside and outside the world of sport.

It also served as the opening salvo of an era when athletes of nearly all types—white and black, men and women, professional and amateur—would use their clout and public presence to agitate for change. Although athletes—Jackie Robinson foremost among them—had certainly engaged in political and social activism prior to Ali's press conference, most had shied away from politics, focusing instead on their athletic careers. Even the great black boxer Joe Louis, with all the national acclaim that came along with his domination of the heavyweight division in the 1930s and 1940s, had trodden very carefully when it came to anything controversial: he refused to have his photograph taken with a white woman, let alone agitate for an anti-lynching bill (the most pressing political issue of the day for black America).[2] But in the ten years or so after Ali's press conference, football player Jim Brown would found the Negro Industrial and Economic Union to boost black entrepreneurship; sprinters Tommie Smith and John Carlos would raise their fists in a demonstration of Black Power on the medal stand at the Mexico City Olympics; tennis players Arthur Ashe and Billie Jean King would fight against apartheid and for gender equity in pay, respectively; college basketball star Charlie Scott would lobby for the goals of the Black Student Movement on the campus of the University of North Carolina; marathoners Bobbi Gibb and Kathrine Switzer would fight for women's equal access to sports; and pro basketball stars like Julius Erving would bring attention to black urban America's ingenuity and spirit in the wake of government neglect.

Ali almost certainly didn't know it, but his declaration of independence from the assembled media in February 1964 marked a turning point in the history of sports in America. No longer would athletes be relegated solely to the realm of entertainment. Athletes' support of mainstream norms—from patriotism, to racial politics, to consumer capitalism, to gender ideals and everything in between—could no longer be assumed. And although the revolution that began that day sputtered out in the next decade, these changes were never undone. Athlete activism in later decades, including that of Martina Navratilova, LeBron James, Megan Rapinoe, and Colin Kaepernick, made clear that the sports world would never be the same.

INTRODUCTION

The Fire This Time

In February 2018, Fox News journalist Laura Ingraham criticized LeBron James and Kevin Durant, two of the biggest stars in the National Basketball Association (NBA), for their disparagements of President Donald Trump. Admonishing the two black players to "keep the political commentary" to themselves, she added, "Shut up and dribble." The backlash was immediate. Many accused Ingraham of racism, believing her comments to be a thinly veiled threat to keep black men in an inferior position. As journalist Martenzie Johnson observed, Ingraham's critique of James and Durant was akin to "blowing her dog whistle like a trumpet" to racist white viewers and fit a long pattern of whites critiquing black athletes like Ali who had used their platform to criticize American culture and politics. James responded by telling reporters, "I will not shut up and dribble. I owe it to my peers. I owe it to my fans. I owe it to the youth. I owe it to . . . everybody that has laid the path for me to get to this point."[1]

Ingraham's jibe and James's response were not isolated events. In the six years leading up to their exchange, a number of athletes had used their platforms to call for social transformation. The tragic 2012 murder of Trayvon Martin by neighborhood-watchman-turned-vigilante George Zimmerman inspired James and his then-teammates on the Miami Heat to pose for a photo wearing hooded sweatshirts (like the one worn by Martin on the night of his death). James and other teammates posted messages on Twitter and scrawled notes like "We want justice" on their sneakers. Two years later, after New York resident Eric Garner died as a result of a New York police officer's chokehold, Chicago Bulls basketball player Derrick Rose wore an "I Can't Breathe" T-shirt to practice. In November 2015 nearly the entire University of Missouri football team pledged to boycott their upcoming game unless the university president resigned in the wake of racist events on campus. Women athletes were involved as well; in spring 2016, star players on the highly successful U.S. women's national soccer team, including Megan Rapinoe and Alex Morgan, filed charges of wage discrimination with the Equal Employment Opportunity Commission. In July of that same year, members of the Women's National Basketball Association's (WNBA) Minnesota Lynx donned "Black Lives Matter" T-shirts in response to the deaths of black men Philando Castile and Alton Sterling in police shootings. And then the most publicized event: San Francisco 49ers quarterback Colin Kaepernick refused to stand for the national anthem in the fall of 2016 to express his opposition to systemic racism in the United States. When Trump criticized his ongoing protests one year later at a campaign rally, calling him a "son of a bitch," numerous athletes in sports across the globe supported Kaepernick and his efforts by taking a knee during the anthem and raising their fists. James's critique of Trump's and Ingraham's dismissive responses, then, were part of a larger story of (mostly black) athletes speaking out against social injustices.[2]

How did we get to that point? After all, the immediately preceding decades had mostly been known for the absence of political and social activism among athletes. Some of the biggest icons in global sports, such as basketball star Michael Jordan and golfer Tiger Woods, studiously avoided controversial political stands. Although there had been examples of athletes engaging in protests in the 1990s and early years of the twenty-first century, most protests had been short-lived and not widely supported. The story of NBA player Mahmoud Abdul-Rauf is a case in point. The Denver Nuggets' leading scorer announced in March 1996 that he would not stand for the national anthem before games because it represented "a symbol of oppression, of tyranny," especially for African Americans.[3] The NBA swiftly suspended him for a game and fined him, and many in the public disparaged him. Although he reached a compromise with the league, in which he stood for the anthem but bowed his head in prayer, Abdul-Rauf found himself traded to a new team after the season. One year later his NBA career came to an end, a fact many attributed to his political stand. Few came to his defense, and he spent the rest of his career with professional teams overseas. Almost no other professional athletes rallied to his cause.[4] Clearly, something had shifted between the time of Abdul-Rauf and the murder of Trayvon Martin.

A look into a longer history past the 1990s and 1980s reveals that the activism of recent years was not so much a shift as it was a rebirth. From the mid-1960s through the mid-1970s, long before the protests of James and Rapinoe, numerous American athletes campaigned for a variety of issues inside and outside the world of sports. From Muhammad Ali's anti–Vietnam War protests to Billie Jean King's fight for pay equity in the world of tennis, athletes in the 1960s and 1970s entered the public consciousness through more than their exploits on fields, or in courts and rings. This past era was an important prologue, a time when athletes used their clout and celebrity across race and gender lines to push for social change. What inspired those protests in that era? What happened to that momentum? These questions lie at the heart of this book.

* * *

American sports have long been a site of contestation for broader social norms regarding race, gender, sexuality, class, and ethnicity. The first several decades of organized sports after the U.S. Civil War provided many opportunities for members of marginalized groups to showcase their skills and humanity in athletic contests. Women at colleges such as Mount Holyoke and Smith formed club baseball teams, defying gender norms against women participating in competitive sports. Although their teams were eventually shut down by nervous administrators who feared the sport was dangerous and unladylike, they were not alone in their desire to play competitively. In the 1870s women eagerly joined the croquet fad, finding delight in a game that allowed them to be physically active, competitive, and dominant over male opponents. That same decade saw the creation of the Carlisle Indian School, where Native American students lobbied school president Richard Pratt to create a football team so that they could demonstrate their skills on the field and challenge notions of inferiority. Their successes against the powerhouse squads of the time, including those of Harvard and Yale universities, generated considerable attention and acclaim. African Americans also sought out athletic opportunities to prove their worth and challenge demeaning stereotypes. In the 1890s, black boxers such as Peter Jackson and Jack Johnson pressed for opportunities to fight for the heavyweight championship of the world against white boxers who drew the color line, and Johnson's claiming of the world title in 1908 marked a major breakthrough. At the amateur level, William Henry Lewis's exploits in football with Amherst College and Harvard University in the late 1880s and early 1890s, where he earned All-American honors and achieved academic distinction, contested widely circulating notions of black male intellectual inferiority.[5]

Many realms of sports remained off-limits to racial minorities at the turn of the century. Major League Baseball's (MLB) infamous "gentleman's agreement" barred the signing of black players by the major professional baseball franchises until 1945, and colleges and universities across the country—especially in the South—remained segregated spaces. In this context, black-run sports at the amateur and professional levels emerged to provide viable options for competition and camaraderie. Historically black colleges and universities offered opportunities for young black men and women to take to fields and courts. Starting with the foundation of the Colored Interscholastic Athletic Association (CIAA) in 1912, spirited rivalries in football and basketball developed between the sports teams of schools such as Howard University, Grambling University, and the Tuskegee Institute. Even as white women saw declining opportunities for college athletic participation in the 1930s as a result of gender norms that promoted womanhood as delicate, graceful, and free from the strains of competition, black women found outlets at colleges such as Bennett College in Greensboro, North Carolina, where a dominant women's basketball program emerged in the 1940s. Women's track and field programs, such as those at Tuskegee and Tennessee State University, provided vital training grounds for black women.[6]

Collegiate accomplishments paved the way for success in the Olympics, which provided a showcase for women and minority athletes to perform on the international stage. The global setting infused their feats with a wide range of political meanings. The modern games debuted in 1896 with only male competitors, but women appeared in the subsequent games and saw a very gradual expansion of sporting opportunities in ensuing years. African American athletes made the U.S. Olympic squad in its early decades as well, with George Poage claiming two bronze medals in track and field events at the 1908 games. The 1936 Olympics took on special meaning for African American athletes. Held in Berlin, Germany, during Adolf Hitler's rise to power, the games provided a testing ground for Hitler's notions of Aryan supremacy. The U.S. squad featured eighteen black athletes, most in track and field. There, with the eyes of the world watching, African American track athlete Jesse Owens rose to international superstardom by claiming gold medals in the 100-meter dash, the 4 x 100-meter relay, the 200-meter dash, and the broad jump. The accomplishments of Owens and other black Olympians, who collectively won fourteen medals, including eight gold, earned plaudits in the mainstream and black press for challenging Hitler's ideals. Yet all of the black athletes—including Owens—continued to face segregation and limited opportunities on their victorious return to the States. By the 1950s the Cold War similarly impacted American athlete opportunities, as the United States sought to keep pace with the Soviet Union by bolstering its women's teams and welcoming the contributions of black athletes to illustrate American national dominance.[7]

At the professional level in the prewar years, the Negro Leagues in baseball offered the brightest possibilities for black athletes hoping to cash in on their talents. The most successful iteration of black-only professional baseball emerged in the 1930s, when the Negro National League and the Negro American League featured teams starring talented players such as Satchel Paige, Josh Gibson, and James "Cool Papa" Bell. With millions of spectators and a network of supporting businesses buoyed by the games, the leagues were a vital part of the black community and the black economy. Although the salaries were lower and the conditions harsher than those of their white counterparts, the leagues did offer opportunities for black players to earn money at the professional level. In basketball, professional traveling teams provided options in the decades prior to World War II. The all-black New York Renaissance squad, formed by black businessman Bob Douglas in the early 1920s, dominated competition, black and white, in the 1930s and 1940s. The rival Harlem Globetrotters—actually formed in the Chicago area by white booking agent Abe Saperstein—would eventually eclipse the Rens. Combining tremendous basketball skills with humorous showmanship, the Globetrotters especially earned acclaim for their victory over the all-white Minneapolis Lakers, one of the nation's premier professional teams, in 1948. The Globetrotters' showboating antics, however, proved controversial, as some worried that they reaffirmed Hollywood stereotypes that depicted black men as harmless buffoons. Even as these professional opportunities existed, they were nonetheless reminders of segregation's limitations and the marking out of African Americans as second-class citizens.[8]

As the twentieth century progressed, black athletes who found access to integrated sports competition tended to pursue a strategy of "muscular assimilation," in which they hoped that their contributions on football, baseball, and track fields; in boxing rings; and on basketball courts would earn white esteem and lead to broadened opportunities, acceptance, and greater equality for all African Americans.[9] However, Jack Johnson's struggles as heavyweight champion were a cautionary tale in this regard. Widely reviled in the white community because of his unwillingness to accede to majority norms of black inferiority, Johnson lived a flashy life that included fast cars, lavish spending, heavy drinking, and, most controversially, white wives. When Johnson defeated former white boxing champion James Jeffries (who had been coaxed out of retirement solely to "restore" the championship to the white race) on July 4, 1910, his victory inspired blacks across the country even as it thoroughly shook many whites. In the wake of the fight, numerous race riots broke out across the nation as white men, threatened by Johnson's symbolic victory, indiscriminately attacked black people. In cities across the country, public officials banned the

Heavyweight champion Jack Johnson generated controversy among white Americans for his refusal to abide by racial norms. Photo courtesy of Library of Congress, Prints and Photographs Division, Washington, D.C.

exhibition of the fight in movie theaters, concerned that images of a black man pummeling a white one would be too upsetting. Small wonder that many whites celebrated Johnson's arrest in 1912 on trumped-up charges of violating the Mann Act, a law meant to fight sex trafficking but used against Johnson when he and a prostitute voluntarily traveled across state lines together. Most white Americans heaved a sigh of relief when Johnson finally lost the heavyweight title to white boxer Jess Willard in 1915. No black boxer was given a chance to compete for the title for more than twenty years.[10]

As a result of the bitter response to Johnson and the fraught racial climate of the early twentieth century, most black athletes tended to shy away from controversial political stands, taking as their model the boxer Joe Louis, who in the 1930s and 1940s followed a code of modesty and subdued political activism in order to generate positive media coverage and support from whites. His strategy paid off; not only did Louis earn the opportunity to fight for the heavyweight championship (defeating Max Baer in 1937), but he also avoided the legal troubles that had followed Johnson.[11] Baseball pioneer Jackie Robinson's debut with the Brooklyn Dodgers in 1947 initially followed a similar footprint, with Robinson agreeing to refrain from responding to any racial abuse he encountered on the baseball diamond. Working closely with Dodgers president Branch Rickey, Robinson sought to provide a model of a black man working with white teammates and competing civilly against white opponents.[12]

As the 1960s progressed, however, that approach began to shift. With the mainstream civil rights movement in full swing, black athletes and entertainers increasingly became involved in the quest for social justice and the end of white supremacy. Black athletes such as Robinson, basketball standout Bill Russell, and, most importantly, boxer Muhammad Ali increasingly used their prominence as public figures to call for political and social change. Ali especially challenged white conventions by defying the military draft, eschewing Christianity, and promoting black nationalism. These athletes and others, such as football star Jim Brown, believed they had an obligation to the black community to speak out on issues relevant to African Americans.[13]

The movement toward increasing activism became especially pronounced in the late 1960s, crystallizing in 1968, the year of the so-called black athlete revolt. Much of the impetus for widespread black athlete protests that year and in subsequent years came as a result of the efforts of Harry Edwards, a former college athlete who became a sociology professor at San Jose State University. Having seen firsthand the exploitation of minorities in sports, he encouraged black athletes at the college and professional levels to fight against racial injustice. As part of this movement, Edwards founded the Olympic Project for Human Rights (OPHR), which sought to contest a wide range of discriminatory practices in Olympic sports, including the participation of apartheid South Africa in the games, the use of discriminatory track clubs for Olympic trials, and the lack of minority coaches in the U.S. Olympic organization. Although an attempt to have black athletes boycott the 1968 games largely failed (with the exception of a handful of athletes), the OPHR gained international attention as a result of U.S. sprinters Tommie Smith and John Carlos. On the medal stand for the 200-meter dash, the two bowed their heads and raised black-gloved fists as the U.S. national anthem played, an image that sent shockwaves across the globe.[14] But Smith and Carlos were not alone. Protests erupted at colleges and universities across the United States in 1968, with athletes calling attention to a wide range of issues, from discriminatory language used by coaches and athletic directors, to unequal medical treatment, to poor wages for minority housekeeping staff.[15] The late 1960s, then, were a time of tremendous upheaval in the world of sports, politics, and society at large.

As black athletes became increasingly involved in political activism over the course of the 1960s, the tenor of the civil rights movement shifted as well. Although the Civil Rights Act of 1964 ended discrimination in public accommodations and the Voting Rights Act of 1965 gave federal protection to African Americans attempting to vote, a number of thorny issues remained unresolved, including economic inequality between blacks and whites and ongoing discrimination in housing, education, policing, employment, and cultural representation. Frustrated by ongoing violence against peaceful black protesters and the continuing misery of life in the ghetto, a number of black activists began to adopt a more aggressive tone in contrast to the moderate language employed by Martin Luther King Jr. and other centrist civil rights leaders. Stokely Carmichael, chairman of the Student Nonviolent Coordinating Committee (SNCC), channeled the frustrations of many when he called for "black power" at a rally in June 1966. Building on long-held notions of black nationalism and racial pride, Carmichael exhorted African Americans to band together and find strength within their own community rather than in mainstream political parties and organizations. Although controversial in both the black and white communities, Black Power represented a decisive shift in the battle against white supremacy and influenced countless groups in ensuing years. In addition to well-known organizations like the Black Panther Party, founded in Oakland, California, in 1966, the shift to Black Power emboldened others to challenge white supremacy and patriarchal domination, including activists in the Chicano movement, the American Indian movement, and the gay rights movement.[16]

Women were another group inspired by this climate of protest. For much of the twentieth century, women faced considerable barriers in their attempts to participate in competitive sports. Although physical educators supported women's participation in calisthenics, "ladylike" sports such as tennis and golf, and noncompetitive "play days," access to competitive team sports proved limited. Even in sports with widespread popularity among girls and women, such as basketball, rule adjustments slowed down the pace of the game and limited physical contact. Intersections of gender, sexuality, and class norms also impacted women athletes in profound ways. Female athletes often earned derision as hypermasculine oddities or as man-hating lesbians. Numerous concerns about the effects of sports participation on women's bodies—in terms of both health and appearance—dominated discourse surrounding female sports. While working-class women such as Betty Robinson and Babe Didrikson, and African American women such as Alice Coachman and Wilma Rudolph, found more space to participate in sports, dominating U.S. track and field teams from the 1920s through the early 1960s, middle- and upper-class white women faced intense pressures to refrain from anything that removed them from ideal conceptions of womanhood. Professional sports opportunities for women were almost nonexistent as a result.[17]

The middle of the twentieth century, though, saw a resurgence in women's rights activism. In the wake of the civil rights movement, a number of women began to clamor for reconceptions of gender and sexual norms. In the United States the 1963 publication of Betty Friedan's *The Feminine Mystique* proved especially galvanizing. Questioning the dominant norms that positioned women solely as homemakers, Friedan's text emboldened many women to seek out new educational and professional opportunities. Groups like the National Organization for Women, representing a liberal feminist approach, worked through courts and legislative halls to fight for gender equity in employment, political representation, and education. While *The Feminine Mystique* registered with white suburbanites in particular, working-class, radical, and minority women felt neglected. Women's liberation groups, seeking more radical change, emerged in the years after the Black Power movement. Affirming that the "personal is political," these groups sought to challenge broad cultural norms by understanding the wide range of women's frustrations and challenges. Although still largely focused on white women's needs and interests, these groups moved beyond employment and education to target broader cultural norms that limited women's intellectual, physical, and emotional well-being. By the early 1970s, black feminist groups were calling attention to the particular challenges faced by minority women at the intersection of gender and racial oppression. Although prominent women's rights leaders largely ignored sports, female athletes responded to the cultural shifts around them and began to fight for greater recognition and more opportunities for women in sports.[18]

In addition to quests for gender, racial, ethnic, and sexual equality, anti–Vietnam War protests, the counterculture phenomenon, and a series of violent deaths and riots also contributed to a sense of unrest. Students, in particular, took to streets in opposition to the deadly war in Vietnam and rejected mainstream cultural norms through drug use, free love, long hair, and outrageous fashions. Assassinations of prominent public figures, including President John F. Kennedy, Malcolm X, Martin Luther King Jr., and presidential candidate Robert Kennedy contributed to a sense of crisis and instability. Urban riots exploded across the country, in which predominantly African American residents protested incidences of police brutality and ongoing discrimination, and uprisings in Los Angeles in 1965; Newark, New Jersey, in 1967; and Washington, D.C., in 1968 garnered significant public attention. Although it received scant national attention at first, the Stonewall Uprising in New York in 1969—when gay, lesbian, and transgender patrons protested police brutality in Manhattan's Greenwich Village neighborhood—proved to be a transformative event in ushering in a vibrant gay rights movement.[19]

Sport's place in American life was changing, too, with the increasing visibility of televised sports. Although the first televised sporting event in the United States had taken place in 1939, the technology was not widely available until the 1950s. That decade, professional baseball, football, and boxing saw increased viewership as more games and bouts became available to home viewers. The 1960s saw an astonishing rise in television contract fees for sports, particularly in football, where the National Football League and its new rival, the American Football League, each sold their games to the highest bidder. Television executives like ABC's Roone Arledge transformed the broadcasting of sports events as well, shifting from simple game coverage to entertainment events, with crowd reaction shots, slow-motion replays, catchy theme songs, and innovative graphics adding extra drama and interest to sports. The debut of *Monday Night Football* in September 1970 marked an especially important moment in this transformation.[20]

Television's rise coincided with athletes' entrance into a new realm of celebrity. Although professional athletes had certainly been popular in previous years and had earned commercial endorsement opportunities, the 1960s marked an expansion of athletes' visibility as popular entertainers. New York Jets quarterback Joe Namath represented this broader shift, as he became almost as well known for his fashions, his New York City nightclub, and his bachelor lifestyle as for his performance on the football field. Black athletes such as Jim Brown, Fred Williamson, and O. J. Simpson also broke out into mainstream American popular culture in the 1960s and early 1970s. Simpson scored major endorsement deals, while Brown and Williamson parlayed their athletic stardom into Hollywood film roles.[21] Women athletes saw fewer commercial endorsement opportunities than their male counterparts, but the televised spectacle of the 1973 "Battle of the Sexes" tennis match between Billie Jean King and Bobby Riggs helped usher in a new era of sports entertainment program that offered some new possibilities for women stars.[22]

By the mid-1960s, then, American society and its sporting life were in flux. Sports stars were gaining more media attention precisely as a series of upheavals regarding race, gender, sexuality, the economy, and war gripped the nation. Athletes, many of them young people whose peers were engaging in various social justice protests, could hardly be unmoved. It would be impossible to document all of the athlete activism of this era. However, the case studies that follow move beyond the medal stand protest of 1968 to spotlight several key moments and trends from 1964, when Ali made his stand, through 1976, when the ABA merged with the NBA and free agency came to Major League Baseball. By cutting across race and gender lines, these examples showcase a wider range of athlete activist efforts and draw connections between events and individuals playing in different sports in locations across the country. Some of the stories here are well known, and some are relatively obscure. This book synthesizes familiar material, such as the work of Billie Jean King with the Virginia Slims Tour and the heightened discourse of the first Ali-Frazier fight, with lesser-known material, such as Charlie Scott's lonely struggles at the University of North Carolina (UNC) and the hip-hop meanings of the American Basketball Association. Together they show what changes took place and what obstacles remained, highlighting the potentials and limitations of sports to effect social transformation in American life.

Chapter 1, "Playing for 'Green Power': Sports and Economic Uplift," explores two efforts to use sports celebrity to create economic change. The first is football star Jim Brown's work with the Black Economic Union (BEU), an organization he founded in 1966 to create economic development in the black community. An outspoken athlete with wide-ranging interests, Brown saw the BEU as an opportunity to bring together African Americans and to promote black-run businesses. Building on a long history of African American plans for economic self-uplift, Brown's work attained considerable acclaim and support across the country and on both sides of the color line. In addition, it made considerable headway during the presidency of Richard Nixon, who promoted "black capitalism" as a solution to the economic woes facing the African American community. The second effort is that of women's tennis star Billie Jean King, who lobbied for women's pay equity in tennis and played a leading role in the creation of the Virginia Slims Tour in the early 1970s. This separate tour for women players offered more money and greater freedom for its athletes than the United States Lawn Tennis Association (USLTA) and put pressure on the USLTA to bolster the meager purses it provided for women's tournaments.

Both efforts for economic growth achieved success in their own right, yet both inevitably failed to fundamentally change the economic structures that led to imbalances across race and gender lines. In exploring these campaigns, we see the limits faced by athletes who wanted to change economics from within the system. The emphasis on a market-based capitalist solution to economic imbalances may have led to small and temporary adjustments, but sustainable transformations proved elusive, and issues of power and control over sports and the wider economy were especially difficult to address.

Chapter 2, "Getting into the Race: Women Runners / Women's Rights," explores the efforts of women distance runners to break through the sex-based restrictions associated with their sports. Even as the women's rights movement made inroads into American culture in the mid-1960s, the world of women's sports remained largely unchanged. The Boston Marathon, the nation's most prestigious race, had never permitted women runners. Indeed, Amateur Athletic Union rules prohibited races of more than 1.5 miles for women. In this context, the efforts of runners Bobbi Gibb and Kathrine Switzer to join the race in 1966 and 1967 had deep symbolic meaning. Both Gibb and Switzer would challenge the race's limiting regulations in their own distinct ways, stirring up public discourse that was both discouraging and disheartening.

In the wake of the 1967 marathon, women's participation in sports and recreational running gradually gained more acceptance in mainstream popular culture. In college athletics, multiple organizations fought to shape the future of women's sports and to promote new opportunities. An exploration of the coverage of distance running in women's magazines, however, reveals the tenacity of conservative gender norms and expectations. While women took to the streets to run in increasing numbers, dominant ideologies regarding femininity, especially related to body shape and competition, continued to constrain women's freedoms.

Chapter 3, "College Athletes Flex Their Muscles," explores the rising tide of college athlete activism—especially among black men at predominantly white schools in the National Collegiate Athletic Association (NCAA)—in the late 1960s and early 1970s. Inspired by Muhammad Ali's defiance, the rise of Black Power, and the activism of athlete-turned-scholar Harry Edwards, black college athletes began to use their prominent places on campuses across the country to advocate for a wide range of changes inside and outside the world of sport. While efforts to boycott the Mexico City Olympics of 1968 and the attendant protest of Tommie Smith and John Carlos were early examples of amateur athlete uprising, they were not alone. On campuses across the country, athletes called for changes to educational curricula, lobbied for minority coaches and staff, critiqued racial stereotypes, and pushed for better social opportunities for black students.

Two case studies showcase the tenuous ground on which black athletes had to operate. Charlie Scott's struggles to balance his desire to engage in activism with his standing as the first black basketball player at the University of North Carolina highlights the challenges faced by athletes who wanted to initiate social change but were isolated as racial pioneers. The saga of the "Wyoming 14," meanwhile, underscores the maintenance of white supremacy in leadership positions in sports and higher education. The suspension of fourteen black players at the University of Wyoming for initiating a conversation about engaging in activism—and the university and town community's support for their banishment—revealed the harsh realities of the power imbalance in college athletics.

Chapter 4, "Black Men / Black Gladiators: Redefining Black Manliness through Sports," uses the Muhammad Ali versus Joe Frazier boxing bout of March 1971 to explore black athletes' efforts to challenge dominant stereotypes of black men. Taking place against a backdrop of anti–Vietnam War protests, the rise of Black Power, and calls for greater athlete empowerment in professional sports, the bout generated considerable rhetoric before, during, and after the fight. Ali's brash persona, refusal to be drafted into the Vietnam War, outspoken criticisms of white racism, and faith in the Nation of Islam made him a potent symbol of 1960s rebellion and Black Power. Frazier, meanwhile, by claiming the heavyweight championship while Ali was banished, endorsing controversial white politicians, and supporting U.S. involvement in Vietnam, represented a worthy foil for Ali's politics.

In responding to the fight, observers thought through two models of black manhood and activism. One leaned toward revolution and outspoken critiques of established norms. The other emphasized working within the system, seeing value in hard work and modesty as a way to rise up. Both sides recognized the inequalities facing African Americans in and out of the ring and sought to use black male celebrities to initiate larger changes. In debating the fight, the fighters, and, particularly, the financing of the fight, a wide range of Americans envisioned a new future for black men—but ran up against serious obstacles in their efforts to claim access to the privileged (and problematic) role of male breadwinner.

Chapter 5, "The ABA and the Origins of Hip-Hop America," analyzes the larger meanings of the American Basketball Association, an upstart professional basketball league in existence from 1967 to 1976. Meant to challenge the more established National Basketball Association, the new league offered innovative rules, on-court flair, and increased opportunities for African American players. Taking pride in its reputation as an outsiders' league, the ABA also encouraged a more wide-open and improvisational style of play that came primarily from black players on urban playgrounds. Players combined this innovative basketball style with personal flair, channeling Black Power's emphasis on black pride and beauty. Wearing their hair in large Afros and exploding for powerful slam dunks on the court, black players in the ABA celebrated an African American aesthetic rooted in rhythmic sophistication, personal style, and improvisation.

These attributes connected ABA players to more than just Black Power. In drawing from urban roots, the athletes also drew attention to the plight of African Americans suffering from the legacies of white flight and urban decline. In effect, the black players in the ABA were contributors to the new genre of hip-hop. Born in the South Bronx neighborhood of New York City, an area decimated by white flight and the failure of urban renewal plans, hip-hop culture (including music, dance, and graffiti) marked an attempt to affirm black individuals' identity and creativity. The changes wrought by pioneering hip-hop artists spilled into sports. By playing in the way they did and by cultivating the fashion styles they wore, black players in the ABA affirmed black identity at a time of government neglect.

* * *

The athletes in these chapters, and the activists inspired by them, set out to change a broad set of issues in American life. These included, but were not limited to, the economic inequalities faced by women and African Americans; the limited access of women to public spaces; the social isolation, poor treatment, and lack of representation of black college athletes at predominantly white schools; the need to revise and challenge demeaning stereotypes of black masculinity; and the material poverty and cultural dislocation of urban residents in the wake of white flight. Significant progress took place. We need only look at the increased presence of black athletes and women athletes in American public life, and the increased earning potential and power of those athletes, to see a marked transformation.

And yet there were underlying issues that time and again thwarted hopes for lasting change and sweeping reform. Of particular note was the rather limited focus of many of the athletes' efforts. Although they did call attention to broader issues in society, very often their activism centered on opening up access to individuals in sports or on improving conditions for athletes as a class. Billie Jean King's campaign for equal pay for women's tennis players fell into this category, as did much of the activism by college athletes, who primarily sought improvements in minority athletes' day-to-day lives. Even efforts to engage with larger issues, such as Jim Brown's work to address wealth inequality in American life, largely eschewed any efforts to make significant changes to the economy. When Ali and Frazier fought in March 1971, for example, they primarily sought to make the most money possible in the existing framework of professional boxing—not to remake that system in a way that benefited members of the broader community. When athletes did seek larger changes, they were often forced to compromise in order to win smaller victories. Charlie Scott succeeded as an integrationist pioneer at UNC, with other black athletes following in his footsteps, but his inability to engage in outspoken activism reflected the challenges of expanding social justice campaigns beyond the world of sports. Indeed, for most women and minority athletes in this time period, their most pressing concerns centered on gaining access to sports institutions and roles and in garnering better treatment as athletes. Such was the case with the women seeking to run the Boston Marathon and the black basketball players fighting for more opportunities in their sport. They sought to level the playing field within sports in comparison to those who traditionally had more access and stardom: white men. Larger, systemic changes, including the nature and control of the American economy, took a backseat to these immediate aspirations. As we will see, the deep-rooted connections of the nation's economy to racial, sexual, and gender-based discrimination meant that these efforts for change often proved limited or fleeting.

Efforts to improve lives for individual athletes, or even groups of athletes, also failed to challenge the larger power structures in the sports world itself—whether in the amateur or professional realm. As a result, while material changes took place for athletes in important ways, whether they were women tennis players or black college football players, the people in charge of the institutions that controlled these institutions remained mostly white, wealthy, male, and entrenched in conservative gender and racial politics. The fact that the NCAA, the USLTA, the NBA, and the MLB all remained under the control of the same leadership despite the activism of women and minority athletes in this era speaks to this reality. In many ways, the struggles of these athletes echoed the limitations of American labor unions throughout the twentieth century. Many historians have argued that organized labor leaders in the United States put so much emphasis on worker hours, wages, and safety that they neglected the larger structural changes that socialists argued for.[23] In claiming access to some basic benefits of American consumer capitalism, both organized labor and athlete activists did little to shift the balance of power in leading institutions. Time and again, the individual efforts made in these chapters encountered the resilience of the dominant hegemony to restrict revolution and to limit gains by those in positions of inferiority. Systemic racism and patriarchy embedded in the nation's economic institutions proved remarkably difficult to undo.

Two terms, "systemic racism" and "patriarchy," deserve special note as underlying concepts for the book. Systemic racism, referred to in 1966 by black activist Stokely Carmichael as "institutionalized racism," speaks to the broad set of institutional structures that relegate African Americans to an inferior place in American life. In Carmichael's words, "the ordering and structuring" of the United States in terms of employment, education, housing, law, medical access, and more has worked to keep the African American "community in its condition of dependence and oppression."[24] Racism, in this formulation, is far more than individual acts of bigotry, prejudice, or even violence. It is a broad set of practices and structures that maintains a racial hierarchy with whites in positions of power.[25] Similarly, patriarchy, as defined by Gerda Lerner in her classic text *The Creation of Patriarchy*, refers to "the manifestation and institutionalization of male dominance over women and children in the family and the extension of male dominance over women in society in general."[26] As with systemic racism, this definition takes into account the ways that patriarchal power circulates widely, and often in unseen ways, in social institutions and practices.[27] Taken together, both concepts help explain the frustrations experienced by athlete activists even as they made headway in creating change in localized and individual cases.

In 1963 African American writer and cultural critic James Baldwin published *The Fire Next Time*, consisting of two essays that assessed race in American life in unflinching terms. The book drew its title from an African American spiritual, "Mary Don't You Weep." One lyric, pointing back to the biblical story of Noah, affirms "God gave Noah the rainbow sign / No more water, the fire next time." Many saw the tumult of the 1960s as a realization of that fire, a time of upheaval and transformation as the nation wrestled with its inequalities and oppression.[28] The story of this book is the story of that fire burning and the many ways athletics contributed to the flames. It is also a story of how that fire burned out, at least temporarily, and the changes wrought in its aftermath. For change did come—not as much or as lasting as many had hoped—but American society in and out of sports saw significant alterations. And if the story of Laura Ingraham and LeBron James is any indication, the fire is burning again. The results of that conflagration remain to be seen.

CHAPTER 1

PLAYING FOR "GREEN POWER"

Sports and Economic Uplift

On October 16, 1968, Tommie Smith and John Carlos staged one of the most memorable acts of protest in sport history. On the medal stand of the 200-meter dash at the Summer Olympic Games in Mexico City, as the U.S. national anthem played, the two bowed their heads and thrust black-gloved fists in the air. In doing so, gold medal winner Smith and bronze medal winner Carlos acted in defiance of an International Olympic Committee (IOC) ban against acts of protest and in support of an Olympic boycott of apartheid South Africa—and for the efforts of Harry Edwards, the Olympic Project for Human Rights (OPHR), and the cause of black equality more generally. The act and its image have become iconic, celebrated in statues, posters, and documentary films. And yet there is a danger to that pervasiveness—something that sociologist Douglas Hartmann has observed in his work *Race, Culture, and the Revolt of the Black Athlete*. Much of what specifically drove Smith and Carlos to make their stand has been forgotten or, even worse, assumed to be only a vestige of a troublesome past.[1]

That lack of clarity mitigates some of the important, wide-ranging issues that the athletes in that protest, and in other activist campaigns in the late 1960s and early 1970s, sought to address. Of particular importance were the economic issues that inspired Smith and Carlos. For when Smith raised a black-gloved right fist and Carlos a left one, they did more than affirm a nebulous idea of black pride, as many seem to think. In specific gestures they addressed issues that were particularly relevant to the broader black community. The badges they wore on their tracksuits promoted Edwards's work with the OPHR. Tommie Smith's black scarf was meant to indicate black pride. John Carlos left his jacket unzipped to express solidarity with all blue-collar workers, and he wore beads around his neck to call attention to the victims of lynching. They also made one further gesture of protest: both athletes took the podium shoeless, in only their socks, changing from white to black ones, a symbol, they said, of black poverty. Tellingly, the image that often appears in books and on the internet leaves out this detail, a sign of its status as the most-ignored and most-forgotten aspect of their stand.[2]

In an era of Black Power activism, when even moderate civil rights leaders like Martin Luther King Jr. were emphasizing the urgent need for economic transformation, and as the federal government increasingly promoted black capitalism as a solution for persistent economic inequalities in the United States, the activities of Carlos and Smith spoke to broader currents in the quest for equality. They joined a wide range of amateur and professional athletes who used their prominent positions to push for sustainable economic transformations. Of particular note was the work of football player Jim Brown with the Black Economic Union (BEU) from 1966 through 1973.[3] As the most celebrated running back in professional football history, and a man with an enormous public presence, thanks to his acting career and other off-the-field endeavors, Brown's campaign for economic uplift generated significant coverage in the mainstream and black press and attracted financial support from private foundations and the federal government alike. But he was not alone. At the same time that Brown pushed for economic change for black Americans, tennis star Billie Jean King and her allies in women's professional tennis conducted their own campaign for economic equality. The establishment of the Virginia Slims Tour in the fall of 1970, a response to the huge disparities in prize money awarded to men and women in the pro circuits, showcased the impact of second-wave feminism. As King and her peers sought to level the wage gap between men and women in their sport, they emphasized messages of considerable importance to women, especially the necessity of achieving economic independence and earning fair market value.

Although their specific end goals were distinct, both Brown and King saw sports as a means to address economic inequality, a sign of the heightened activism of the era. There were certainly many differences between Brown and King, including their race, gender, and sexuality, and the sports they played. Brown's troubling history of violence against women makes pairing him with King problematic.[4] However, the ideological affinities between the two, their conservative approaches to the economy, and their shared interests in athlete financial empowerment speak to larger trends at work. Both fully embraced the U.S. capitalist economy, bowing to the pressures that came with the changing political climate of the late 1960s and early 1970s and the dominance of consumer capitalism in American life. In doing so, their economic missions achieved great successes but also fell far short of their lofty goals.

Jim Brown and the BEU

Brown's political awakening coincided with changes in the tenor of the quest for racial equality. Brown's plans for economic uplift through the BEU began the same year Carmichael issued his call for Black Power, and the more assertive and nationalistic overtones of that movement certainly influenced Brown and his allies. Wealth inequality proved an especially vexing issue for African Americans, and a number of black leaders, including those affiliated with Black Power, attempted to chart out new courses of economic uplift for the black community. Of course, attempts to address income and wealth inequality were hardly new; as historian Michael Ezra notes, "The black freedom struggle has always had a significant economic component, and economic concerns have guided its direction," including boycotts of businesses that did not hire black employees and long-standing efforts to create black-run companies of various types.[5] Jackie Robinson's leadership in founding the Freedom National Bank in Harlem in 1964 was one example of these early efforts. Robinson sought, in his own words, "to establish a first-class, commercial bank to serve the interests of" the Harlem community, believing that capital investment in the area would boost the quality of life for its mostly black residents.[6]

As the Black Power era took shape, efforts at economic reform varied, "from independent Black ownership to collective Black entrepreneurship, to grassroots attempts to rebuild inner city markets in the wake of disinvestment."[7] The Nation of Islam, for example, employed a conservative approach that built on the efforts of past black leaders such as Alexander Crummell and Marcus Garvey to nurture a blacks-only capitalist economy. On the other hand, the Black Panthers argued for more radical change, believing that "the capitalist economic order . . . rested on the racial division of exploited peoples."[8] In the last years of his life, Martin Luther King Jr. also argued for a transformation of the capitalist American economy, telling an audience in early 1967, "We are called upon to help the discouraged beggars in life's marketplace. But one day we must come to see that an edifice which produces beggars needs restructuring."[9] For many black Americans, a thorough revision of the economy seemed necessary for upward mobility.

As various leaders debated these and other ideas, the concept of black capitalism began to gain momentum. The Economic Opportunity Loan Program, initiated under President Lyndon Johnson, went into effect in 1965 and was meant to provide loans and technical assistance to the urban poor to integrate themselves into the larger economy. At the same time, a number of grassroots initiatives emerged under the leadership of black Americans. Dr. Thomas W. Matthew, for example, organized the National Economic Growth and Reconstruction Organization (NEGRO) in New York City. Around the same time, Freedom, Independence, God, Honor, and Today (FIGHT) started up in Rochester, New York, and worked to connect community resources in order to aid black businesses.[10] Black capitalism emphasized the need for black Americans to participate more equitably in the American capitalist marketplace, although programs varied from those focused on a black nationalist economy to full integration. As historian William L. Van Deburg notes, "There was a black capitalism to fit almost any ideological predisposition," and the push for black capitalism influenced a wide range of supporters.[11] Floyd McKissick's "Soul City" program, intended to create a black-owned, black-run community in Warren County, North Carolina, picked up on black capitalist ideas.[12] Whitney Young, director of the National Urban League, also "called for the creation of more black capitalists" and secured funding from several white foundations and corporations.[13]

Although many black leaders remained suspicious of capitalism's potential for fostering equality and uplift, black capitalism continued to gain momentum, especially after the election of Richard Nixon as U.S. president in 1968. Nixon promised that he would oversee policies that would, in his words, lead to "an expansion of black ownership, of black capitalism" that would lead to "black pride, black jobs, black opportunity and, yes, black power, in the best, the constructive sense of that often misapplied term."[14] To that end, Nixon promoted initiatives like the Minority Small Business / Capital Ownership Development Program and the Minority Business Development Agency (MBDA).[15] He also appointed two wealthy black women, Gloria A. Toote and Jewel Lafonte, to key positions in his cabinet in order to promote the virtues of black economic entrepreneurship.[16] Although Nixon believed his programs would lead to black empowerment, others were more suspicious. Instead of leading to black residents having control over health services, police, and businesses, black capitalism, critics argued, tended to produce black businessmen who did little for the benefit of the community.[17] Still, by the time of the 1972 election, a number of black entrepreneurs had benefited from Nixon's policies and thus endorsed him for president.[18]

The shift to Black Power, then, necessarily involved an engagement with economic issues but one fraught with division and tensions; some argued for economic revolution and others for integration into the mainstream economy. Still, as historians Laura Warren Hill and Julia Rabig have noted, most programs and activists ascribed to "commonly held goals—self-determination, community control, and economic independence."[19] For black leaders of nearly every political persuasion, sustainable economic growth controlled by the black community was central to the quest for black uplift. The role that black athletes could, or would, play in that quest—and how women athletes might be affected—remained unclear.

The mantle for economic activism among black athletes fell especially on Jim Brown, the thoughtful, rugged, talented, and temperamental fullback for the National Football League's Cleveland Browns. Over time, he would become one of the most prominent public faces of the new spirit of black athlete activism, and his organization, the Negro Industrial and Economic Union (later renamed the Black Economic Union), came to represent one of the most noteworthy efforts of black athletes to address economic uplift in the black community at large. Brown's faith in the capitalist market—buttressed by his own successes in the worlds of business and entertainment—informed his activism to considerable degrees.

For most of Brown's amateur and professional career, there were few signs that he would become an activist. Born in St. Simons, Georgia, Brown moved with his family at an early age to Manhasset in Long Island, New York. There, he quickly earned a reputation as a star athlete, excelling in a number of sports, including football, baseball, basketball, lacrosse, and track. A local Manhasset attorney solicited funds to pay for Brown to attend his alma mater, Syracuse University, where Brown earned a place on the football team as a freshman despite racial bias from the team's coaches. After showing off his considerable skills, Brown was given a scholarship and eventually earned first-team All-American honors as a running back for the football team and as a star with the lacrosse team. Drafted with the sixth pick of the NFL draft in 1957 by the Cleveland Browns, Brown played nine years of professional football, setting numerous records in the process and earning acclaim as one of the greatest running backs in the sport's history. He also led the Browns to an NFL championship in 1964. As Brown triumphed on the field, he also began to attract attention from companies eager to cash in on his fame, talent, and good looks. He signed endorsement deals with Pepsi-Cola and other corporations and began an acting career by appearing in the 1964 western film *Rio Conchos*.[20]

Yet as Brown's athletic achievements led to increased stardom, some of his actions off the field revealed an activist temperament that made him a more controversial figure, especially among whites. According to biographer Mike Freeman, Brown, even early in his professional football career, "inspired black players to brook no discrimination—from the Browns or anyone else."[21] He also showed a savvy awareness of his importance to the Browns, using his clout to negotiate larger and larger contracts with the team. In the spring of 1960, for example, Brown started rumors that he was going to quit football in order to take up boxing, using the threat as a negotiating ploy to get more money from the Browns. That summer, Brown signed a two-year contract that made him the highest-paid player in the sport. Although he continued to attain athletic and financial success, the 1964 publication of his autobiography, *Off My Chest*, riled a significant portion of the general public. Unflinching in his assessment of racism in sports—including on his own team, the Cleveland Browns—Brown's book unsettled many white Americans who looked to sports as an arena of life free from racial and political strife. An unrepentant Brown made it clear that he was his own man, with his own opinions on matters ranging from interracial relationships, to racial stereotypes, to civil rights.[22]

Brown did more than talk about racism in sports, however; in January 1966 he also cast his lot with one of the most controversial figures in sports—Muhammad Ali—by becoming a partner in Main Bout Inc. Ali established Main Bout, a promotional company for his boxing career, as a way for black Americans to enter a potentially lucrative realm that had been previously dominated by whites. This new outfit would be, according to Ali, "one in which Negroes are not used as fronts, but as stockholders, officers, and production and promotion agents." Brown and two other black men—Herbert Muhammad and John Ali, both affiliated with the Nation of Islam—were among the group's five stockholders.[23] Brown was clear that the company had interests beyond the boxing ring, vowing that the organization's profits would "be invested in Negro businesses and organizations to try to bolster the economy of the Negro."[24] When the company encountered opposition as it tried to schedule Ali's fights, Brown publicly accused white boxing organizers of discriminatory treatment of the black-run company and solicited the aid of black New York congressman Adam Clayton Powell Jr. to help the group overcome opposition.[25] Eventually, Main Bout Inc. successfully promoted a number of Ali's fights before the boxer's conviction and loss of boxing licenses doomed the company to failure.[26]

More was to come soon. Only six months after announcing his participation in Main Bout, Brown shocked the sports world when he announced his retirement from professional football on July 13, 1966. Brown's decision to retire while still in the prime of his career further showed his determination to follow his own life plan and marked a new chapter in his career as a social activist. After the conclusion of the 1965 season, Brown had agreed to act in his second major motion picture: the World War II action film *The Dirty Dozen*. As a result of scheduling delays, Brown was unable to report in time for training camp with the Cleveland Browns. Pressured by Browns owner Art Modell to report to the team, Brown instead decided to retire. Saying he had "gotten almost everything [he] could get out of football," he explained that there were "other things I would like to accomplish." Thanking the Browns and expressing his admiration for the team, Brown emphasized the permanence of his decision and his desire to begin a new phase in his life, specifically noting his burgeoning acting career and his newly formed BEU.[27] And it was that organization, the BEU, that would thrust Brown squarely into the center of black athlete activism in the late 1960s and early 1970s.

Brown's creation of the BEU stemmed from his frustrations with the difficulties that black entrepreneurs faced in starting new businesses. While still playing in the NFL, Brown was asked by John Daniels, an African American Los Angeles–area businessman, to help produce a fashion magazine called *Elegant*. Although he was eager to get involved, the publication, according to *Washington Post* writer Dave Brady, "folded after about ten issues for lack of sustaining financial help." Frustrated by the magazine's failure and the attendant loss of jobs for African Americans, Brown sought out a solution. Conferring with business leaders and other athletes, including Maggie Hathaway, an actress and activist, he created the BEU believing that the organization could provide a network of business experts to help aspiring black entrepreneurs, aid in the securing of start-up loans, and offer African Americans expanded opportunities.[28] As he explained, the group would enable "Negroes to participate in the economy of the country so that they can stand on their own feet and won't have to beg anybody to give them a little of this and a little of that. What could be more dignified than that?"[29]

The occasion of Brown's retirement generated a significant amount of discussion regarding the BEU, and nearly all of the press coverage of the organization in the mainstream and black media was positive. A story in the venerable African American newspaper the *Chicago Defender* emphasized Brown's dedication to the "private anti-poverty program aimed at helping Negroes launch and run small businesses."[30] A widely circulated Associated Press story, meanwhile, devoted time and attention to Brown's economic plans, describing the BEU as "an organization dedicated to bringing the Negro into the full stream of the American economy." Brown expressed his belief that the BEU would help to "instill pride" in black Americans and would emphasize "self-help."[31] Although Brown had opened the organization's first office in Los Angeles in February 1966 and their national headquarters in Cleveland the following month, his retirement in July of that year added new momentum to the group's work.[32]

Brown officially incorporated the BEU as a nonprofit on May 31, 1966, and the black press was especially eager to publicize the organization's positive efforts.[33] On New Year's Eve 1966, *New Pittsburgh Courier* sports editor Bill Nunn Jr. included in his list of hopes for the coming year that "Jim Brown's Negro Industrial and Economic Union prospers and enables numerous Negroes to open their own businesses."[34] As support for the organization grew, Brown quickly expanded to other cities across the country. By fall 1970 the BEU had more than twenty thousand members, with offices in four cities across the country.[35] These field offices initiated a number of programs, from a summer youth program in New York; to a Los Angeles summer program that linked government, labor organizations, entertainers, and business leaders; to a minority business exposition in Kansas City.[36] When the BEU opened its office in Harlem, the *Amsterdam News* eagerly promoted the event: "The organization is dedicated to assisting black people to increase their economic standard of living through establishing new businesses, lending management planning to public and private economic projects in black communities and providing other community services relating to the upgrading of the economic standards of black Americans."[37] A wide range of businesses, from factories dedicated to producing prefabricated housing, to Cleveland's Way Out Records label, to clothing shops and hair-care products, benefited from the BEU's advice and financial assistance.[38] If most in the mainstream press missed the economic aspects of Smith and Carlos's medal stand gesture in 1968, Brown and the BEU did not. In Los Angeles the BEU manufactured medallions featuring the two sprinters "carved in their fist-brandishing power-salute pose."[39] This was one small way to use black athletes to bolster small black businesses.

But the BEU did more than aid local and national companies. From the outset, community outreach was a key component of the organization, and Brown and his team made a number of efforts to connect with local community members. As one story in the *Philadelphia Tribune* reported, Brown hoped that the group could make use of the "image value of black athletes" to inspire urban-dwelling African American children and teens toward greater achievements in and out of school.[40] Sports stars like basketball player Lew Alcindor met with ghetto youth in various programs, offering advice and guidance.[41] In April 1967 the BEU teamed up with the Greater Cleveland Associated Foundation to open the Hough Progressive Youth Center in one of the city's black neighborhoods. The previous summer, riots had broken out there, and Brown saw the center as a first step in addressing the economic woes and injustices facing the city's black residents.[42] One year later, in the days following the assassination of Martin Luther King Jr., members of Cleveland's BEU joined the city's mayor, Carl Stokes; players from the Cleveland Browns football team; and various black leaders in the community to travel through the Hough section of the city in an effort to quell any impending riots.[43]

The connections between the BEU and professional athletes went beyond simply athlete participation and support of the organization. The BEU also lobbied for increased empowerment of professional athletes as a way of redressing economic imbalances in the world of sports. Brown talked with pride about the United Athletic Association, a part of the BEU that, according to him, was "the first organization to represent athletes negotiating contracts, and to help them in planning investments, endorsements, personal appearances and off-season employment." He argued that, contrary to popular belief, "athletes are an exploited class, bought, sold, and traded whenever their owners care to."[44] Brown also used his public prominence as an actor, athlete, and BEU leader to speak out in favor of athletes who attempted to fight for greater empowerment in the sports world. When five of Brown's former black teammates decided to go on strike from the Browns in July 1967, he publicly supported the efforts of John Wooten, John Brown, Mike Howell, Sydney Williams, and Leroy Kelly. Attempting to shield his former teammates from backlash against the civil rights movement and Black Power, Brown said that economic issues, not racial ones, were the prime motivators for the players, and he indicated that all had legitimate grievances. Believing that owners had too much power, he asked rhetorically, "Should the owners be complete dictators in salary negotiations? Is it wrong to have legal representation when dealing with legal problems?"[45] When Browns owner Art Modell rebuked the players, Brown took their side, dismissing Modell's criticisms.[46] Although Brown sided with the players, he shied away from race-based analysis, using fundamentally conservative arguments about economic imbalances to support his claims. Brown's color-blind rhetoric failed to address the role of systemic racism in perpetuating economic imbalances.

Nonetheless, Brown continued to push for black athlete empowerment in a variety of ways. One such effort came in November 1967, when Bernie Parrish, a former teammate of Brown's, mailed a brochure to 640 NFL players detailing a proposal to form the American Federation of Professional Athletes. In response, Brown sent out a letter on BEU stationery in support of the idea.[47] He also acted in 1971 as a mentor for Dallas Cowboys running back Duane

Thomas, who believed that he was underpaid as a star player.[48] In addition, Brown sponsored black athletes in traditionally white sports such as golf and tennis, hoping to expand their professional career possibilities.[49] Although the BEU's primary focus was on small business development in the black community, Brown clearly saw the relative powerlessness of professional athletes—and black athletes in particular—as an issue that needed to be addressed. In 1973 he became co-owner of a professional football franchise in Detroit as part of the fledgling World Football League. Although the league collapsed in only its second season, Brown's involvement signaled his interest in changing the power dynamics of the sports world.[50]

Brown's efforts and Ali's inspirational stand inspired other athletes to pursue economic activism. In the college ranks, athletes like Charlie Scott, the first black basketball player for the University of North Carolina at Chapel Hill and one of the first black star college players at any predominantly white Southern school, became involved with the Black Student Movement on his campus, fighting in part for higher wages for the school's mostly minority housekeeping staff.[51] A number of black athletes, including five members of the Super Bowl–winning Kansas City Chiefs 1969 team, invested some of their earnings from their playing careers into businesses meant to aid their local black communities. Curtis McClinton, for example, helped establish a bank in Kansas City geared toward investing in black businesses.[52] Former Washington Redskins wide receiver Bobby Mitchell took up a career as an insurance agent, expressing his hope for "more money going into the ghetto area." He wanted the insurance premiums paid by poor people to come back to them in the form of investment and services.[53] Other athletes, such as former pro basketball player Willie Naulls, started restaurants and nightclubs aimed at the black community.[54] In these varied ways, black athletes picked up on the BEU's ideas regarding black athlete presence and ownership in the capitalist market economy.

One of the BEU's most notable programs, and one that earned significant media attention, was its "Food First" initiative. In early 1970 Brown gathered a number of professional athletes at his home in Los Angeles to announce plans for Food First. According to Jim Toback, a white writer who was staying with Brown while writing a biography of the athlete, Brown explained that he wanted "to institute a program that starts with essentials—food and clothing." Brown asked the athletes in attendance to spend a few weeks garnering support—financial, food, and clothing donations—and then prepare to travel to Holly Springs, Mississippi, a largely black community with widespread economic woes. The athletes would pay their own way and then meet up to distribute the materials and meet local community members. Brown indicated that "designated BEU workers will remain down there and will begin job training, educational assistance and voter registration as soon as the minimal point of health has been reached." He asked the athletes to pay their own way to make it clear that this was not "a publicity tour or a pleasure trip." Everyone in the room, Toback reported, including noted athletes Curtis McClinton, Paul Warfield, and Leroy Kelly, agreed to participate.[55]

The project started in February 1970. The athletes, who also included Kelly, Warfield, Russell, Gale Sayers of the Chicago Bears, Ray May of the Pittsburgh Steelers, Bob Hayes of the Dallas Cowboys, Carl Eller of the Minnesota Vikings, Irv Cross of the Philadelphia Eagles, and Mike Garrett of the Kansas City Chiefs, first met in Memphis, Tennessee, visiting the Lorraine Motor Inn, the site of Martin Luther King Jr.'s assassination. From there the group traveled to Holly Springs, where they met with local residents and community leaders. According to media reports, they were stunned by the poverty they encountered. Although blacks outnumbered whites by a significant margin, almost no black residents held any political position of consequence. Jobs were scarce, and many were on welfare; threats to take away their government financial support prevented most residents from getting involved in any kind of activism. As a result, the BEU decided on a three-phase plan to invigorate the community and boost the economy. First the organization would provide food donations through the Food First initiative, including school breakfast and lunch programs. Then it would make use of federal funds "to provide work and employment programs for the area." The third phase was to encourage other black organizations, such as the NAACP, the Urban League, and CORE (Congress of Racial Equality), to adopt their own counties and engage in similar efforts.[56]

The media, especially the black press, reported enthusiastically on the group's efforts. Stories in the *New Pittsburgh Courier*, the *Chicago Defender*, the *New York Amsterdam News*, and the *Baltimore Afro-American* eagerly publicized the group's efforts, with syndicated sports columnist A. S. "Doc" Young praising Brown's efforts to address "the racial need for economic development."[57] George Caldwell, the executive secretary of the local NAACP chapter in Holly Springs, celebrated "the endorsement of nationally known people" as a way to improve conditions in the area.[58] The Los Angeles Board of Supervisors, led by supervisor Kenneth Hahn, publicly praised Brown for his efforts with the Food First campaign.[59] Even national politicians lauded the initiative. The efforts of the BEU in Mississippi earned a tribute in the House of Representatives from Ohio representative Louis Stokes, the first black Congressman in the state's history, who praised Brown for making time in "his busy schedule . . . to help those who need help."[60] This initial positive buzz surrounding the program led to plans for expansion.

In March 1970 the *Washington Post* reported that the Anacostia neighborhood of Washington, D.C., had been selected as another site. A. D. Whitfield, a former member of the Washington Redskins, was tabbed as the project director, and another Redskins player, Brig Owens, was chosen as the director of the Washington office. The BEU hoped to raise $150,000 to fund the program in Anacostia; other locations were targeted for Kansas City; the Compton section of Los Angeles; East Oakland, California; and the Glenville section of Cleveland.[61]

The positive coverage of the Food First campaign in 1970 spoke to the group's ability to attract positive attention and to secure financing for its efforts. In March 1968 the Ford Foundation announced a $520,000 grant for the BEU, a major donation that enabled the organization to expand into Chicago and New York.[62] A grant from Nixon's Economic Development Administration followed soon after.[63] Other individuals and organizations contributed as well. In April 1968 singer Nancy Wilson announced that she would donate all of the proceeds of a one-week engagement at Harlem's Apollo Theater to the organization.[64] One month later, *Playboy* magazine donated $10,000 to the group. Various entertainers, including singer Lou Rawls, football star O. J. Simpson, and black golfer Curtis Sifford, participated in fund-raising golf tournaments.[65] When the BEU returned to Holly Springs after their initial visit in 1970, they brought with them, according to historian Robert Bennett, "more than thirty tons of food and clothing to disperse," along with $25,000 in donated money.[66] The success of these events, coupled with the personal contributions made by the many athletes involved in the Food First campaign, showed the widespread appeal of the BEU.

In part, that appeal stemmed from Jim Brown's emphasis on the theme of self-help in articulating the group's goals and aims. Pursuing a familiar strain in programs for black advancement, most notably the turn-of-the-century efforts of Booker T. Washington, Brown emphasized the capacity of black Americans to lift themselves up through a commitment to the American economy. As historian W. Fitzhugh Brundage observed, "Washington envisioned black advancement flowing from the individual labors of individual blacks who had embraced the gospel of work and wealth." For Washington, the American marketplace "was both rational and color-blind" and offered an avenue for black advancement in an era when commercial enterprise was fast becoming the new American religion.[67] Brown envisioned his program in similar ways. Even though he started the BEU during the heyday of President Lyndon Johnson's Great Society programs, Brown appeared to anticipate the changing political climate and the vagaries of public support for black uplift. As a result, he promoted a relatively conservative message, one based on opening economic access, not affirmative action or the institution of racial quotas. Nearly every time Brown discussed the group, he emphasized the importance of African Americans being able to pull themselves up into mainstream American society. In October 1966, in a guest columnist role for the *Los Angeles Sentinel*, he argued that the BEU would work for "the common welfare" of African Americans even as it emphasized "self help."[68] Only through economic growth within the black community could equality be achieved: "Black Power has got to mean green power—money. . . . The only answer is for us to help ourselves and to help one another."[69] As the group expanded and worked with a number of businesses, he repeated that theme, telling reporters in August 1969 that the BEU would enable African Americans "to become self-supporting and most important, determine their own destinies."[70] And he was clear that the BEU was a superior alternative to revolution: "In the BEU, we keep our manhood. We don't sell out. We're not going into guerilla warfare, and that's significant. We're going to compete and we're going to manage our own affairs."[71]

Brown's emphasis on manhood spoke to the fundamentally patriarchal nature of his work and many of his attitudes about gender and sexuality. Brown was accused of assault and battery against a woman in July 1965 but was found innocent in a jury trial. In the spring of 1968, authorities arrested Brown for assault with intent to murder after a female companion named Eva Marie Bohn-Chin was found bruised and battered on the ground fifteen feet below the balcony of Brown's apartment in Los Angeles. Neighbors had reported hearing scuffling and arguing, and Brown forcibly removed one police officer from his apartment when the authorities first arrived. Charges were dropped after Bohn-Chin refused to name Brown as her assailant.[72] Brown later averred that Bohn-Chin had fallen while trying to flee the arrival of police because of visa issues.[73] These disturbing events, which would be echoed in later years, were largely glossed over by both the black press and the mainstream media. Patriarchy's roots reached deep in American culture, and many civil rights activists supported a vision of American society that put the male breadwinner in an elevated position.[74] As a result, the media largely ignored these incidents as writers focused instead on Brown's economic uplift efforts.

While journalists largely shied away from Brown's violent behavior, his emphasis on self-help resonated with many inside and outside the world of sports. In the black press, many applauded Brown's efforts. Veteran columnist Doc Young was especially enthusiastic about the BEU, writing in January 1968 that Brown and the BEU might even eclipse Jackie Robinson's trailblazing efforts. Young believed "that Jim Brown, fellow athletes, and associates have struck out on a course which very well may be, in the long run, if not in the short dash, the most important move toward equality by any group in the history of Negroes in this country."[75] In another column, Young praised Brown for not dwelling on entrenched grievances—a familiar refrain for Washington and his supporters decades before. Young argued that "progress would come more quickly to Negroes if the race quit harping on the negatives of the past, canned its anger and bitterness (both real and the professional variety) and concentrated on thinking and acting more positively." He supported Brown's emphasis on "green power" as a practical response to the economic inequalities facing black Americans across the country.[76] White writers often supported these goals as well; for example, Gene Handsaker's November 1967 story in the *Atlanta Constitution* praised some of the multiple ways that Brown sought to help black Americans: "It's overseeing college kids . . . lending youngsters money to buy books or sneakers . . . instilling pride, teaching economics, getting dropouts hired, staging a golf tournament—and remaining friends with Negro leaders from Black Power advocate Rap Brown to moderate Whitney Young." On the whole, Handsaker supported Brown's emphasis on African Americans working together to develop businesses that would provide jobs and boost self-esteem in the black community.[77]

Nonetheless, Brown's emphasis on the marketplace rankled many critics. Just as Washington had faced significant criticism because of his embrace of capitalism and his unwillingness to broaden his push for social equality and political rights, some believed Brown put too much faith in the color-blindness of the American economy. In Toback's memoir, for example, he recounts an unnamed SNCC veteran approaching him after a meeting and criticizing Brown's emphasis on individual wealth. The man argued that the BEU would not "make a bit of difference" because it was still participating in the corrupt economic system, and he indicated that Brown was out of touch because he was "individual instead of collective."[78] Although Brown attempted to couch his self-help program in the language of Black Power, emphasizing community strength and pride, the tensions between radical black sloganeering and relatively conservative economic planning were difficult to keep under control.

Given these circumstances, the BEU especially appealed to a range of black athletes who had been leery of more controversial and radical Black Power ideology. Even as black athletes had garnered more public power and presence as a result of previous trailblazers and the impacts of the civil rights movement, many still refrained from fully engaging in controversial political stands. Tennis star Arthur Ashe, who had been hesitant to get involved in outspoken activism as his career took off in the mid-1960s, celebrated the message of the BEU at a speech in Baltimore in March 1968. The tennis superstar emphasized the need for a "do-it-yourself" approach to improving life for black Americans, citing Jackie Robinson, Bill Russell, and Jim Brown as positive examples of black athletes. And he specifically praised the BEU because of its "network of do it yourselfers."[79] Eric Allen Hall's biography of Arthur Ashe notes this speech as an especially important moment in Ashe's evolution as a civil rights activist. In celebrating Brown's focus on creating "producers instead of consumers, achievers instead of orators," Ashe spoke out on behalf of black athlete activism but from a politically moderate position.[80]

Other athletes followed suit. Kansas City Chiefs football player Curtis McClinton lauded the BEU's focus on "making consumers into producers and employees into employers, producing essential services that are meaningful within the general economy."[81] Similarly, Baltimore Colts tight end John Mackey emphasized the need for black Americans to get "into the mainstream of the American economy." When Brown launched his Food First initiative, he even told the assembled athletes that the apolitical nature of his efforts would shield them from any fan or media criticism; because the initiative would help poor blacks and whites, the athletes didn't "have to worry about accusations or recriminations over 'black power,' 'black militance,' 'black separatism,' 'black racism,' or any of the other bullshit that lightweights like to throw out."[82] Instead,

Jim Brown's conservative economic policies made him popular with President Richard Nixon, who gladly accepted Brown's endorsement for president in 1972. Photo courtesy of the Richard Nixon Presidential Library and Museum.

athletes could support an initiative that promised to help the needy and build up capitalist infrastructure so that community members could work to lift themselves out of poverty.

That emphasis on self-help fit well with the political atmosphere. With Richard Nixon's election in 1968, federal government and public support for the welfare state began to slip. Nixon's emphasis on black capitalism reflected this shift; instead of programs dedicated to providing better-quality housing and community-controlled economic cooperatives, his policies pushed for greater black ownership of small businesses in urban ghettos. The hope was that such changes would lead to "an increase in political power, improvements in the physical and social infrastructure of black communities, reduced dependence of African Americans on whites, and an increase in employment opportunities."[83] This retreat from Lyndon Johnson's Great Society was, of course, more amenable to fiscally conservative Republicans, and Brown's work with the BEU fit well with this focus. The Los Angeles branch of the BEU was one of four black-owned organizations to receive contracts in the summer of 1972 from the Office of Minority Business Enterprise (OMBE) of the Department of Commerce. When the director of the OMBE, John L. Jenkins, announced the awards, which included one hundred thousand dollars to the BEU, he indicated that all four groups were "fine organizations" who represented "President Nixon's expanded minority business enterprise program."[84] Other black business benefited from Nixon's administration, including Motown Industries and the Johnson Publishing Company.[85] Civil rights leader Jesse Jackson's founding of Operation PUSH (People United to Save Humanity), which focused on entrepreneurial uplift for black Americans, fit this political climate as well.[86]

But there was a danger to this dependence on Nixon and his advisors. As rank-and-file black Americans and leaders became frustrated with the select few who received political support, Brown and other black entrepreneurs found themselves on shakier ground. Before the 1972 presidential election, Brown announced his endorsement of Nixon, arguing that "this administration has emphasized black capitalism and economic development," in contrast to "Democratic rhetoric [that] hasn't proven anything."[87] Other prominent black entertainers and leaders joined him, including entertainer Sammy Davis Jr., singer James Brown, and Black Power advocate Floyd McKissick. Some leaders in the black community, however, believed that these celebrities had sold out their race. The black editors of the *Los Angeles Sentinel* argued that Nixon had caused division within the black community by creating a subset of African Americans—like Brown—who were beholden to him because they "feel threatened with loss of federal contracts or grants." As a result, black audiences began to promote boycotts of Brown's films.[88]

Although Nixon won reelection in the greatest landslide in modern electoral history, the political benefits for Brown and others dwindled soon after as a result of the scandals that plagued the Nixon administration and eventually led to his resignation in August 1974. By the fall of 1973, as investigations into corruption in the Nixon administration gained intensity, his minority business initiatives came under scrutiny as well. Investigations in the U.S. Senate discovered political pressure in the Nixon administration to funnel money intended for minority businesses solely to those aligned with the Republican Party. As a result, well-planned and well-meaning minority businesses suffered, and failing businesses aligned with the president received money that went to waste. Even within the administration, infighting occurred, as Jenkins resisted efforts to reward businesses along party lines. One sticking point for him was a request from Brown for $1.2 million, which Jenkins believed was intended to fund a film, not a legitimate minority business enterprise. In other cases, African Americans were exploited as fronts for white-run organizations to gain federal funding and support.[89]

As Nixon's power waned in the face of scandal, and as an economic recession continued to bog down the economy, black capitalism began to falter. Funding for federal programs stagnated; the momentum for "black is beautiful" campaigns diminished; and the BEU began to fade into oblivion, its significance and legacy unsettled.[90] By 1974 almost all coverage of the BEU vanished from mainstream and black media alike. Although offices in Cleveland and Kansas City would continue to engage in behind-the-scenes efforts to boost economic development, with the Kansas City office garnering national attention in the black press on occasion over the years, by and large the momentum of the BEU had stalled.[91]

They've Come a Long Way: Billie Jean King and the Virginia Slims Tour

If Brown's work with the BEU showcased the potentials and pitfalls of athlete economic activism for the broader community, Billie Jean King's struggles in establishing the Virginia Slims Tour showed the challenges of creating economic change within the world of sports. King's efforts to empower female tennis players stemmed from the reinvigorated women's rights movement of the 1960s and fit well in the broader framework of economic activism led by Brown and others. Starting in fall 1970, King and tennis impresario Gladys

Heldman defied the United States Lawn Tennis Association (USLTA) by creating a renegade professional circuit for women that offered increased pay and freer working conditions. Encountering resistance from tennis establishment leaders, male professionals, and even some cautious fellow women stars, King nonetheless persevered, in the process boosting media coverage of women's tennis—and prize payouts—considerably. Focusing her efforts on economic worth and market value, and initially distancing herself from the more radical "women's liberation" movement, King accomplished a great deal for women's sports—and eventually felt herself pulled headlong into broader challenges to cultural norms, despite her initial hesitance. Nonetheless, by emphasizing market worth and self-help, her efforts showcased the challenges of extending athletic economic activism into the broader community, especially with regard to achieving economic parity in the nation as a whole.

Billie Jean King's ascension to the most prominent activist voice in tennis came slowly. Born and raised in Long Beach, California, Billie Jean Moffitt took an early liking to sports. Frustrated by the limited options available to girls, she turned to tennis at the suggestion of a school friend and found herself hooked. Ascending through the ranks of amateurs in California, Moffitt became a national sensation as a teen, playing in major tournaments in the United States and abroad and earning special acclaim for winning the doubles championship at Wimbledon in 1961 as a seventeen-year-old. After marrying fellow UCLA student Larry King in 1965, her new husband encouraged her to focus on her tennis career full-time, despite the limited financial rewards for players and the societal pressures on women to enter motherhood. With her total attention on her tennis career, King began her climb up the rankings in women's tennis, claiming her first singles title at Wimbledon in 1966 and earning the number one ranking for the first time ever that same year.[92]

King's ascension in tennis came at a time of important transition for women in the United States. The 1950s had been marked by a time of conservative gender roles, with countless cultural forms espousing the ideal of the stay-at-home suburban mother in the climate of the Cold War—ideals that focused almost exclusively on white, middle- to upper-class families.[93] King came of age in this era, and her parents ascribed to these values wholeheartedly, including the decade's widespread homophobia.[94] However, the 1960s reinvigorated long-standing debates regarding women's place in society, especially following Friedan's publication of *The Feminine Mystique* in 1963. In her text Friedan interviewed suburban housewives about their dissatisfaction with their isolated suburban lives, an affliction she called "the problem that had no name." Many women, Friedan wrote, yearned to do more than stay at home, raise the children, and keep house, and she urged a transformation in American life that would open up more educational and professional opportunities for women. Friedan's text, and the empowerment experienced by women who participated in the civil rights movement and antiwar protests, spilled out into a broader social movement for women's equality that was usually called second-wave feminism. By 1966 the National Organization for Women (NOW) had formed, naming Friedan as its first president. Focused on legal, educational, and political equality, NOW promoted measures such as the Equal Rights Amendment to the Constitution, which would guarantee legal equality for men and women, and they campaigned tirelessly against barriers to women in the workforce and in classrooms.[95]

Although NOW marked an important development in the quest for women's rights, detractors quickly came to criticize the organization's limited reach. Minority women, working-class women, and gay women often felt underappreciated (and even outright rejected) by the predominantly middle-class leadership of NOW. They accused the group of focusing on middle- and upper-class topics while neglecting issues that mattered to those who were less fortunate. They also felt that NOW's focus on working within the system to enact legal and political change was too conservative, and they argued for more sweeping changes to American cultural norms and social practices. By 1967 numerous groups were holding "consciousness-raising" sessions in which women could discuss the obstacles they faced and find shared comfort and power in the experiences of their peers. Out of these sessions, women's liberation groups began calling for an end to patriarchy in all of its forms, criticizing advertising norms, fashion standards, dual standards on sexuality, and limited support for women in leadership positions. Even those sessions left some feeling alienated. By the mid-1970s, groups such as the Combahee River Collective expanded the terms of women's liberation, staking out a position for gay black women who felt neglected and abused by men and white women alike (even white feminists, who could still be blind to the privileges of race and class). By expanding beyond issues of legal and political access, women's liberation groups called for a reassessment of cultural ideas regarding men and women in total. For these women, society needed to reconceive notions of women's bodies, intellects, desires, and interests, to open up vast new possibilities for women's lives.[96]

Even as ideas of gender and sexuality were changing dramatically, the sport of tennis was also in transition. The year 1968 marked the beginning of the so-called open era of tennis. Previously, the four major Grand Slam championships (the Australian Open, the French Open, Wimbledon, and the U.S. Open) had prohibited professional players from participating, as had many other major tournaments, including the Davis Cup. Amateur players could be compensated with travel expenses (and top players were often given significant cash payments under the table to appear in tournaments), but outright payment and cash prizes for tournament victories were prohibited. By 1968, though, after activism by many of the top male players, the major tennis circuits capitulated and opened up to professional players.[97] King, like many others, celebrated the shift. At a press conference in April 1968 announcing her decision to turn professional, she said it was "a great deal for me, and a great deal for tennis. . . . I have always wanted to be a pro. In this country, if you're a pro, you're somebody. If you're an amateur, you're nobody."[98]

However, King's elation at turning professional was short-lived. Although she continued to succeed at the highest levels—capturing two singles titles and finishing as the runner-up four times out of the twelve Grand Slam finals between 1968 and 1970—she became increasingly frustrated by the disparity in prize money available to women players in comparison to men. The first Wimbledon championship to offer prize money, in 1968, awarded Rod Laver, the male champion, $4,800; King, the female winner, claimed only $1,800. Those disparities continued at ensuing tournaments. Increasingly frustrated, King and some of her peers reached their breaking point with the Pacific Southwest Open, scheduled for fall 1970. At that event, promoter Jack Kramer offered the female winner only $1,500 in comparison to the male prize of $12,500. Not only would the woman champion earn just 12 percent of the amount the male champion earned, but only women who reached the quarterfinals or higher would receive any money at all.[99] Aghast, King and a number of other players plotted a response to the inequity. Fellow player Ceci Martinez, a college graduate with a major in sociology, created a survey for fans at the September 1970 U.S. Open to gauge their interest in women's tennis. With responses from 94 women and 184 men of the 13,000 in attendance, the survey results indicated that men and women enjoyed watching women tennis players, and many thought they deserved pay equal to that of their male counterparts. More than half of both men and women said they would pay to watch an all-women's tournament. Given the lack of publicity for women's tennis, these were surprising results, and a story in the *New York Times* spread awareness of the growing frustration of the women players.[100]

Weeks later, when Kramer refused to listen to the women players' grievances about the prize money disparity, they took action. Gladys Heldman, the founder of *World Tennis* magazine and an avid fan of the sport, announced the creation of a new, eight-woman tournament in Houston to take place the same week as the Pacific Southwest Open. Heldman had staged three women-only tournaments in 1969, but the stakes were higher this time around, since she would be competing with an established USLTA event. Making use of her business connections, Heldman convinced Joe Cullman, an executive at Philip Morris, to be the lead sponsor for the new tournament. Seeing an opportunity to promote the Virginia Slims brand of cigarettes—one marketed to women—he signed up as a sponsor and boosted the prize money for the Houston tournament from five thousand dollars to seven thousand, five hundred dollars. The response from the established institutions was predictable: the USLTA demanded that the women not play in the tournament as professionals and threatened that they would lose their standing in the group. But the "Original Nine" women—King, Peaches Bartkowicz, Rosie Casals, Judy Tegart Dalton, Julie Heldman, Kerry Melville, Kristy Pigeon, Nancy Richey, and Val Zigenfuss—refused to be intimidated. They signed symbolic, one-week, one-dollar contracts with Heldman, posed for the cameras, and took their chances.[101] A defiant King announced, "We knew this would happen. This is no surprise and it is fine with us."[102]

Although King, who was making her first return to the court following a knee injury, lost in the first round of the tournament to Dalton, the tournament went off with nary a hitch and propelled the women forward.[103] Writing decades later about the event, King observed that the Houston tournament "would forever change tennis and open the doors for generations of women professional tennis players to make a living playing the sport they love."[104] Change came relatively quickly. By October 1970, Gladys Heldman and King announced the funding of five more tournaments sponsored by Virginia Slims and the addition of two more women players to the Original Nine: Mary Ann Curtis and Denise Carter.[105] In subsequent years, the tournament expanded even further. By 1971 there were nineteen tournaments on the Virginia Slims Tour, with purses totaling more than $300,000. One year later, there were twenty events and more than $500,000 in prize money. By 1973 these figures were up to twenty-two events and $775,000. The total prize money for men that year was $1,280,000.[106] In an effort to keep up with the rival tour, the USLTA increased its payouts for women players as well, setting off a bidding war of sorts between the two organizations that would eventually result in a merger.[107]

As the Virginia Slims Tour launched, King, along with Gladys Heldman and her daughter Julie, was quick to make it clear that they were not trying to take down the USLTA. King insisted the issue was simply related to prize money, about creating better opportunities for themselves. Julie Heldman agreed: "The women's pro group wants every woman player who works hard to make money to make some money. . . . If you can't even make enough money to cover expenses of traveling unless you make the quarterfinals, then it isn't fair." The women were "not fighting the U.S.L.T.A.," according to Gladys Heldman. They were "protecting themselves. You've heard of women's lib. This is women's lob."[108] The emphasis on economic equality and not broader social change fit well with Nixon's focus on capitalism as a tool for uplift and also resonated with King's outlook at the time. King wrote that her "first reaction" to the women's liberation movement "was pretty negative." She "thought it was a collection of fanatical, bra-burning women who hated men," and she "didn't have too much use for it."[109] Instead, she emphasized a message of economic fairness. Even as late as December 1972, when she was honored by *Sports Illustrated* as one of the two "Sportsmen of the Year," King explained her interest in seeing equal pay in sports:

> We do not want equal pay for equal work. . . . We only want what we're worth. For two years we've out-drawn the men at Forest Hills by whatever criteria they've used, but this year the men's money was 2½ times the women's, and at Wimbledon it is twice as much even though I know we draw at least as many people there as the men every year. We think our tournaments should be apart from the men's so we can be judged. If we don't draw as well, we shouldn't be paid as much.

She justified her quest for better pay, then, strictly on capitalist assessments of market value. This tactic fit right in with the "black capitalism" atmosphere promoted by Nixon and with dominant liberal capitalist ideals.[110]

The emphasis on economic equality, on earning fair pay for the work they put in and the entertainment they provided, seemed to resonate with many. Although David Gray of the *New York Times* called the chain of events "the women's rebellion in lawn tennis," he seemed to support the players, arguing that the USLTA "acted unjustly in provoking the dispute" by telling the players they couldn't accept money for participating in the Houston tournament.[111] Robert Wussler, CBS Sports vice president, agreed in 1974 that "the women's game has become just as popular with viewers as men's tennis" and that women therefore deserved the higher compensation they received.[112] President Nixon himself offered words of support to King. After winning the Thunderbird tennis tournament in Phoenix in the fall of 1971, King became the first woman to earn one hundred thousand dollars for tennis in a year. She talked to President Nixon over the phone, who said, "I just wanted to congratulate you on your successes. . . . I'm glad to see a fellow Californian do it."[113] In distancing themselves from the more radical aspects of women's liberation and focusing on the more prosaic goals of workplace equity, King and her peers carved out a relatively safe space from which to fight for better treatment.

Yet, just as Brown's efforts to fit in with black capitalism proved unwieldy and ultimately unsatisfactory, King and her peers ran into their own challenges in trying to base their "rebellion" on solely monetary terms. Although King had said from the outset that the Virginia Slims tournament was "not a women's Liberation Movement," there were undeniably larger social and cultural issues involved in the players' protests.[114] The Original Nine had to calculate their worth so that they could pitch appropriate prize money for their new circuit. That, according to historian Selena Roberts, pushed them outside of gender norms: "Making financial demands—even in polite discourse—was a brand-new experience for these women. To flout authority, to gamble on the public's interest, to slap a dollar figure on their talent, these were necessary steps if they wanted to achieve independence from the men and inclusion in the mainstream."[115] These steps required a rejection of mainstream norms regarding women's submissiveness and secondary status as breadwinners—the same norms that had allowed Brown's violence against women to go relatively unchallenged. Even as Casals noted that the fight was primarily about the players' "livelihood," their ability "to earn a living," she also acknowledged that there were larger issues at play regarding women athletes: "We wanted to play sports, be accepted," she said in later years.[116]

In addition, the decision to focus on monetary factors for the women's tour led to complications regarding marketing. The sponsorship of Virginia Slims came with financial benefits but also controversy. The company's slogan, "You've come a long way, baby," spoke to the gains made in women's rights, even as it seemed to demean women by infantilizing them. Meanwhile, growing awareness of the health risks associated with smoking cast a (literal and) metaphorical cloud over the company's promotion of women's sports.[117] But King largely waved off such concerns. According to a September 1971 story by writer Mark Asher, King thought "the Virginia Slims ad that says 'You've come a long way, baby'" was "great." "I love it," she said; "I think it's true."[118] Indeed, although she had come to appreciate more of the women's rights movement in later years, she still criticized *Ms.* magazine for turning down an ad deal from Virginia Slims "because it didn't like the slogan, 'You've Come a Long Way, Baby.'" She thought this was "ridiculous. . . . Why lose all that good dough that could be used to spread the word?"[119] For King, almost nothing trumped the financial benefits the company provided. While King did have her reservations about the dangers of promoting tobacco use to young people—"That hits home. . . . I don't drink or smoke," she once acknowledged—she argued that the financial benefits nonetheless outweighed the drawbacks. Turning down

Virginia Slims' sponsorship, she argued, would have scuttled the tour and, in effect, would have deprived "80 girls of a living."[120] But in sacrificing message for money, King failed to challenge the links between patriarchy and the capitalist economy—links that black feminist leaders like Angela Davis targeted in their analysis.[121]

The focus on monetary success also potentially conflicted with women's liberation ideals regarding the objectification of female bodies for male pleasure. One of the innovative features of the tour was its embrace of more adventurous outfits for the players. Designed by British fashion designer Ted Tinling, his ensembles brought color and style to the matches that was lacking from the USLTA tour.[122] But there was a fine line between style and substance. Many in women's liberation had campaigned against fashions that played up women's bodies in order to attract male interest, especially those that led to discomfort. Indeed, one key event that thrust women's liberation into mainstream awareness was the protest of the Miss America Pageant in 1968. Led by a group called the New York Radical Women, the protests were meant to call attention to the objectification of women, to their reduction to sexualized body parts. The best-known feature of the protests was the "Freedom Trash Can," where protesters encouraged women to deposit any and all "instruments of torture"—from girdles to eyelash curlers to sexist magazines like *Playboy*.[123] Some of these critics might well have objected to the idea that women tennis players should flaunt their bodies in order to attract more male fans. But King argued that sex appeal would only help women's tennis by bringing in additional viewers, noting that having "young" players "with excellent bodies, clothed in relatively little" would attract viewers, something that the players needed to "use to our advantage."[124] If women's liberation had concerns about the objectification of women's bodies, the ogling of the female form by male viewers, King seemingly didn't agree. With a paramount goal of financial empowerment, King was perfectly willing to sell sexual appeal on the women's tour.[125]

In the end the Virginia Slims Tour marked a triumphant economic moment for women's tennis and women's sports in general. The financial success of the tour validated women athletes' economic worth as performers and entertainers and forced the USLTA to come to terms with these athletes. By the spring of 1973 it became clear that the Virginia Slims Tour was not going to go away. In fact, the tour had grown in its first three years and had even added star player Margaret Court to its cohort. Feeling the pressure to end the feud, the USLTA and the Virginia Slims Tour began merger discussions. John Granville, the head of Virginia Slims, led the negotiations and terms were agreed upon on May 1.[126] The results were significant. The USLTA promised equal purses for men and women at the upcoming U.S. Open, a first for a major tournament.[127] Prize money continued to increase for women players. From 1971 to 1973, the minimum purse for tournaments grew from ten thousand dollars to thirty-five thousand dollars. After the merger, that figure had risen to fifty thousand dollars.[128] But merger between the two tours was not a complete victory for the women who led the charge for greater equity. One casualty was Gladys Heldman, the spirited tennis fan and entrepreneur who had led the charge for the separate tour in the fall of 1970 and who had served as director of the tour. The merger eliminated her position, retaining USLTA executives in positions of power.[129] While the financial payoff for the players was significant, power remained in the hands of the male-led tennis establishment—the same individuals who had fought so hard against women's professional endeavors.

One last event would crystallize the struggles for equity in tennis later that year: the so-called Battle of the Sexes match between King and retired male champion, self-proclaimed chauvinist, and hustler Bobby Riggs. Not only would the event thrust King and tennis into the public spotlight more prominently than ever before, but it also marked King's evolution from a focus on economics to one based on broader, gender-based concerns. The match was the brainchild of Riggs, a former Wimbledon champion. Fifty-five years old in 1973, and long out of the limelight, the attention-starved Riggs promoted a match with King to prove the superiority of the male sex. When King initially refused the offer, Riggs took on Margaret Court instead. The two met on May 13, 1973. Court, unprepared for the spectacle of the event, and for Riggs's soft lobs and drop shots, fell easily to Riggs in straight sets, an event the press dubbed the "Mother's Day Massacre." At that point, frustrated by Court's failure to play up to her potential and recognizing the potentially damaging public relations regarding women's athletics, King agreed to take on Riggs. The match was scheduled for prime time in the Houston Astrodome on September 20, with the winner to claim a one-hundred-thousand-dollar purse.[130]

The buildup to the match made clear that much was at stake symbolically. Riggs engaged in banter with the press, proclaiming himself a male chauvinist and declaring that women belonged only in the kitchen and in the bedroom. King parried his verbal shots, calling attention to her superior skills. At stake for many was nothing less than the legacy of second-wave feminism. Riggs represented the old order, in which male supremacy in professional spaces, including sports, went largely unchallenged. King represented the new order, in which women had increasing (if not entirely equal) access to educational, professional, and athletic opportunities. With press coverage reaching a fever pitch in the buildup to the event, the public latched on; about fifty million Americans, "more than one-quarter of the population" in the United States at the time, tuned in to watch the match.[131] Some of the celebrities in attendance were artist Salvador Dali; actors Robert Stack, Rod Steiger, and Janet Leigh; and, appropriately, Jim Brown.[132] Although Court had been thrown off by the spotlight, King delighted in it: "This was what I had always wanted: arenas, sequins, nighttime tennis." She loved the huge crowd and the knowledge of the huge numbers watching on television.[133] The result was convincing: although Riggs fared well early on, King breezed to a straight-sets victory, leaving Riggs looking sluggish and outclassed. King, and women in general, had emerged triumphant.[134]

And they had done so in many ways. As much as King had focused her rhetoric on financial equity first and foremost, it was undeniable that others attached broader cultural meanings to her campaigns in tennis. For women observing of and participating in societal transformations via second-wave feminism, King's exploits on and off the court spoke to new possibilities for women. As *Austin American Statesman* writer Eve Sharbutt noted in a year-ending column of 1973 dedicated to American women, King's triumph "bolstered liberated women everywhere."[135] Even King had come around in this regard. By October 1972, just less than a year before her match with Riggs, King was one of the guests of honor at a meeting of the Manhattan Women's Political Caucus. At the fund-raiser, held at a ritzy townhouse in Manhattan, King expressed her disbelief at her stardom: "I really don't believe that I'm here. . . . I mean, these are the women I read about. . . . I'm here to see them, but now they're here to see me." Guests included Gloria Steinem; Muriel Siebert, the first woman on the New York Stock Exchange; and Bella Abzug. King was presented with an honorary membership in the group. Although she had shied away from embracing women's liberation, she acknowledged that her husband, Larry, had started her "thinking about it in sports a long, long time ago."[136] Indeed, as historian Susan Cahn has noted, whether or not King or other female athletes acknowledged their connection to feminism, they "shared an agenda and an activist spirit" with the women's movement and the many issues it tackled at the time, including reproductive rights, women's health, antirape efforts, self-defense, and gay rights.[137]

Within the world of sports, King pressed forward—and beyond her initial focus on pay equity. Even as Jim Brown's work with the BEU was fading out due to Nixon's troubles and the growing backlash against anything affiliated with Black Power, King retained her position of power in the world of sports. The passage of Title IX of the Education Amendments of 1972, which guaranteed equal funding to male and female students in colleges and universities, ushered in transformative changes to women's sports in the United States.[138] Although King did not have a role in the creation of the legislation, she participated in

Billie Jean King's success and liberal feminism earned her an invitation to the White House in 1975. Here she pals around with First Lady Betty Ford. Photo courtesy of the Gerald R. Ford Presidential Library.

the efforts to support it. In 1974 the so-called Tower Amendment came up for debate. Sponsored by Texas senator John Tower, it "would have exempted revenue-producing sports from Title IX's coverage," effectively undermining the impact on women's sports programs. In response, King drafted a letter to select senators, asking them to drop the amendment because it would "allow intercollegiate athletics to continue to discriminate against women." She reminded senators of the huge disparities between men's and women's sports programs across the country. Eventually, the amendment was dropped during a House-Senate conference committee. In addition, King founded a sports magazine for women called *womenSports*, which debuted in June 1974. Perhaps her most lasting contribution was her role in helping to create the Women's Sports Foundation, a nonprofit advocacy group that was "dedicated to encouraging women of *all* ages and *all* skill levels to participate in sports activities for health, enjoyment, and development." The organization focused on changing negative attitudes about women's participation in sports and advocating for political changes that would ensure increased access and equity for women athletes. In later years it played important roles in defending Title IX and in promoting women's sports participation at all levels.[139] The early efforts for equal pay had emboldened King and, picking up on the spirit of women's activism, she had pushed beyond that limited stance into a broader spirit of reform.

Economic Uplift, Race, Gender, Sports, and American Life

The common threads of the BEU and the Virginia Slims Tour—and their divergent outcomes—speak to the tangled complexity of American life in an era of social change and pronounced activism. Both organizations sought to bring about economic equity through sports. Brown attempted to make use of athletes' clout and presence to foster entrepreneurship and uplift in the black community, while King sought to take advantage of women tennis players' popularity to bring about fairer wages and increased opportunities for women in her sport and, by extension, in sports and society in general. Gaining prominence during the era of Richard Nixon and his enthusiastic support of black capitalism and entrepreneurial uplift, both saw the benefits of playing up rhetoric that emphasized self-help, market worth, and an equal opportunity job market. Civil rights and Black Power, women's rights and women's liberation, all promoted societal change even as Brown and King navigated the changing political realities of American life as the 1960s ended and the 1970s began.

The reality, however, was that both groups faced new possibilities and new obstacles in this changing climate. For women, there was no denying that access to athletics and increased resources for women's education and women's sports improved tremendously in the wake of King's activism and as Title IX came to be put into practice. In 1972 fewer than 300,000 girls participated in high school sports; by 2011 that number had reached 3.2 million. The number of women college athletes showed a similar increase, going from fewer than 50,000 to a current total in excess of 200,000.[140] Events such as the 1999 International Federation of Association Football (FIFA) Women's World Cup, which featured a U.S. national team victory and placed the team on the front page of newspapers and magazines nationally, spoke to the increased prominence of female athletes and the legacy of Title IX's increased access to sport.[141] Nonetheless, as will be discussed in chapter 2 and in the conclusion to this book, serious inequities remain when it comes to access and financial empowerment for women athletes. Although King certainly achieved a great deal in her quest for women's pay equity in the world of sports, that victory was far from complete. The NCAA resisted Title IX as much as possible, delaying enforcement of the law so much that "not a single institution was fined for failure to comply" during the 1970s.[142] King's efforts to overcome the Tower Amendment were part of a broader pattern of resistance to the legislation, one that meant Title IX's impacts would be significantly delayed.[143] The disparity in pay for women and male athletes continues in a wide range of sports. Unequal pay for U.S. women's national team soccer players has been especially disheartening: despite their superiority on the global stage in comparison to the U.S. men's national team, women players earned less money and were subjected to poorer accommodations and travel expenses for decades until a 2022 agreement with the U.S. Soccer Federation finally granted them full parity with men.[144] Even tennis has proved surprisingly recalcitrant in terms of pay equity. Wimbledon did not feature equal pay for men's and women's champions until 2007. Meanwhile, in 2017 a major tennis promoter and top men's player Novak Djokovic both questioned the value of women's players, arguing that men outdrew women and that men deserved more pay as a result.[145]

One last aspect of King's life (and of a significant number of athletes, male and female alike) remained largely untouched by her efforts at pay equity: her closeted sexuality. For decades, women athletes had to negotiate the homophobic climate of the United States, especially in the years following the 1930s. While sports had offered a safe haven for many lesbian women—a place where they could feel comfortable and meet other like-minded women—heterosexual women athletes often went out of their way to emphasize their femininity in hairstyle and dress in order to "prove" their conformity to mainstream norms.[146] Growing up in the 1950s to very traditional Catholic parents, King distanced herself from homosexuality, even as she came to feel sexually attracted to other women. After her marriage to Larry, King had short-term affairs with women. Saying in later years that she "had very soft boundaries when it came to sexuality," she struggled to make sense of her conflicting feelings about sex.[147] In 1971 she began an affair with Marilyn Barnett, a hairdresser who became her traveling personal secretary. Although many close to the tour were likely aware of the relationship between the two, King remained in the closet, maintaining her marriage with Larry and publicly denying her homosexuality in a 1974 interview in *Playboy*.[148] No matter how prominent she had become, and no matter how much economic clout she had as the star of women's tennis, King was unwilling (and psychologically unable at this point) to embrace her true identity. While King would later become a champion for gay athletes, the cultural pressures of the early 1970s, and her own rhetorical choices in emphasizing market equity, restrained her considerably.[149] Once her affair did come out in the open—in 1981—King wrote that she "was damaged financially" as a result. A number of clothing sponsors pulled back from, or out of, endorsement deals, and she estimates that she "lost almost $1,500,000" because of dropped endorsements, coaching opportunities, and public appearances.[150] Clearly, the economic revolution envisioned by King was not entirely successful, a reflection of the deep ties between the capitalist market and heteronormative patriarchy.

Meanwhile, the BEU's grand aspirations fell short as well. The group faded as a national organization as the 1970s progressed, a victim in part of its close ties to the disgraced Nixon administration. Of course, black athletes retained a heightened interest and awareness in economic empowerment. But perhaps the most lasting legacies of black athlete interest in the market economy came not from business ownership for African Americans, as Brown and others had hoped, but rather from increased power as performers. Arguably, the largest and most lasting shift to come out of this era in sports economics came in the empowerment of player unions in professional sports. And both Brown and King played pioneering roles in both, one final way that their stories overlapped.

Brown had made early and important forays into athlete empowerment through his own negotiating ploys and his support for unionization efforts and players who held out. As mentioned previously, in August 1967 Brown supported five black players for the Cleveland Browns who held out for better contracts and the right to negotiate their deals as a group. Despite public backlash, Brown criticized owner Art Modell's dismissive statements regarding the players' rights.[151] Two months later, Brown wrote a letter on BEU stationery to support the formation of a players' union in the NFL.[152] King, too, had done more than organize the Virginia Slims Tour. She also lobbied for and helped create the Women's Tennis Association (WTA), a union to represent professional women's tennis players, in 1973.[153] Both King and Brown saw the potential for athletes to band together and fight for economic empowerment. Doing so would increase their pay as entertainers and performers. Indeed, the greatest advances for athletes in this regard came in the sport of baseball. There, the efforts of Marvin Miller, elected as executive director of the Major League Baseball Players Association (MLBPA) in 1966, and Curt Flood, the disgruntled St. Louis Cardinals outfielder who filed suit against the league in 1970 in an effort to negotiate with any team, helped to empower the players' union and eventually usher in the era of free agency. The resulting increases in players' rights and salaries were immense.[154] However, as will be discussed in the conclusion, there were real limits to the gains made—limits that emphasized individual uplift over the community and failed to undress systemic inequities built into the U.S. capitalist economy.

In many ways the BEU's emphasis on self-help, in its attempts to straddle the divides of Black Power and black capitalism, foretold these outcomes. Although Brown consistently emphasized the group's efforts to lift up the black community through economic empowerment, his focus on self-help and entrepreneurship did little to correct the wealth gap that existed in the country or to create a sustainable economic foundation for the black community. Discovering shortages of capital in comparison to that of white investors and entrepreneurs, most aspiring black business owners faced a steep uphill climb.[155] Although Brown promoted "green power" as a way to raise up the whole black community, his emphasis on black entrepreneurship fit in well with a capitalist marketplace in which an exceptional few profited while the majority saw little improvement in their finances and wealth. Even for those who did manage to earn more—such as King and her female cohort, and Flood and subsequent free agents—the power structure remained largely the same, with white men continuing to dominate the sports world and to hold the purse strings. In that way, the increasing salaries for black professional athletes and women tennis players showcased self-help's limitations as a tool for community uplift.

* * *

The activist spirit of the 1960s and 1970s was not isolated to the economic realm, of course. Numerous athletes, especially women, sought to push through cultural limitations that had historically restricted access to sports participation. In the next chapter, we will explore how women's activism in the sport of running, especially distance running, helped open new doors in the world of sports and beyond.

CHAPTER 2

GETTING INTO THE RACE

Women Runners / Women's Rights

In the summer of 2019, the U.S. women's national soccer team traveled to France to participate in the eighth edition of the FIFA Women's World Cup tournament. The competition was intense; apart from one easy victory over Thailand, the United States faced formidable opposition, with narrow, one-goal victories over France, Spain, and England. Off the field, controversy swirled, as U.S. star midfielder Megan Rapinoe openly criticized U.S. president Donald Trump, indicating she would not visit the White House if invited. On the night of the final, the fifth time the team had made it to the championship game, the U.S. women squared off against the Netherlands. After ninety hard-fought minutes, the United States emerged triumphant, claiming a 2–0 victory. Stars Rose Lavelle, Alex Morgan, Christen Press, and Rapinoe led the team to America's fourth World Cup title, completing the latest chapter in U.S. women's excellence on the global soccer stage.[1]

The success of these remarkable women owes much to traditional athletic values of hard work, resilience, camaraderie, and competitive spirt. But it also marked the continuing impact of the legislation usually referred to as Title IX, passed by the U.S. Congress in 1972. Part of a series of amendments to the Higher Education Act, Title IX reads: "No person in the United States shall, on the basis of sex, be excluded from participation in, be denied the benefits of, or be subjected to discrimination under any education program or activity receiving Federal financial assistance."[2] Primarily intended to eliminate unequal funding for male and female students in medical schools, law schools, and academic programs, the act has become better known for its effects on sports. The mandate to prevent discrimination in *any activity* receiving federal assistance in education led to huge shifts in the allocation of resources for women's athletics. Although funding for men's and women's sports in high school and college remains unequal, the gap has closed significantly, and there has been a transformation in women's sports in the last forty years. Increased participation of girls and women in high school and collegiate sports, better facilities and training programs for female athletes, and, yes, U.S. dominance in soccer on the global stage—all can be, and have been, traced to this monumental piece of legislation.[3]

But the focus on Title IX, important as it was, obscures the deeper roots—and specifically the grass roots—of women's increasing presence in the world of sports. Although this legislation and the efforts of high-profile figures like Billie Jean King and her victory in the Battle of the Sexes tennis match against Bobby Riggs in 1973 mattered a great deal, they both benefited from the groundwork laid before them.[4] A number of individuals helped pave the way for Title IX and everything that came after, most notably several pioneering African American women track stars of the 1940s, 1950s, and 1960s, and two women marathon runners of the late 1960s: Bobbi Gibb and Kathrine Switzer. African American women such as Alice Coachman, Wilma Rudolph, and Wyomia Tyus broadened public support for women athletes through their success in Cold War–era competitions. Meanwhile, by ignoring race rules that barred women from running the Boston Marathon, Gibb in 1966 and 1967 and Switzer in 1967 called attention to women's desires for sports participation and challenged long-held ideas about women's athletic capabilities. Despite their modest goals in entering the race, Gibb and Switzer played a pivotal role in a slow transformation of public attitudes regarding women in sport. Mainstream media coverage of these women, and simultaneous changes in how women's magazines engaged with sports and fitness, reveals how these runners bridged multiple gaps in the 1960s and 1970s.

Politically, distance runners like Gibb and Switzer linked the fight for legal equality that was the hallmark of groups such as the National Organization for Women with the broader cultural critiques of women's liberation. In addition, the increasing prominence of distance running for women provided a way to navigate gender norms regarding competition and body type while still pursuing sport and fitness. The revolution remained unfinished: entrenched gender norms and a moderate feminist approach often left men in positions of power. But the public discourse about these women, and contemporaneous changes regarding Title IX and women's sports organizations, gradually transformed cultural attitudes about women athletes, long before Title IX's effects would be fully realized in American culture. By the late 1970s the growing acceptance of women's distance running revealed that women's participation in sports was no longer limited to "ladylike" pursuits for the wealthy and vigorous activities for the working class; the physically active woman had arrived in American mainstream culture. Global soccer dominance would not be far behind.

Women's Sports, Women's Activism: Complicated Cultural Terrain

Historically, women's access to sports had been severely limited by dominant gender norms, entrenched medical beliefs, and concerns relating to female sexuality. As organized sports emerged in the United States in the decades after the Civil War, influential Americans viewed athletics as the province of men, and they circulated cultural norms that cautioned women against participating. Although calisthenics might be acceptable for women to foster health and to attract a desirable male suitor, more competitive sports and more exhausting activities were to be avoided.[5] Many feared that participating in sports would make women too masculine in temperament and physique and would damage their reproductive health.[6] These concerns were more likely to be expressed among Victorian elites, whereas lower-class women could not afford to fetishize "physical frailty."[7] Concerns about women's role in sports continued in ensuing decades. Women athletes in the 1920s and 1930s faced accusations of being "molls"—oversexed, promiscuous women undeserving of respect. As anxieties about homosexuality heightened in the 1940s and 1950s, critics tarred women athletes as "mannish" lesbians. Both of these critiques, which circulated widely in mainstream American culture, depicted athletic women as unnatural and unfeminine. Although women's participation in some "country club" sports such as golf and tennis earned grudging acceptance, most Americans rejected their involvement in competitive sports.[8] And schools did little to inculcate athleticism in their young charges: even women physical educators worried that competition-focused sports, instead of those centered on leisure, would leave out less-gifted athletes, encourage illicit recruiting in college sports, and undermine women's role as community-centered caretakers.[9]

Given these circumstances, running could potentially have found a niche among women, as it did not involve the physical contact of baseball, basketball, and football. But it did not: male critics and female physical educators alike felt that running was too competitive for women. As the Olympics opened up opportunities for women in track and field in the 1920s, many elites in the United

States protested. Prominent leaders in the Women's Division of the National Amateur Athletic Federation advocated against women's track and field events, and many colleges deemphasized or eliminated competitive track and field programs as a result. Instead, minority and working-class women dominated the sport.[10] In 1928, for example, Chicago native Betty Robinson, a product of the city's playground programs for working-class residents, claimed the first-ever Olympic gold medal in the women's 100-meter dash.[11] The women's track team from Tuskegee Institute, the all-black school founded in the 1880s by Booker T. Washington, dominated U.S. amateur competition in the 1930s and 1940s.[12] And working-class Texan Mildred "Babe" Didrikson emerged as one of the most successful female athletes in American history in the 1930s. Playing basketball and track in an industrial league for the Employers Casualty Insurance Company of Dallas, Didrikson went on to become the star of the U.S. women's Olympic team in 1932, claiming gold in the javelin and the 80-meter hurdles and silver in the high jump.[13]

The 1928 Olympics—and reactions to one of its events—proved a key moment in shaping popular attitudes toward distance running. When newspaper reporters indicated that half of the runners in the women's 800-meter race failed to finish, and that the other half collapsed soon after crossing the line, critics howled. Although exaggerated and inaccurate, these media reports roused opposition to the sport, and the Olympics removed the race for women until 1960.[14] The concerns about women's capacity to engage in distance running were ironic, given that two of the most celebrated women celebrities of the 1920s earned notoriety for their participation in endurance activities: Gertrude Ederle, who swam the English Channel, and Amelia Earhart, who flew solo across the Atlantic Ocean.[15] Nonetheless, concerns over the effects of distance running on women's supposedly frail bodies and reproductive systems limited women's access to distance running in the United States and abroad. Indeed, even as late as the mid-1960s, Amateur Athletic Union (AAU) rules stipulated that women could run races no longer than 1.5 miles.[16]

The Cold War—in which American national leaders tried to best the Soviet Union in all aspects of life—provided an opening for women to participate in both the Olympics and in track and field.[17] African American women played an especially important role in this regard. Alice Coachman's gold medal win in 1948—the first gold claimed by an African American woman—was an important milestone and one that spoke to the legacy of the Tuskegee Institute's track team.[18] But it was the starring role of Wilma Rudolph in the 1960 Olympics that many credit with transforming American attitudes. Many Americans, black and white, celebrated Rudolph's Olympic triumphs in 1960—when she earned gold medals in the 100-meter and 200-meter races and the 4 x 100-meter relay. The federal government and mainstream media trumpeted this success. As Rita Liberti and Maureen Smith argue, "Images and stories of successful African American athletes, including Rudolph, provided the US mainstream media and government with a narrative of opportunity contrasting with those that underscored racial inequality, oppression, and brutality."[19] In this way the Cold War helped validate some aspects of women's athletics and opened up new opportunities for black Americans to earn public acclaim.[20] But it also reflected the ongoing dominance of persistent gender norms. Part of Rudolph's wide-ranging appeal, many argue, had to do with her ability to fit into dominant norms of femininity, as many in the media celebrated her long legs and slender physique along with her successful performances. "By introducing the possibility of a feminine American woman athlete," historian Cat Ariail writes, "Rudolph opened a space for white women to earn acclamation as athletes." Rudolph's accomplishments, and those of other black track stars, led to increasing opportunities for white women in track, and eventually, as Ariail argues, to more white women running marathons.[21]

Altogether, the combination of black women's success and Cold War pressures amplified support for women's athletics in the United States. By the

Wilma Rudolph, shown here getting an award from the Fraternal Order of Eagles in 1961, played a pivotal role in making women runners more popular in mainstream culture. Photo courtesy of the Fraternal Order of Eagles Photo Archive.

1960s educators held "a series of National Institutes on Girls' Sport" to instruct coaches, teachers, and administrators in best policies and practices for implementing competitive girls' sports programs.[22] However, although women could participate in sprints at the Olympics and other major track and field events, distance running remained off-limits. Not even President Kennedy's Cold War–inspired calls for improved physical fitness, and the associated invigoration of physical fitness programs across the country, could fully break through concerns about women's capacities to engage in arduous distance running.[23]

Social changes outside the realm of sports in the 1960s, though, spurred debates about these outdated notions. As noted in chapter 1, although popular media and politicians in the 1950s espoused conservative gender roles, the 1960s saw the emergence of second-wave feminism, which challenged many conservative ideas about women's place in society. Two dominant strains shaped women's activism in this era. *Liberal feminism*, embodied by NOW and its first president, Betty Friedan, focused on legal, educational, and political equality by working within existing systems of law and politics. By focusing on increasing access to existing institutions, these women sought to improve women's plight by granting them the same legal, economic, and political privileges enjoyed by men. Meanwhile, *radical feminism*, manifested in the many groups affiliated with women's liberation, expanded beyond issues of legal and political access, calling for an all-encompassing reassessment of legal, political, social, and cultural ideas pertaining to men and women. For these radical feminists, a thorough revamping of society was needed in order to fully liberate women's bodies, intellects, desires, and interests. Believing that existing institutions would never fully be equitable for women because of their roots in a patriarchal world, these women envisioned a more thorough reformation of American culture.[24]

However, no matter their goals, neither strain of feminists thought much about athletics—and athletes, by and large, refrained from joining in feminist activism. Leading feminists in the 1960s and early 1970s, most scholars agree, paid little attention to sports.[25] Few had personal experience with competitive athletic endeavors and thus felt little personal investment in them.[26] Others saw sports as a masculine world driven by competition instead of collectivism, one that offered little value to women.[27] At the same time, female athletes and athletics administrators had their own misgivings about the burgeoning feminist movement. Since many athletes did not have direct experience with feminist activism and saw little recognition of sports and physical education in early activist campaigns, they often hesitated to get involved.[28] Women coaches and administrators often avoided outright links to feminism, fearing that such associations would weaken their already tenuous positions within their institutions. This context led to many female athletes and coaches engaging in "an apologetic rhetoric, striving to emphasize their femininity in order to maintain social acceptability."[29] Indeed, Billie Jean King's reticence to identify herself as a part of women's liberation, even as she participated in the Battle of the Sexes, made clear this gap between athletes and activists.[30] Although historian Allen Guttmann argues that King was a key figure in bringing these two worlds together through her activism in terms of pay, decades later many women athletes continued to avoid an identity as a feminist.[31]

The Boston Breakthrough: Gibb and Switzer Go the Distance

Women distance runners, then, were caught in the crosscurrents of multiple forces: growing social movements that argued for women's increased opportunities, misgivings about the competitive and supposedly masculine nature of sports, and conventional medical and social norms that dismissed women's athletic possibilities. In these circumstances, two American women, Bobbi Gibb and Kathrine Switzer, entered the national consciousness when they competed in, and completed, the Boston Marathon.

Gibb made her mark first. Growing up in the Boston suburbs, she enjoyed running as a pastime, not as a competitive pursuit. When she reached college, her boyfriend at the time, a cross-country runner for Tufts University, encouraged her to take up distance running, and she began to run the 8-mile commute from home to school. Watching the Boston Marathon for the first time in 1964, at the age of twenty-one, she became intrigued. By 1966 she attempted to enroll in the race, only to be rejected on the basis of her sex. "I was stunned," Gibb later said, but added, "All the more reason to run."[32] Married by then and living in San Diego, Gibb came home for the race despite the rejected application and, avoiding detection by wearing a blue hooded sweatshirt that covered her hair, slipped onto the course with the other runners. Completing the race in a time of roughly 3:21:00, Gibb outpaced more than half of the field, definitively proving that women could complete a marathon.[33]

Gibb's feat earned local and national media attention, and the initial responses to her 1966 run were largely positive. In *Sports Illustrated*'s coverage of the annual race, writer Gwilym Brown noted that Gibb's performance "should do much to phase out the old-fashioned notion that a female is too frail for distance running." The story made clear that Gibb prepared arduously for the race, noting that she "trains in the hills and on the golf courses around town, two hours a day, seven days a week, with an occasional five-hour tour thrown into the schedule to keep her from getting lazy."[34] This story and others like it praised

Gibb's efforts. A United Press International (UPI) photograph showed Gibb after the race, smiling and resting in a chair with a blanket over her shoulders. The accompanying caption indicated that she "outran 300 male rivals" at the Boston Marathon and that she was "the first woman ever to finish the 70-year-old-marathon and possibly the first to ever participate."[35] *Time* magazine praised her impressive time in its coverage, dubbing her "Queen of the Marathon."[36]

The following year, 1967, Gibb returned to the race and followed the same routine—slipping onto the course without a number. This time, though, she was joined by a second woman: Kathrine Switzer. And it was Switzer's race experiences that would draw even more attention to women's distance running and the challenges they faced. Switzer, a junior from Syracuse University, grew up in Virginia and had earned notoriety during her two years at Lynchburg College when she and another woman ran on the otherwise all-male track team. After transferring to Syracuse, Switzer began to work out with the men's track team (there was no women's team), becoming friendly with an older team manager named Arnie Briggs. Briggs had run the Boston Marathon in the past and waxed poetic about the race. Inspired by Gibb's run the previous year, Switzer began to train for the race with Briggs, and two other Syracuse men—including Switzer's boyfriend, hammer thrower Tom Miller—decided to join them. Registering as "K. V. Switzer," she received a race bib and number from race officials, who were unaware of her sex. The day of the race, she and her racing partners started the marathon. Although several of her fellow runners noticed her gender, they expressed their enthusiasm and support.[37]

However, when race officials caught wind of her presence in the marathon, their reaction, and the ensuing publicity it generated, thrust women's running and broader issues of women's participation in sports into public consciousness. With many runners wearing bulky sweatshirts and hats to combat the cold, rainy weather, Switzer's presence initially went unnoticed. However, a writer on the press bus spotted Switzer, reportedly yelling, "No. 261 is a broad!"[38] Race director Will Cloney and longtime race official Jock Semple sprang into action.[39] The aged Semple, who had been involved in managing the race for decades, ran onto the course and attempted to remove Switzer's number. When he lunged for the bewildered Switzer, shouting, "Get the hell out of my race and give me that number," the bulky Miller body-checked Semple off the course, allowing Switzer to continue her run.[40] A photographer captured the events in a three-shot photo sequence that circulated in newspapers across the country. The first showed Switzer turning back to see the grimacing Semple close on her heels as he eluded the grasp of Briggs. The second depicted the moment when Miller launched himself into Semple as the official grabbed her. The third showed Semple stumbling off the course as Switzer pressed on with her run. Although Switzer finished nearly an hour behind Gibb, with a time of approximately 4:30:00, the dramatic confrontation brought her experiences—and the issue of women distance runners in general—into the spotlight.[41]

Much of the initial coverage of Switzer and Gibb depicted the women in positive ways. *Sports Illustrated*, for example, called attention to the performances of Gibb and Switzer in its coverage, praising the two for finishing the grueling race.[42] An Associated Press (AP) story, calling Gibb a "freckle-faced, 23-year-old redhead," indicated that she "was greeted with a roar of approval by the sleet-soaked crowd" when she crossed the finish line.[43] Three days after the race, the *New York Times* followed up Switzer's race experience with a feature story, and the article indicated that "her presence in a men's race drew cheers from the crowd" and "delighted the male runners."[44] In the *Boston Globe*, writer Bud Collins agreed that most in attendance seemed to support women running, including Walter Bingham, a *Sports Illustrated* editor, who praised Gibb's performance.[45] The recollections of Gibb and Switzer support these accounts of positive reception. According to Switzer, when Semple appeared again later in the race, yelling at her to get off the course, the men running around her "gave him the finger and shouted obscenities back at him." Fans, too, tended to shout encouraging words to her, including some women who yelled, "'C'mon, honey, do it for *all* of us!'"[46] Gibb, similarly, indicated that when her fellow runners discovered her identity, most were supportive, with one commenting, "It's a free road."[47]

But as Semple's actions demonstrated quite vividly, not everyone responded positively. A number of publications reported on the women's runs in ways that were both demeaning and outright hostile. Some viewed women's presence in races like the Boston Marathon as an invasion of a sacred male space. Cloney, for example, said he was "terribly disappointed when American girls force their way into something where they're neither eligible nor wanted."[48] A story in *Newsweek* about the 1967 marathon focused on an aging male runner and mentioned only in passing that two "girls" had "sneaked into the pack" and run the race that year as well.[49] One writer, according to a later recollection from Switzer, complained that she and Gibb "were posing an 'unnecessary problem' for the race organization."[50] A story about the race in the *Atlanta Constitution* featured the headline "Male Refuge Shattered."[51] Even some who admired the effort made by the runners still felt that these women were pushing into spaces where they didn't belong. After Gibb's first race, Michael Spring of Yonkers, New York, a winner of the marathon in 1904, wrote to *Sports Illustrated* to comment on her feat. Although impressed by Gibb's accomplishment, he also cautioned her against doing it again, citing his own sense of the race as a kind of "physical torture": "My congratulations to a game girl in a man's game, and it is my sincere hope that she does not attempt it again." Clearly, for Spring, a woman running the marathon seemed too dangerous, too extreme.[52] In this way, Spring rehashed traditional concerns about women's athletic limitations and health concerns.

Similarly, although some in the media mocked Semple for his attempts to grab Switzer's race number—the image of him being knocked off the course by Switzer's boyfriend didn't help — some also defended him. A 1968 story about Semple in *Sports Illustrated* described how Switzer's "deception" to run in the race (she skipped a pre-race physical by having a doctor sign off that "K. Switzer" was fit to run and had a male friend pick up her race forms) "outraged" Semple. Legendary Boston Celtics coach Red Auerbach, whose players received physical therapy from Semple, defended him as well: "The Boston Marathon is a big part of that man's life. He didn't want a mockery made of something he believes so strongly in." In that same story, writer Myron Cope linked women's attempts to run the race to other "jokers and oddballs," including "college freshmen" subjected to "fraternity hazing; fat men who look as though they might have trouble climbing a flight of steps; [and] saloon braggarts trying to win a bet."[53] For these commentators, defending the males-only space of the marathon was appropriate, a retention of a tradition that celebrated only male athletic performance. Indeed, that attitude was so prevalent that Switzer never considered suing Semple for his attempts to grab her on the course, believing that doing so "would have made everyone in the running community and in Boston angry and set women's running back forever."[54]

However, overtly hostile responses were relatively rare. A more common and especially troubling trend surfaced in the ways that male writers and runners sexualized Gibb and Switzer. The *Sports Illustrated* story about Gibb's first run noted that the "last barrier" to full participation in the Boston Marathon fell with Gibb's performance in the race, but the article emphasized her femininity and physique in ways they would never have dreamed for a male. In different moments, the story described Gibb as a "shapely blond housewife" and "a tidy-looking and pretty 23-year-old blonde."[55] Publications the following year picked up on that trend in describing Gibb and Switzer. In the *Globe*, stories referred to Gibb as "beautiful" and referred to her and Switzer by their first names, while using last names for male race organizers. One runner was mesmerized by Gibb's legs and kept thinking, he told the *Globe*, that he ought to ask her out to dinner.[56] The AP story about the race concluded by noting that one male runner ran behind Switzer for eight miles because he was "enchanted . . . by her flowing stride and those lovely, lovely legs."[57] Similarly, the *New York*

Times described Switzer's appearance in positive terms, noting that she was "a former beauty contestant" with "soft brown hair and [a] winsome look," and featured a glamorous head shot along with her race picture.[58] In focusing on the runners' appearance, these publications diminished their athletic accomplishments and made them the objects of male desire. These trends validated the long-standing concerns of some opponents of women's athletics, who feared that women's participation in sports would invite unwelcome and dangerous attention from men.

Comments by Cloney in the days following the race highlighted just how demeaning this language could be. In defending the race against the inclusion of women, and in criticizing Switzer's acquisition of a race number, Cloney observed, "We have no place in the marathon for any unauthorized person, even a man. If that girl were my daughter, I would spank her." The follow-up from the unnamed *New York Times* writer was even worse: "Not if you gazed into those big, brown eyes, you wouldn't."[59] The infantilization (and sexualization) of Switzer by Cloney is, of course, appalling, as is the *Times* writer's unwillingness to outright reject the idea. Apparently, Switzer's good looks would make the writer think twice about spanking her—but not the fundamentally patriarchal and demeaning nature of the idea itself. Switzer's mother was outraged by the "spank" comment from Cloney, and he later tried to backtrack from his comments, but his initial response speaks to how women athletes, and women in general, were denied equal status with men in nearly every aspect of life.[60] Even the *Times*'s headline about the 1967 race showed these problematic reactions to women's participation: "2 Girls in Marathon Don't Have Lovely Leg to Stand On," the newspaper declared.[61]

Despite these negative responses, the two runners both used the attention generated by the race to call for change. However, the tenor of their comments suggested varying degrees of an activist spirit. In the wake of her first run, Gibb kept her comments largely focused on women's fitness potential. She told *Sports Illustrated* that she was "just in it for the fun . . . but I want to make people see something different that would shake them up a little bit, maybe change some traditional attitudes." Later in the same story, she added, "It's silly that there aren't more distance races for women. . . . They may not be as fast as men, but I think it's been proved many times that they have just as much endurance and stamina."[62] Gibb observed in later years that she "hadn't intended to make a feminist statement" by running the marathon. For her, she saw the race as a challenge to unlock her full "potential."[63] After her 1967 race, she again distanced herself from overt activism, instead emphasizing the athletic significance of her feat: Gibb, who divorced her husband during the previous year, proved wrong the "skeptics" who did not believe that she had run the race as fast as she did the previous year. Gibb indicated that she was not trying to cause trouble: "I'm kind of shy by nature and I don't want to cause a furor."[64] In this way, Gibb avoided overt activism and emphasized an individualistic, sports-focused approach.

While Gibb kept her comments limited to the realm of running, Switzer went slightly further in her comments after the race. Interviewed after crossing the finish line, she explained to the assembled reporters that "women deserve to run too. Equal rights and all that, you know."[65] When talking with the *New York Times* later that week, she reemphasized that point: "A lot of people said women couldn't run a marathon. . . . But I'm glad I ran—you know, equal rights and all that kind of business."[66] Although hardly a ringing endorsement of NOW or any specific activist issue, Switzer did indicate some connection to women's broader concerns. For her, running the marathon afforded an opportunity to call attention to women's lack of access to all realms of society in the form of "equal rights." That resonated with NOW's affirmation in their founding "Statement of Purpose," which affirmed: "NOW is dedicated to the proposition that women, first and foremost, are human beings, who, like all other people in our society, must have the chance to develop their fullest human potential." Although NOW made no mention of sports, fitness, or athletics in their founding statement, a sign of their lack of connection with the sporting world, Switzer implicitly extended their hopes for professional, legal, and educational access to athletics.[67] As scholars Oren Renick and Lea Robin Velez note, Switzer's efforts to acquire an official race bib spoke to her desire to challenge the "unjust system" in a more direct manner than Gibb.[68]

Although Switzer had those larger goals in mind, much of the positive commentary in the media centered on Gibb's more limited, sports-focused perspective. In particular, some media commentators took the race as an opportunity to ridicule traditional thinking about women's abilities as distance runners. Gibb's run in 1966, according to *Sports Illustrated*, "should do much to phase out the old-fashioned notion that a female is too frail for distance running." When Cloney told the publication that Gibb had not run the race, since she did not have an official race number, the story called him "a staid New Englander to the last codfish."[69] In the *Globe*, Bud Collins's defense of the women runners stayed largely focused on the question of access to this specific event: "It is everybody's race, isn't it, so why shouldn't they be received politely?" Although noting that Cloney and Semple showed "devotion" to the race over the years, Collins wrote of them, "Like many people entrusted with maintaining a tradition, and preoccupied by it, they have forgotten what year this is." Women "got the right to vote in 1920," he pointed out, "and they should get the right to run in 1968."[70] Tradition—when it came to running—seemed obsolete.

Would that same perspective extend outside of sports? Many women certainly hoped so. Although Gibb acknowledged that she didn't intend to make "a feminist statement," in later years she nonetheless observed that her response to being denied a race number was: "They thought the world was flat, so I was going to teach them it's round."[71] In this way she envisioned her run as a way to change attitudes about women's capabilities. As Switzer ran the marathon and heard women cheering her on, she realized that many of the women watching "believed all those myths about women's fragility and limitation." She had an epiphany that she needed to spread the word about running to other women, to show them that they could do it.[72] Running could bolster women's self-confidence and could inspire them to take on new challenges. One runner who embodied this link between the sport and larger issues of economic and political access was Jacqueline Hansen, who won the Boston Marathon in 1973 and broke the 2:40 mark at a marathon in Eugene, Oregon, that same year. When she discovered that there was no women's marathon in the Olympics, she was stunned. In 1977 Hansen attended a NOW conference in Houston, Texas, and "realized how many bigger issues there were for women in the world—like simply the right to equal pay and jobs." But she also realized that making breakthroughs in the world of running could lead to changes elsewhere.[73]

In this way, Gibb, Switzer, and the numerous runners who followed in their footsteps, tended more toward the focus on legal, economic, and social equality espoused by NOW than toward the more radical cultural assault suggested by women's liberation. Scholars of women's activism in the realm of athletics have noted this as a broader pattern. NOW's approach, often defined as liberal feminism, has been popular with supporters of athletics because of its emphasis on individual opportunity and uplift. For feminists who "embraced a fundamental individualism" seeking "the same inalienable rights" of men, access to existing athletic opportunities was a sufficient goal.[74] Commentators had long posited American sports as a model for meritocracy, an arena where individual worth and effort, not race, class, gender, or other markers of identity, determined one's success.[75] However, radical or socialist feminists argued for a cultural revolution and thus did not see an embrace of existing athletic practices and institutions as useful.[76] For them, the structure of sports—like the structure of society as a whole—needed reimagining in order to improve conditions for women. Media scholar Pamela J. Creedon refers to these two perspectives as either "*reform*," which means making changes to the existing systems to accommodate women, or "*transform*," which entails changing "the fundamental values on which the system is based."[77]

For most women runners, liberal feminism's emphasis on reform was as far as they were willing to venture. In the wake of the Switzer incident, many activists in the world of running used language that focused on issues of equality within sport. According to historian Annemarie Jutel, "In 1970, at a prominent Californian race, the Bay-to-Breakers, women demonstrated with placards that read 'AAU Unfair to Women!' and 'Who Says Women can't run?'" Indeed, Jutel has argued that "the emergence of the women's marathon did not hinge upon radical activity." Instead, she believes that "the changing attitudes towards women's long distance running were the result of reassuring the public that running did not upset traditional gender roles and values."[78] One criticism leveled at some sports activists—including those who led the charge for Title IX's implementation in the world of sports—was their acceptance of a "masculine model of sport" that reaffirmed gender divisions and kept men in positions of power.[79]

Switzer's own attitudes reflected some of that mind-set. Although Switzer embraced an activist mind-set when it came to running, believing it would open doors for women and would inspire them to fight for more access in other areas of life, she nonetheless clung firmly to many traditional gender norms and ideals. In the opening of her autobiography, published in 2007, she remembered watching the 1960 Olympics as a girl and being put off by "the . . . photo of Tamara Press, the Soviet shot-putter" who had "arms like ham, a jelly roll on her midriff, and grimy bra straps showing." That image proved "scary" to her, because she feared that being a female athlete would mean looking like that.[80] Running appealed to her because it did not necessitate a transformation of her body. One week after her first appearance in the Boston Marathon, she observed, "Women can run, and they can still be women and look like women."[81] Little surprise, then, that early key sponsors of women's races, including marathons, were Bonne Bell, a cosmetics company; L'eggs pantyhose; and Avon cosmetics, all geared toward a kind of female beauty that did "not upset traditional gender roles and values."[82] Because many women runners emphasized gaining access to sport without engaging in broader cultural critiques, they operated from the assumptions of a liberal feminist approach to change in American life.

"Is Aerobic Exercise Fit for a Lady?" Women's Magazines and Women's Sports

One way to see this tension—between the liberating possibilities of women entering into these new spaces and the ongoing conservatism regarding key ideals of femininity—is through popular media directed at women, especially contemporary women's magazines. Most sports publications of the time, such as *Sports Illustrated*, focused almost entirely on men. The first publication devoted to female athletes—*womenSports*, founded by Billie Jean King, debuted in 1974, well after the marathon controversy.[83] Women's general interest magazines, then, such as *Redbook*, *Ladies' Home Journal*, *Cosmopolitan*, and *Essence*, offer a window into how women's athletic accomplishments infiltrated the broader culture. As women's general interest magazines first ignored and then gradually came to cover women's increasing participation in sports, especially running and the implications of Title IX, they worked through new representations and possibilities of femininity. Although few magazines formulated anything like a radical feminist critique, they nonetheless revealed how individual efforts like those of Gibb and Switzer could come to change public attitudes about women's capabilities in and out of sport.[84]

Although change would occur over time, women's magazines on the whole were slow to come around to the idea of women distance runners (and women athletes in general), a result of the genre's general conservatism. British sociologist Marjorie Ferguson, who published one of the earliest analyses of women's magazines, argued that the publications created a "cult of femininity" in their readers.[85] This focus on femininity tended to be relatively conservative, geared toward an ideal of the stay-at-home caretaker. Attuned to the interests of readers and the desires of advertisers, most women's magazines, according to business scholar Mary Ellen Zuckerman, "generally reflected mainstream thinking" and "did not try to radically reconfigure women's lives or society."[86] Many second-wave feminists like Betty Friedan disdained women's magazines for precisely that reason, and they were a target of derision in *The Feminine Mystique*. Too focused on a hegemonic articulation of femininity centered on marriage, child-rearing, sex, and physical appearance, these magazines, according to critics like Friedan, held back feminist causes.[87]

Those dominant attitudes usually left physical activity—whether competitive or leisurely—out of these magazines. If they did address sports and fitness, they often parroted traditional concerns about the impacts of exercise on women's health—especially with regard to reproductive functions.[88] In addition, in the decades leading up to the Boston Marathon breakthrough, women's magazines largely ignored women runners, even those who achieved national and international acclaim. The coverage of Didrikson's remarkable athletic career offers a useful example of dominant tendencies. In the years immediately following her Olympic success, Didrikson received scant attention in women's magazines. Even as she earned considerable acclaim in national newspapers, none of the major women's publications reported on her remarkable success at the Olympics, and no follow-up biographical articles appeared in ensuing months.[89] Even the stories that engaged with Didrikson and her remarkable athletic achievements did so in a way that emphasized her as an aberration, a violator of conventional femininity. A September 1933 feature story in *Redbook* by William Moulton Marston, a psychologist who would go on to later fame for his creation of the comic book *Wonder Woman*, set out to "know the secret" of Didrikson's remarkable success as an athlete. The photos accompanying the story depicted her competing in a wide range of sports, including basketball, swimming, hurdling, golf, and the high jump. Marston praised Didrikson for defying expectations, noting that her "*general* athletic ability" contradicts "the theories of many doctors and psychologists." And he rejected the notion that Didrikson was a "masculine type of girl" and instead painted her as an "ordinary, nice, un-self-conscious country girl." Yet, even in praising Didrikson for her wide-ranging accomplishments, Marston still characterized her as an outsider, believing that Didrikson had "an unusual amount of male dominance in her particular mixture of personality traits." He cited her preference for male friends and her lack of romantic attachments to men. He believed that Didrikson had a "male hunger drive" for domination and immediate gratification.[90] While meant to be laudatory of Didrikson, the article nonetheless made her out to be a man in a woman's body.

Paul Gallico offered a far more demeaning assessment of women athletes, including Didrikson, in a July 1937 issue of *Cosmopolitan*. The article, an excerpt from his book *Farewell to Sport*, opened: "For all their occasional beauty and unquestioned courage, there has always been something faintly ridiculous about the big-time lady athletes." What followed was almost entirely focused on women athletes' physical attractiveness, or lack thereof. Even in praising Didrikson as the "best all-around woman" athlete, Gallico described her as "a hard-bitten, hawk-nosed, thin-mouthed little hoyden." During her successful performance in the Olympics, Didrikson was "the muscle moll to end all muscle molls," caring only about sports. Her lack of attention to her appearance led Gallico to describe her as "hatchet-faced." Although allowing that Didrikson had improved her physical attractiveness when she turned professional, coming into "her woman's birthright" in rejecting her "tomboy" persona, he clearly positioned women's primary value in their status as objects of male desire. He closed his article by writing about women swimmers, who he believed to be "the only group of girls who have ever been able to couple complete femininity with genuine athletic achievement." All others were "trying to be imitations of men."[91] Articles like this one trained *Cosmopolitan*'s readers to view female athleticism with deep suspicion.

That suspicion perhaps explains the lack of coverage of the Boston Marathon in the 1960s. None of the major women's magazines—including *Cosmopolitan, Ladies' Home Journal,* and *Redbook*—mentioned Gibb's and Switzer's feats. Indeed, these magazines had no stories at all about running or jogging through the early to mid-1960s. Even Wilma Rudolph's star turn at the 1960 Olympics, which generated significant national and international press, made almost no impact in mainstream women's magazines.[92] A 1967 story in *Woman's Day* did mention jogging as a way to stay healthy, but it was in an article headlined "Longer Life for Your Husband" that discussed physical fitness activities to keep *men* active and healthier.[93] However, starting in 1968, one year after Gibb and Switzer earned attention at Boston, these magazines began to cover the trend. The first article of consequence appeared in the August 1968 issue of *Cosmopolitan*. Although hardly revolutionary in its rhetoric (the first reason cited for why women should take up jogging is that "*men* are doing it," and women can use this activity to spend more time with their beaux), it nonetheless offered support for running, noting the health benefits of a better cardiovascular system.[94] By December 1968 *Town and Country* promoted the "Indoor Jogger"—an early treadmill—in a story listing "Beauty Secrets" for its readers. The machine would enable "all the cardio-pulmonary effects of jogging in the park without the inconvenience of "rain or rubberneckers."[95]

While those stories in 1968 were limited in scope, 1969 saw a change. That year, *Seventeen, Cosmopolitan, Redbook, Woman's Day,* and *Better Homes and Gardens* printed stories or photo spreads that promoted women joggers and runners. Although these were still often couched in emphasizing running as a way to promote heterosexual mingling, they also increasingly began to praise exercise's positive effects on women's own psychological well-being and confidence. For example, while a fashion spread in *Seventeen* urged readers to "jog, jog and away (to a slimmer figure)" in stylish canvas sneakers,[96] a story in *Woman's Day* promoted the benefits of running, including a "slimmed down" figure, "pep and energy that lasts all day long," and better sleep and "less tension."[97] This flurry of stories in 1969 came as Switzer and other women distance runners increasingly agitated for more opportunities. And they predated the significant media coverage that Billie Jean King would occasion with her leadership of the Virginia Slims Tour for women tennis players, which started in fall 1970, as well as her starring role opposite male tennis player Bobby Riggs in the famed 1973 Battle of the Sexes match.[98]

Running, specifically distance running, thus marked an important bridge between the 1960s and 1970s. It gave women an avenue into sports and fitness activities, paving the way for the countless women who would traverse that path in the wake of Title IX and the Battle of the Sexes. In addition, it also provided a conduit between the battles for legal equity sought by NOW and others with the more radical social and cultural transformations called for by women's liberation. Jutel's caution that "running did not upset traditional gender roles and values" is well worth remembering,[99] but it seems clear that running also opened the way for many women to challenge sports and society at large, albeit staying in the more conservative lane paved by moderate feminists. By April 1972 a story in *Cosmopolitan*—the magazine that had previously recommended that women start running only so they could spend more time with their men—now lauded women athletes, including Switzer, who were breaking through barriers and proving assumptions wrong. It further argued that women had been "bamboozled by men and culture patterns" and that they were "victims of a massive hoax that presupposed girls weak and frail."[100] Even the middle of the road had become a channel for previously unheard-of ideas.

To Compete on What Terms? Title IX, the AIAW, and Resistance to Women in Sports

Only two months after that story in *Cosmopolitan*, lawmakers passed Title IX. Although the legislation had tremendous impacts inside and outside the world of sports, women's magazines remained mostly silent about it. Initially, *Ladies' Home Journal* was the only magazine to call attention to the amendment's passage in 1972. However, its analysis emphasized not sports but "freedom in the choice of occupations, and equality of pay and equal job opportunity."[101] By 1974, as awareness of the amendment's relevance to athletics became more apparent, coverage picked up in select publications. *Seventeen* included a blurb about the law in its "Hot Lines" section in September 1974, noting, "The controversial federal law Title IX, calling for an end to sex bias in the schools—regarding athletics, the awarding of scholarships, recruiting, courses—is creating havoc from coast to coast."[102] That pessimistic tone seemed to anticipate later, antifeminist objections. By February 1975, though, *Seventeen* more fully embraced the potential of an athletic revolution, with a three-page article by Robert Peterson pondering the increased opportunities for girls to play sports. He spotlighted the impact of Title IX as especially important. Because "schools will have to offer equal opportunity to girls and boys in interscholastic sports," he noted, there was "no doubt" that girls' opportunities for participation in a wide range of sports would increase at the high school level.[103] *Seventeen* was at the forefront, publishing two additional articles in 1975 that referred to the impending changes to come from Title IX and celebrating the new possibilities in sports for girls.[104]

Seventeen's focus on a younger audience, who would benefit most from increased scholastic athletic opportunities, undoubtedly played a part in the magazine's coverage of Title IX. Other publications shied away from engaging with its impacts on sports. Although *Redbook* mentioned Title IX in a May 1975 story, it emphasized educational programs, not athletics. The only mention of sports came when author Susan Edmiston noted that "feminists have . . . criticized the act because it does not require schools to spend equal amounts of money on athletics for the two sexes."[105] Edmiston and her editors were apparently still uneasy with aligning themselves with the "feminists" advocating for increased athletic opportunities.

But that was changing. As the 1970s progressed, women's magazines began to embrace women's sports participation more fully, and women runners played a key role in this evolution. A lengthy October 1975 story in *Woman's Day* extolled the virtues of aerobic exercise, quoted numerous physicians, and outlined a healthy exercise program.[106] By March 1975, *Ladies' Home Journal* was sponsoring a televised athletic competition called Women Superstars. The following year, Billie Jean King cohosted the show along with noted broadcaster Keith Jackson. Editor Lenore Hershey celebrated "the new visibility and achievements of women in the area of sports" and noted the importance of Title IX in pressuring high schools and colleges "to desegregate athletic programs and to offer equal opportunities for girls to participate, win athletic scholarships, etc."[107] Her magazine featured a lengthy article about the second annual entry of the Women Superstars competition and offered advice on exercise, commentary on coed sports, and other issues related to women and athletics. The article, which contained a number of different sidebars, veered between celebrating athletic progress, providing daily stretching routines, and offering tips on the best hairstyles for exercise. On the whole, it celebrated the progress women had made as a result of Title IX and noted the importance of women participating in sports and receiving more equitable treatment.[108] *Ladies' Home Journal* was not alone in embracing women's participation in competitive sports: *Redbook* and *Seventeen* also sponsored athletic competitions in the mid-1970s.[109] And a September 1976 story in *Woman's Day* featured testimonials from eighteen women athletes about "how they win." The athletes included tennis star Chris Evert, swimmer Diana Nyad, golfer Jane Blalock, and Switzer.[110] Clearly, women's magazines were opening up to sports, even competitive sports, and Switzer was one of the key figures in this transition.

However, journalist Jane Leavy, writing for *womenSports* in 1977, still found much lacking in the attention that women's general interest publications paid to women athletes. She cautioned that even as women's magazines had begun to include more sports coverage, they had "been resourceful in finding ways to leave sports—and especially sports events—out of their sports articles." Instead, they offered "sports-related articles on fashion, beauty, travel, or sex discrimination." Articles didn't discuss specific athletes and competitions as much as they described "tailgate picnics, the Dorothy Hamill look, equal pay for equal play, and exercises to flatten your tummy."[111] There was a tenuous transition taking place—even as sports became more popular among women, and as access to sports became more of a reality, thanks to Title IX, traditional gender norms and biases continued to impact sports coverage in these publications.

Women's magazines were not alone in trying to balance women's increasing interest in sports with the maintenance of traditional gender norms. Women physical educators also struggled in this regard. The rise and fall of the Association for Intercollegiate Athletics for Women (AIAW) is a case study of the tensions that came with increasing women's sports participation. The AIAW formed in 1971 as a replacement for the Women's Division of the National Amateur Athletic Federation. Although AIAW leaders clearly supported women's athletics, they had deep reservations about the state of men's college sports in the early 1970s and sought to create an alternative student-centered and women-led organization. Many leaders were especially suspicious of overemphasizing competition, fearing that doing so would undermine schools' academic mission, promote illicit recruiting practices, lower the moral standards of female athlete participants, and raise questions about athletes' and coaches' sexual orientation.[112] To these ends, many leaders in women's sports and physical education "accepted restrictions placed on women athletes." They saw sports for women as a way "to enjoy the spirit of play while experiencing sport as a means of physical, intellectual, and emotional growth," not as a means to equality or the worrisome developments that came along with it.[113] For these leaders, too much emphasis on competition would undercut, not promote, what they saw as the virtues of women's sports. In this way they clung to traditional gender norms and stereotypes.

Although the AIAW hoped to chart out a different model from that of the NCAA, pressures soon forced the organization to lean into commercialized and competitive sports. First, the lawsuit of *Kellmeyer, et al. v. NEA, et al.* forced the AIAW to permit the awarding of athletic scholarships to women, something the group had hoped to restrict.[114] Although debates continued within the AIAW about whether to follow the male college sport model or embrace "a women's alternative," the AIAW grudgingly expanded the number of women's sports championships.[115] In 1972, the year the AIAW took charge of women's intercollegiate competition, it sponsored national championships for collegiate women in golf, tennis, track and field, gymnastics, swimming and diving, basketball, and badminton.[116] Gradually, the AIAW also began to accept more commercial links to women's sports, including the naming of sponsored All-American teams, television broadcast rights, and acceptance of alcohol advertising at events.[117] Although many leaders remained uneasy about these initiatives, the movement toward a model similar to men's collegiate athletics seemed inexorable.

Women's magazines also reflected these tensions and debates. As Leavy noted in *womenSports*, coverage of women's athletic endeavors did not mean a wholesale embrace of sports. Sports articles typically fell into one of six categories: "Personalities," "How-To's," "A Pretty Face," "From Slim to Trim," "Issues," and "Muscle Phobia." Sports competition, Leavy observed, took a backseat in all of these. For example, the how-to articles involving sports were less about "how to do a sport" and more about social activities connected to sports. Stories showed "readers how to catch a man while playing sports; how to be a sports spectator (and look good doing it); [and] how to find the 'in' ski resorts and tennis camps."[118] Similarly, a 1976 article in the *Journal of Communication* explored advertising regarding women in sports and found that many advertisements, if they did depict sports, tended to show women in "recreational rather than competitive situations." One ad showed women with baseball bats and gloves, but instead of being in the field, they were socializing "in informal, picnic-type settings."[119] Likewise, *Cosmopolitan*'s October 1969 issue featured a five-page article dedicated to "Girl Athletes: what makes them skate, fence, swim, jump, run?" And while the story focused on competitive desires of top women athletes, it made sure to couch its analysis in language that indicated that women athletes could still be "appropriately" feminine and heterosexual. For example, the story described tennis player Nancy Richey as "delicate" and "ladylike"; introduced figure skater Mary Lynn Gelderman as a "blonde, blue-eyed teenager", and described British fencer Janet Wardley Yarbrough as "a voluptuous brunette." The story featured a number of quotes from women track and field athletes, including long jumper Willye White and Tennessee A&I University track coach Ed Temple, defending their femininity. In addition, the story quoted psychologist Bruce Ogilvie, who assured readers that "girl athletes exhibit a *higher* heterosexual interest" than their non-athletic peers. Clearly, anxieties about women as competitors remained, and the author's vow to "start jogging" showed how noncompetitive running could soothe some of those concerns.[120]

Competition of a different sort ultimately led to disaster for the AIAW. As the organization sought to stave off the NCAA model for sports, the NCAA itself became increasingly interested in women's sports. Although NCAA executives initially fought against Title IX's implementation, arguing that it would doom men's sports, by the early 1980s the writing was on the wall: women's college athletics were here to stay. A power struggle between the NCAA and the AIAW ensued, but the NCAA, with its much larger budget and existing television and sponsorship arrangements, won out. Although the AIAW filed an antitrust lawsuit, they lost their case and collapsed.[121] Although NCAA control did lead to enhanced media exposure and more women's sports opportunities, there were a number of negative outcomes. Black women's colleges suffered, for example, as schools with better resources began to attract the best talent. The NCAA's takeover also removed many women from positions of power at the administrative level, with AIAW leaders left out in the cold. Meanwhile, as women's sports expanded, more men moved into coaching positions, depriving women of leadership and power closer to the field.[122] On the whole, then, even as more women moved into playing fields of various kinds, "it was men, and not women," Jaime Schultz has written, "who increasingly governed their sports."[123] While many AIAW leaders clung to conservative ideas about women's sports, still resisting commercial pressures and a total focus on competition even into the early 1980s, competitive sports won, and the woman-led, student-centered sports organization vanished.[124]

The increasing participation of women in sports, however, did not. And distance running continued to play a vital role in easing women into greater acceptance of sports participation. Although early leaders had worried about running and track and field events because of their emphasis on competition, many found value in distance running because it focused more on personal fulfillment than a race against the clock—or against others. After Gibb made her breakthrough at the Boston Marathon, her reasons for running stayed in line with conventional ideas regarding women's temperaments: "Competition never interested me. . . . I liked running just as a way of relaxing and of absorbing the beauties of nature."[125] In a 1977 article in *Newsweek* that addressed the growing popularity of the sport, journalist Susan Cheever Cowley observed that "the noncompetitive nature of running" was key to its popularity among women and its role in boosting self-esteem.[126] Although women's magazines worried about depicting "stress and strain" in their depictions of women engaging in sports, believing their readers wanted something more "glamorous," running offered a compromise of sorts.[127] Guidebooks for women's runners by authors such as Gayle Barron played up the feminine appeal of women runners, noting that running could lead to healthy lives and appealing physiques. Similarly, *Runner's World* magazine offered encouraging words for women runners in a 1978 book titled *The Complete Woman Runner*. The book assured women that the sport would not render them "tomboys" and encouraged them to balance home life with running.[128] This, of course, fit well with Switzer's concerns about body type and Gibb's dismissal of competitive desires. In these varied ways, distance running could be promoted as a healthy activity that did not overemphasize competition or overtly challenge hegemonic feminine norms regarding body shape and type.

Those assets also potentially hindered the sport's capacity to engage in the cultural revolution hoped for by radical feminists. In promoting health and shape, while minimizing competition, the popular discourse around distance running anticipated the rise of a new strand of women's magazines—those dedicated to health and fitness. These new magazines, such as *Self, Shape*, and *Fit*, all emerged in the late 1970s and 1980s, targeting women's increasing interest in sports and fitness.[129] However, unlike *womenSports*, these magazines focused on dieting and achieving normative desirable body shapes. They did not promote the joy of playing sports or women's sports competition. Comparative literature scholar Ellen McCracken argues that most of these magazines "focus readers' attention on their bodies," emphasizing sexual desirability, not personal health.[130] Simon Barber's 1982 review of these new magazines, which also included *Slimmer* and *Pretty Body*, criticized the publications for finding faults in women's physical appearance, mindlessly praising the sexual benefits of exercise, objectifying fitness models, and making readers feel guilty about food and lifestyle choices.[131] While the new magazines certainly did support women's participation in exercise, they did not shake off traditional gender norms.

Still, despite those limitations, popular media coverage increasingly encouraged some level of women's fitness as the 1970s progressed. In June 1974, *Newsweek* devoted a ten-page article to the increasing presence of women athletes at all levels. Impressively, the story argued that these women were "smashing the stereotypes that have held them back for so long."[132] A lengthy November 1974 article by Grace Lichtenstein in *Redbook* linked Switzer, Billie Jean King, and other women athletes to a broader set of social changes in which women were defying expectations and getting positive benefits from their new activities.[133] Even Leavy, who had been skeptical of women's magazines' coverage of sports in her review for *womenSports*, had to acknowledge that progress was being made, that more magazines were publishing articles encouraging girls and women to get involved in sports.[134] By the time of her article in 1977, these kinds of stories had become more and more common, seeing running as a victory against outmoded ways of thinking and calling attention to women's varied interests and talents.[135] The slow but steady acceptance of running for women, the increasing awareness of Title IX's implications, the struggles of the AIAW, and the flawed representations of women's sports in fitness magazines—all spoke to the challenges many faced in adjusting their sense of gender to incorporate new sports opportunities for women.

An Unfinished Race

Change came to running, and to women's sports in general, in the years after 1967. In Boston the growing clamor for women's participation in the marathon eventually led to a breakthrough. Nineteen seventy-two marked the first year women entrants were allowed, with New Yorker Nina Kuscsik easily outpacing the competition to take the title by nearly ten minutes.[136] That same year, at the New York Marathon, twelve women "staged a sit-down strike on the starting line" to protest an AAU ruling that required them to start ten minutes before the male runners.[137] Switzer returned to run Boston in 1972 and in 1973 posed for a photograph with Semple before the start of the race, a sign of the changing times. Switzer became an accomplished marathoner in her own right, winning the New York Marathon in 1974 and finishing second at Boston in 1975.[138] In her professional life, she also helped to create the Avon Running series for women. In 1978 the company put on the Avon Marathon in Atlanta, Georgia, and women from nine countries participated. The following year, that number grew to twenty-five countries. As the series expanded across the globe, it laid the groundwork for establishing a women's marathon in the 1984 Olympics. Although by that point Switzer had finished her career as a competitive marathoner, she was on the broadcast team when American Joan Benoit claimed the first-ever gold medal at the Los Angeles Games.[139]

The growing acceptance of women runners showed up in a variety of ways as the 1970s ended and the 1980s began. Runner Gloria Averbach published a celebration of the sport in 1984 called *The Woman Runner: Free to Be the Complete Athlete*. In it, she recalled the challenges she faced when she took up the sport in the early 1970s: "Going for a run was like surviving a war. Even in the most progressive parts of the country I was hooted at, mocked, and mimicked. I was even spit at, chased by drunks, and had a bottle thrown my way."[140] When she ran the New York Marathon in 1979, conditions had improved dramatically. Although still subjected to the occasional heckler, public support for women runners had clearly grown.[141] By 1978 and 1979, women's magazines were publishing more and more positive articles about running and jogging and encouraging women to participate in sports. In April 1978 *Ladies' Home Journal* featured a story called "The Beauty of Running."[142] By November 1979 *Seventeen* encouraged readers to seek out athletic scholarships, since Title IX was now mandating that schools equalize funding for men and women athletes.[143]

Of course, funding did not equalize between men's and women's sports—neither in 1979 nor in the decades to follow. While the gap closed, inequalities remained. Women's groups are still obliged to protest and sue in order to make universities comply with their Title IX obligations.[144] Media coverage of women's sports remains spotty, well into the second decade of the twenty-first century: women's sports are neglected, and the coverage they get is frequently sexist, racist, or both.[145] The issues exposed in magazine coverage in the 1970s continued for decades. A 2002 study, for example, found that representations of sports in men's magazines tended to emphasize "power and performance," while those in women's magazines focused primarily on "pleasure and participation."[146] Meanwhile, distance running in the United States has remained predominantly white. African Americans' participation rates in marathons and other distance events are astonishingly low, a direct result of the fact that black runners continue to receive the harassment and threats that many white women runners no longer do.[147] That pattern extends to Title IX, which has had the biggest impact on middle-class white women's athletic possibilities.[148] The liberal feminism of pioneering runners, with an emphasis on fitting into previously defined spaces and minimizing direct assaults on conventional gender norms and other social constructs, such as race, might well explain some of these ongoing issues.

But few would argue that nothing has changed. Although Title IX's impacts have not been as equitable as many hoped, sporting opportunities for girls and women at the high school and college levels have increased exponentially. Public acceptance and even celebration of women athletes in a range of sports, including soccer, gymnastics, tennis, and even boxing, reveals a remarkable transformation of public attitudes. If media coverage is still problematic in numerous ways, the celebrity status of athletes such as Megan Rapinoe and Serena Williams marks a new era for fiercely competitive female athletes.[149] And there have been important positive health consequences as a result. Numerous studies have shown that sports participation for girls has a wide range of benefits, including better physical health, improved self-esteem, and better academic performance. Organizations such as Girls on the Run have sprung up to encourage girls to get involved in sports at an early age.[150] Gone are the days when races for girls and women were limited to 1.5 miles.

The women who ran the Boston Marathon in 1966 and 1967, then, did more than run one race. They played an important role in changing attitudes toward women's sports participation in general and in getting men and women to think differently about women's potential in numerous aspects of life. A 1977 story in *Newsweek* showcased both transformations. According to the story, nearly 500,000 women engaged in running or jogging that year, as compared to only 25,000 in 1972. More than 280 women ran the New York City Marathon that year, only ten years after Gibb and Switzer ran Boston. Although the story noted multiple reasons for why women ran, it emphasized that women especially liked the "feeling of personal strength" that came from running. The comments of Henley Roughton, a thirty-three-year-old from Washington, D.C., were especially powerful: "Running has given me the feeling I can do other things. . . . Before that, I was just a housewife who married at 18 and felt guilty about not going to college."[151] No doubt inspired by the examples of Gibb and Switzer, Roughton's access to a previously male-only space and her story of personal growth and transformation signified the broader effects occasioned by women distance runners and the women athletes who followed in their footsteps. While they did so in a way that soothed anxieties about women's increasing role in sports—one runner in that same *Newsweek* story indicated she would "plan recipes" while she ran—they nonetheless chipped away at cultural norms regarding women athletes.[152] Although the battle for women's equality—inside and outside the world of sports—remains unfinished, the growing acceptance of women runners marked an important, lasting, and often unremembered, cultural shift.

* * *

The subtle activism of women distance runners played an important role in altering dominant hegemonic norms. For male athletes in big-time college sports, however, more direct engagement would be necessary. Hemmed in by limiting scholarship arrangements, bigoted coaches, and systemically racist institutions (among other forces), college athletes in the late 1960s and early 1970s fought for change more directly. The stakes were high for both individual athletes and entire teams as we will see in the next chapter.

CHAPTER 3

COLLEGE ATHLETES FLEX THEIR MUSCLES

In the winter of 1969, things were going well, on the surface, for college basketball star Charlie Scott. He was in the middle of a great season on the hardwood, leading his team at the University of North Carolina (UNC) to the top of the standings in the Atlantic Coast Conference (ACC). This was familiar territory: the previous year, as a sophomore, Scott had teamed with All-American Larry Miller to win the ACC championship and earn a trip to the NCAA men's basketball tournament finals, where they fell to a powerhouse UCLA team. In the 1968–1969 season, with Miller graduated, Scott, a wiry, 6'6" shooting guard, took charge. He led the team in scoring and had the Tar Heels poised to make another deep run in the NCAA tournament. He was popular with many fans, who marveled at his agility, leaping ability, shooting, and all-around game.[1]

But things were seldom easy for Charlie Scott. As the first black basketball player at UNC, a school with a rich basketball tradition and devoted fans, he faced constant pressure and strain. Being a star athlete always comes with scrutiny; being a pioneering black athlete in the South during the era of Black Power only intensified that attention. In February 1969, members of the school's Black Student Movement (BSM) approached Scott for help in their efforts to transform the campus. They had submitted a list of demands to UNC chancellor J. Carlyle Sitterson and had gotten nowhere. Sitterson largely dismissed the BSM's demands, which included the establishment of a Department of African and Afro-American Studies, intensified recruitment of black students, better

Charlie Scott, the first black scholarship athlete at UNC, had to navigate the contours of racial politics in a turbulent time. Photo courtesy of the *Yackety Yack*.

financial aid packages for minorities, and improved wages for the mostly minority housekeeping staff. Would Scott join the cause? Would he use his celebrity as a basketball star to generate support for the movement?[2] These were tough decisions for Scott; he had loyalties to his teammates and coaches, to his race, to his school, and to the legacy of black athletes on campus. In a bygone era almost no athlete would have acceded to the request. But in 1969 the time was ripe for all athletes—professional and amateur alike—to channel the activist spirit of the times. On February 18, 1969, Scott and black freshman basketball player Bill Chamberlain joined a group of four BSM members to discuss their cause with Sitterson.[3]

Scott's decision was part of a broader upswell in activism among college athletes in the late 1960s. Galvanized by civil rights, Black Power, and the inspiring actions of Ali and others, college athletes across the country began to use their platform to call for change. While, as we will see, most of the activists focused on inequities within the world of sports, others, like Scott, lobbied for broader institutional and social change. Exploring the wide range of change sought by college athletes—especially black male college athletes—and taking a closer look at Scott's story and the black press's responses to the so-called Wyoming 14 showcases these varied reform attempts. The efforts of college athletes to change society inside and outside the world of sports spoke to the tremendous shifts in sports activism but also highlighted the especially precarious nature of supposedly amateur athletes in the NCAA landscape. The possibilities for change—and the fierce resistance to college athlete activism—offers new insights into both the untapped potential of college sports stars and the paternalistic power of the NCAA's leadership.

The Olympic Uprising and Beyond: The Roots of College Athlete Activism

Like their peers in the professional sports world, college athletes in the 1960s were not immune to the upswell of activism against white supremacy and patriarchy. Indeed, as members of the younger generation, athletes had the potential to be especially prominent and dedicated activists, as young people played especially important roles in movements for civil rights, Black Power, and women's liberation, along with protests against the Vietnam War.[4] By 1967 the first signs of widespread college athlete activism appeared. Influenced by Ali's refusal to be drafted into service in Vietnam and the budding Olympic Project for Human Rights (OPHR), established by sociology professor Harry Edwards at San Jose State University, black athletes in particular began to agitate for change inside and outside the realm of sports.[5]

The OPHR was especially galvanizing, and it attracted athlete engagement across racial and gender lines. As a Division 1 track athlete at San Jose State, Edwards had experienced firsthand the racial discrimination common to black athletes in predominantly white schools. White coaches disregarded black athletes' academic advancement, encouraging them to take classes that were easy to pass but did not contribute toward a degree. Coaches "stacked" black players at certain positions to maintain a majority of white players on teams. Socially, black student-athletes were denied access to many campus groups and events and were especially cautioned against dating white women. Teammates used derogatory language and then chided black players for lacking "team spirit."[6] By the fall of 1967, a wizened Edwards was working as a professor in the school's sociology department while he completed his Ph.D. Together with graduate student Kenneth Noel—another former athlete at the school—and inspired by the National Conference on Black Power held the previous summer in Newark, New Jersey, Edwards decided to use athletics as a way to challenge the widespread racism present at San Jose State and in higher education in general. At a rally at the start of the semester, Edwards and Noel threatened to have black athletes boycott the opening football game of the season unless the school agreed to meet their demands, which included university policies outlawing discrimination in any campus groups (including fraternities and sororities), intensified recruitment efforts for minority students, and concrete steps to provide equitable treatment for black and white athletes. When the university capitulated, Edwards wrote, "We had learned the use of power—the power to be gained from exploiting the white man's economic and almost religious involvement in athletics."[7]

That success emboldened Edwards to broaden his reach, founding the Olympic Project for Human Rights in October 1967 to explore the idea of organizing a boycott of black athletes from the Olympics to protest ongoing racism. While many white Americans (and some black Americans, such as track and field legend Jesse Owens) criticized the effort to boycott the Olympics, Edwards began to build support. Civil rights leaders Martin Luther King Jr. and Floyd McKissick pledged to aid Edwards and his plans for boycott, and a number of prominent athletes, including track stars Tommie Smith, John Carlos, and Lee Evans, and college basketball sensation Lew Alcindor (later renamed Kareem Abdul-Jabbar) became active supporters. The group had six demands: (1) the restoration of Ali's title and boxing licenses; (2) the removal of American Avery Brundage (a well-known racial bigot) as head of the International Olympic Committee (IOC); (3) the banning of South Africa and Southern Rhodesia from the games; (4) the addition of black coaches to the U.S. track and field team; (5) the appointment of black members to the U.S. Olympic Committee; and (6) the desegregation of the New York Athletic Club (NYAC), a prestigious club often used for Olympic trials and other national events. Although the group's efforts to boycott the NYAC were successful, and they succeeded in getting the teams from the apartheid regimes in South Africa and Rhodesia banned from the games, the boycott ultimately failed to take hold among black Olympians. Alcindor stayed home in protest, but the vast majority decided to compete in the 1968 Summer Olympic Games in Mexico City.[8]

It was at those games, of course, that Smith and Carlos made their iconic protest on the medal stand of the 200-meter dash, a story that has been told many times. As described in chapter 1, the two bowed their heads and thrust their black-gloved fists in the air as the national anthem played. Clad in black socks and wearing OPHR buttons, the two were joined by Australian sprinter Peter Norman, the silver medalist, who wore an OPHR button on his tracksuit. Reactions to the protests were swift and divided. Most Americans were aghast, irate at Smith and Carlos's apparent lack of patriotism and militant symbolism. The IOC, headed by Brundage, ordered the two sent home for violating rules against political demonstrations by athletes. Readers sent outraged letters to the editor in local and national publications, and Smith and Carlos received threatening hate mail. Back on the campus of San Jose State, however, Edwards and his supporters cheered, as did black activists across the country. Fellow black athletes at the games (and many white athletes) expressed their support for Smith and Carlos, and runner Lee Evans followed up with his own gesture by wearing a black beret on the medal stand after winning gold in the 400-meter event.[9]

Two groups outside of the prominent black male athletes at the heart of this story bear mentioning, especially with regard to college activism. The first is the Harvard crew team, which comprised the U.S. national team for the Olympics. Early in 1968, five of the all-white members of the team signed a statement in support of the OPHR and worked to generate enthusiasm and publicity for the movement.[10] Indeed, on the day of Smith and Carlos's fateful protest, it was Harvard coxswain Paul Hoffman who gave his OPHR badge to Norman, enabling the Australian to display his support for the cause on the medal stand.[11] Black college women, too, played an especially important part. Although denied an active role in the boycott discussion before the Olympics because of the male-centric leadership, they participated in the discussions held in Mexico City regarding possible protest activities.[12] In fact, a black woman track star had provided a much earlier blueprint for anthem-related activism: high jumper Eroseanna "Rose" Robinson, who refused to stand for the national anthem during the 1959 Pan American Games, protesting the use of athletes as political pawns during the Cold War and the "violence and war" inherent in U.S. foreign policy.[13] Two days after Carlos and Smith made their protest in 1968, Wyomia Tyus, who had already won gold in the women's 100-meter dash (in the process becoming the first athlete to win the event in back-to-back Olympics), wore black shorts instead of the normal white ones as a sign of solidarity with the controversial Carlos and Smith. After winning gold in the 4 x 100 relay, Tyus, on behalf of team members Barbara Ferrell, Margaret Bailes, and Mildrette Netter, told the assembled media that the team wanted to "dedicate our relay win to John Carlos and Tommie Smith."[14] As historian Amira Rose Davis has argued, the contributions of black women like Tyus have been too long neglected in histories of athlete activism, and her protest contributions while still a member of

Wyomia Tyus joined in the 1968 protests by wearing black shorts and dedicating her relay gold medal to Smith and Carlos. Photo courtesy of Wikimedia Creative Commons.

the Tennessee State University track team deserve recognition.[15] As the Harvard crew team and the black women of the U.S. track and field team show, while black male athletes played the largest part in campus protests in this decade, they did not operate alone.

The uprising associated with the 1968 Olympics was also not an isolated phenomenon. College athletes responded vigorously to Ali's anti–Vietnam stance, the Olympic boycott movement, and the Mexico City protests in a variety of ways in the late 1960s and early 1970s. Emboldened by their fellow athletes' activism, athletes across the country rose up in protest starting in 1967 but really gathering momentum in 1968 and the immediate years that followed. Although white athletes engaged in protest, especially with regard to the Vietnam War, the vast majority of the protests centered on African American athletes.[16] Edwards estimated that thirty-seven black athlete revolts took place on the campuses of predominantly white institutions in 1968 alone.[17] During that year, as historian David Wiggins has argued, "black athletes in unprecedented numbers became participants in the civil rights struggle."[18] Some of the schools where protests occurred included the University of California at Berkeley, Western Michigan University, Princeton University, Michigan State University, Oklahoma City College, the University of Texas at El Paso (UTEP), San Francisco State College, Marquette University, the University of Kansas, and the University of Oklahoma.

Stretching from coast to coast and from north to south, the wave of protests deluged campuses with demands for a broad range of changes in regard to sports and campus life more generally.[19]

The peculiar status of "student-athletes" in NCAA sports complicated their status as activists. By the mid-1960s, the NCAA had established the concept of the "student-athlete" as a legal term to differentiate college athletes from their professional counterparts. As Taylor Branch and others have exposed over the years, the concept of the student-athlete was created so that universities could avoid responsibility for workmen's compensation claims by injured athletes. The case of Fort Lewis A&M football player Ray Dennison in the 1950s was a pivotal event. His widow filed for workers' compensation after Dennison died as the result of a head injury suffered during a game, but the court denied her claim on the grounds that he was not an employee—instead, he was a "student-athlete." The "deliberately ambiguous" term enabled colleges and universities to treat their prize athletes as different from ordinary students but did not require them to pay them as employees.[20] Historian Johnny Smith notes that another key moment came in December 1964, when the NCAA altered "the language of athletic scholarships, crafting an agreement that compelled athletes to accept the NCAA's definition of amateurism," which prohibited any remuneration for play and gave control of likenesses to the NCAA.[21] Amateurism became a sacred cow for the NCAA, and the organization trumpeted the relative purity of its athletes because of the supposed lack of financial corruption. As a result, NCAA athletes occupied a nebulous position: even as college sports (especially the revenue-generating sports of men's basketball and football) became increasingly popular and financially lucrative as the result of television deals, they were beholden to rules that limited their rights and denied them financial benefits beyond scholarships and basic expenses.[22] That lack of power and status underlay many of the protests of the 1960s and early 1970s.

The Wide Range of Black College Athlete Activism

The so-called black athlete revolt that took place on college campuses engaged with a number of issues, as will be explored, but often centered on unequal treatment of black athletes in comparison to their white peers. In early May 1968, for example, a group of black athletes at the University of Oklahoma boycotted an end-of-year banquet to protest the treatment of black athletes at the school. They argued that coaches sought out only black stars and then filled out rosters with white athletes, and they pointed to disparities in treatment and hiring practices.[23] Similarly, black athletes at Western Michigan University in

June 1968 called for "more equitable treatment" by the school, and those at the University of Washington demanded a voice in how the school treated them.[24] That same summer, black athletes at the University of Iowa called for a number of changes, including "an assurance that injured black players" were given adequate time to heal and the dismantling of a "quota system" that limited the number of black athletes.[25] The problems did not disappear overnight. Black football players at Princeton University in early 1969 accused their head coach of racism and argued that they were denied starting positions because of their race.[26] Edwards raised this issue in his *Revolt of the Black Athlete*, criticizing the "common practice on many white college campuses . . . to 'stack' black players in one position or another in order to limit the number who actually make the team." The net result, he noted, was "a de facto quota system."[27]

Unequal treatment extended beyond playing time issues or positions on the team. Often, unequal access to food, money, and other resources proved to be essential issues for black athletes. At Nevada Southern University, five black members of the football team lodged a protest with the Nevada Equal Rights Commission over their treatment by the school, arguing that they were treated poorly in comparison to white athletes, noting particularly that the school did not provide them with adequate food.[28] Similarly, at the University of Iowa, improved "expense money" for athletes had been one of the central proposals they had brought to the administration. Improper medical care was another common complaint from black athletes, one raised by not only the Iowa protesters but also black football players at Indiana University.[29] While the means of protest varied, as sometimes players boycotted practices, threatened boycotts of games, or simply issued demands to coaches and university officials, the common themes of inadequate support and biased treatment in comparison to their white teammates emerged consistently.

Those specific, sports-related issues quickly spilled out into broader cultural ones. Of particular importance to black athletes in the western half of the country were contests against Brigham Young University (BYU). Black athletes called for cancellations of games against the school, which had been established by the Church of Jesus Christ of Latter-Day Saints, citing Mormon beliefs in the inferiority of African Americans and policies that permitted African Americans to be members but prevented them from serving as priests. Athletes at UTEP initiated the wave of protests when eight track athletes at the school, including long jump world record holder Bob Beamon, boycotted a meet at BYU to protest what they described as the school's "belief that blacks are inferior and that we are disciples of the devil." UTEP responded by indicating that they believed the athletes had quit the team and made no mention of whether they would be welcomed back to the squad.[30] At San Jose State University, seven football players refused to play in the school's final game of the 1968 season against BYU in protest of the school's "racist policy."[31] A number of schools followed suit in some fashion in ensuing years, with black athletes at the University of Arizona, Arizona State University, the University of Wyoming, and the University of New Mexico among those to call for boycotts, protests, and symbolic gestures against BYU.[32] The situation was so fraught that Western Athletic Conference (WAC) commissioner Wiles Hallock called for a conference-wide meeting to discuss the situation of black athlete protest. BYU was at the center of the issues, and the commissioner acknowledged that protests would likely continue and intensify.[33] Although, as we will see, the protests at Wyoming would be especially controversial and disheartening to many in the black community, the activism did lead to change. In November 1969, Stanford University announced that it would schedule no more games with BYU, after getting confirmation that African Americans were banned from Mormon priesthood.[34]

Mormonism's beliefs and practices were not the only ideologies under assault by activist athletes. In many protests, issues of cultural bias assumed paramount importance. Facial hair proved to be an especially thorny issue. The goatee, along with the Afro, had become symbols of Black Power, reflecting a rejection of white standards of beauty and style.[35] Yet many white coaches across the country had strict no-facial-hair policies, seeing beards as a reflection of an undisciplined and "beatnik" lifestyle. Collision was inevitable. The most high-profile controversy took place at Oregon State University in February 1969. Successful head football coach Dee Andros chastised a black football player named Fred Milton in February 1969 to shave off his mustache and beard or be dismissed from the team, even though the squad was not in season. Milton stood his ground, and the campus Black Student Union rallied behind him. A long saga emerged in which black students and athletes protested what they saw as unfair infringement on their rights to choose their own culturally meaningful style, and the white coaches and players who saw the issue as simply a matter of team unity and discipline. Coaches like Andros, Wiggins argues, saw football as "one of the last bastions against long hair, drug freaks, and a world generally gone mad."[36] But black players saw the restrictions against facial hair as one more infringement on expressing their identities as black men. Eventually, the situation with Milton spilled out into protests, a university fact-finding committee, and public debates. But the coach prevailed: although the school found that Andros had unknowingly violated Milton's rights and called on him to consider permitting facial hair, there were no mandatory changes. Andros's successful record and broad public support insulated him from being forced to change. Milton, meanwhile, left the team in frustration. And he was not alone; athletes at a number of schools, including the University of Kentucky and Cal-Berkeley, also called for the right to grow facial hair.[37]

Surely the desire to grow facial hair spoke to larger issues of black manliness, as Simon Henderson has argued.[38] As will be discussed in chapter 4, the Black Power era marked an important moment for redefining black masculinity to oppose long-held caricatures and stereotypes. But the battle for control over hair also emerged out of frustration with a wide range of coaches' and administrators' behaviors. Accounts of coaches using degrading language and employing stereotypes frequently circulated in players' critiques. This issue surfaced in mainstream media circles following Jack Olson's series on the "Black Athlete" in *Sports Illustrated*, published over five issues in July 1968.[39] In the third part of the series, titled "In an Alien World," Olson spotlighted the University of Texas at El Paso (previously known as Texas Western University), where an all-black starting five for the men's basketball team made history in the school's 1966 national championship victory over the University of Kentucky. Even there, Olson reported, racial problems ran deep. Football player Bob Wallace called out the use of racial slurs by athletic director George McCarty and his assistant Jim Bowden: "It's always 'nigger' or 'nigra'" when the coaches were speaking about athletes, the frustrated Wallace told Olson. Bowden responded to the reporter that his language use was unintentional and that "McCarty's done more for the nigger race than Harry Edwards'll do if he lives to be 100."[40] Such language was galling, of course, and athletes at campuses across the country noted similar problems with coaches and administrators. It was a key point in the protests at Indiana University, for example, and the regular use of racist language by coaches and staff certainly undercut aspirations that integrated sports were a race-free meritocracy.[41]

The broader campus climate also showed how black participation in sports did not necessarily lead to changes in racial attitudes, and many protests called attention to the need to change racism at an institutional level. The hiring of black coaches was one of the most frequent demands made by college athletes. When black football players at the University of Colorado announced in December 1970 that they would boycott spring practice as the result of coach Eddie Crowder being "insensitive and indifferent" to the particular issues faced by his black players, they were giving voice to a larger issue, one that could be best rectified by hiring African Americans for coaching positions.[42] Nearly every school that saw black athlete protests included demands for the hiring of black coaches or black administrative staff.[43] The protests at Syracuse, which generated significant media attention, began over the failure to hire a black coach for the football team.[44] A racially integrated team was one thing; a racially integrated team with a black man in a position of authority was another. Black sportswriters across the country picked up on athletes' calls for the hiring of black assistants and head coaches, noting the symbolic and practical benefits.[45] Combating systemic racism required a fundamental restructuring of all institutions, especially at the leadership level.

Beyond the realm of sports, athletes also sought to change the racial climate on their campuses in two key ways: through an acceptance of interracial dating and the promotion of black studies and black history programs. The subject of interracial dating was a potentially explosive one; long-held cultural taboos against black men dating white women held sway across the country. For black male athletes, this proved especially challenging. As Wiggins notes, many predominantly white schools "were guilty of condemning black athletes to an inadequate social life . . . by deliberately recruiting them to their schools but failing to attract a large number of other black students."[46] As Edwards put it, "The warning of 'Don't be caught even talking to a white girl, much less dating one'" was widespread. "Prescribed by white coaches and enforced by white teammates," this policy seriously limited black athletes' social lives and reminded them of their status as a suspicious racial other.[47] Ongoing segregation of fraternities similarly denoted a second-class status while simultaneously cutting down on possibilities for socializing.[48]

In the midst of these abuses—racist language, segregated campuses, biased coaches, and indifferent white peers—black athletes united with other black students to call for the creation of academic programs that affirmed their heritage and identity. At Marquette University in Milwaukee, twenty black students, including six members of the men's basketball team, protested institutional racism at the school and threatened to leave the university. After meeting with school officials to discuss their grievances, they ended the protest because, according to student Lucien Moolenaar, the university had committed to hire an administrator to coordinate a scholarship for black students and because of the university's pledge to add "black and minority courses."[49] Athletes at the University of Kansas, the University of North Carolina, and many other schools pursued similar goals.[50] As Wiggins notes, these efforts were part of a broader trend in high schools and colleges across the country as black students pushed for the hiring of more black faculty, the introduction of African American Studies programs, and the recruitment of more minority students.[51] Indeed, the first Black Studies program in the country emerged in 1968 at San Francisco State College, where a group of student activists pushed for the creation of the program.[52] That so many athletes committed to changing the educational curriculum and the makeup of their campus communities spoke to the widespread impacts of Black Power. In affirming black culture and challenging dominant hegemony through their protests, black athletes played their part in contesting systemic racism in their schools.

An Individual Pioneer in a Time of Upheaval: Charlie Scott at UNC

It was in this context of activism and unrest that Charlie Scott made the difficult decision to support the BSM at UNC. As a racial pioneer on the campus of a Southern historically white university, Scott faced considerable pressures and constant scrutiny. His story—and the complications that emerged as he tried to use his athletic clout to challenge racism outside of sports—shows the significant resistance that college athlete activism occasioned. And it provides a closer look at the difficult choices individuals had to make during this era of upheaval.

Scott had arrived as UNC's first black scholarship basketball player in the fall of 1966 following a recruiting battle with Davidson College. A star at Laurinburg Institute, an all-black school near Charlotte, Scott had earned national attention for his skills on the basketball court. UNC head coach Dean Smith had, for years, been seeking a good candidate to break through the color barrier on his team, and Scott fit the bill as an excellent student and a remarkable basketball player. His signing made local and national headlines, adding extra scrutiny to his pioneering role. He made an immediate impact on the basketball court for the Tar Heels. During his sophomore season of 1967–1968, his first season of eligibility for the varsity squad, Scott started and averaged more than seventeen points a game for the Tar Heels, helping to lead the team, with senior Larry Miller, to an ACC championship and a runner-up finish in the NCAA Men's Basketball Tournament.[53]

After the season, Scott was selected for the U.S. Olympic basketball team, and he pondered boycotting the event in support of the OPHR. He ultimately decided to play in order to show his faith in integration. Scott explained in later years, "Well, if you go to North Carolina, and you turn around and boycott, you really defeat the purpose of why you went there. You go there to show you can integrate. If you boycott, what are you trying to show? If I boycotted, it would be counterproductive to what I was trying to do."[54] At the Olympics, Scott averaged eight points a game for the team, which won all nine of its contests and claimed the gold medal with a fifteen-point victory over Yugoslavia in the final.[55] Scott supported Smith and Carlos's decision to protest on the medal stand, seeing it as an important way to call attention to the ongoing issues facing African

Scott celebrates with his teammates after winning the ACC championship in 1968. Photo courtesy of the *Yackety Yack*.

Americans. When the U.S. Olympic Committee sent in Jesse Owens to try to talk other black athletes out of participating in protests in the wake of Smith and Carlos's actions, Scott did not heed what Owens had to say. He saw the legendary track star as the "compromising black," while 1968 "was the time of the militant black."[56]

To what extent, though, was Scott willing to take that militancy back to Chapel Hill? Things had changed on campus since Scott's arrival in 1966. When Black Power emerged the summer before Scott's first semester, its influence spread far and wide, especially on college campuses. At UNC student Preston Dobbins started the BSM in 1967 when he grew frustrated by the cautious and conservative campus chapter of the NAACP.[57] By the fall of 1968, the organization was beginning to make waves on campus, inviting provocative speakers and calling attention to examples of racial injustice on and off campus. That December, Dobbins and several members of the group presented UNC chancellor J. Carlyle Sitterson with a list of twenty-three demands. Only two (more recruiting of black athletes and the hiring of black coaches) dealt with sports; the others focused on black student and staff well-being. Some of the demands included the establishment of an Afro-American Studies program, the creation of a dean of black students, the abandonment of the use of standardized tests for admissions decisions, and higher wages for minority housekeeping and food service workers.[58] Sitterson waited until January to respond—when he did, in a nineteen-page document, he rejected all of the group's demands, except those related to the recruitment of black athletes.[59]

When the BSM came calling to ask Scott to support their efforts, he felt torn, and the pressures he faced offer compelling insights into the experiences of college athletes, especially those in the South. Scott struggled to balance his desire to help fellow black students and still be a moderate enough figure, in his words, "that other blacks could come [to UNC] after" him.[60] Heading into his junior year, Scott was the established star, the player on whom UNC's basketball fortunes would depend. It was the first time in UNC's history that a black player would be the leading figure on a team, and he had a chance to change people's conceptions of African Americans as athletes and to open up more opportunities for other black players in the future. To get to that point, he had suffered racial abuse from fans on the road and faced social isolation on campus at UNC. Although he got along with his teammates on the court, integrated socializing was extremely rare in North Carolina.[61] Should he try to maintain his tenuous position, or push for broader social change?

Ultimately, Scott and Chamberlain agreed to join the BSM leaders in their meeting with Sitterson in February 1969. Coming in the wake of violent confrontation at nearby Duke, where black students occupied a campus building and fought with local police, Scott's involvement in BSM activities generated considerable media coverage. The *Durham Morning Herald*'s front-page story about the meeting published thumbnail photographs of Scott and Chamberlain with its story and highlighted Chamberlain's statement at a rally afterward: "If I'm going to represent this university on the basketball court, I think the university should go to bat for me and take some positive action soon." Scott said nothing at the actual event but released a more diplomatic statement later in the day from Maryland, where he had traveled for a game. Saying that he and Chamberlain participated "to serve . . . in helping to close the communication gap" between the BSM and university administrators, Scott emphasized that he was happy at the school and that his "concern grew out of the situation in which black students have found themselves at universities throughout the country."[62] In the aftermath of the Olympic protest and the climate of social activism, Scott felt compelled to act—and not just on behalf of athletes and black students. Instead, Scott participated in a campaign designed to help the local black community gain access to higher education, a more nuanced understanding of history and culture, and better wages. Scott's participation in the

BSM protests thus underscored the broader activist role being played by black college athletes.

At one point, members of the BSM asked Scott to boycott a game in support of their efforts. An anguished Scott approached Smith about the matter. Although the head coach had publicly supported Scott's role in the meeting with Sitterson, he hesitated to give his blessing to a one-game boycott, fearful that he would be fired if he condoned such an action. Scott, too, worried how his teammates and others would respond to such a dramatic step.[63] He knew that he was being cautious, but he also knew the reality of his situation: "I always had a lot of pressure [from the BSM]. But I had a commitment, I had a responsibility to make it so that other blacks could come after me. I wasn't there to close doors, I was there to open doors. To open doors sometimes means compromises, and it didn't always mean doing what I wanted to do." Scott believed that his reserved stance toward activism enabled Chamberlain to get more directly involved: "Billy could be an activist because I was the buffer and was doing the proper things so whites felt comfortable."[64] Even in staking out that rather moderate position, Scott received no support from the local mainstream press. The major newspapers in the area printed editorials that ridiculed the demands of the BSM and praised Sitterson and UNC system president William Friday for taking a firm line against on-campus activism.[65]

The BSM refused to give up when Sitterson dismissed their demands. Recruiting black athletes, the one point that Sitterson approved, would not be enough: the BSM wanted substantial change and vowed to fight for it. One week after the meeting with Sitterson, the BSM started a boycott of campus dining facilities. Believing that the mostly minority employees were underpaid and denied access to supervisory positions, the group encouraged black workers to stay home, and they set up their own food service at Manning Hall on campus. Shutdowns of some dining facilities ensued, and the makeshift restaurant at Manning Hall had steady business.[66] Although Scott refrained from publicly supporting the boycott, this engagement with the broader black community was surely what he had in mind when he decided to lend support to the BSM.

Scott's limited activism came with consequences: despite being the best player on the best team in the conference in 1969, Scott failed to win the ACC Player of the Year award and was left off of five ballots for the ACC first team altogether.[67] The latter was an especially outrageous slight—no objective observer would have chosen five other players over Scott. Clearly, his activism and his race mattered in the media voting. The ACC Player of the Year went to John Roche, a white sophomore guard for South Carolina. Roche had certainly played well that season and had scored thirty points in leading South Carolina to an early season victory over UNC. Traditionally, however, the Player of the Year award had been awarded to the best player on the best team—in this case Scott. The Tar Heels had also bounced back to win the rematch with South Carolina later in the season, a game in which Roche committed a crucial late-game gaffe that helped UNC clinch a 68–62 victory.[68] Given Scott's more advanced status in school—another factor that voters usually considered—Scott appeared to be a shoo-in for the award. When the votes were tallied, however, Roche earned fifty-six votes to Scott's thirty-nine. Scott publicly fumed at the decision and indeed almost boycotted his team's NCAA tournament games, feeling that the vote was racially motivated.[69] In a story in the *Morning Herald*, Scott expressed his anger that voters had selected Roche "because he's white."[70]

Few supported him publicly. Head coach Dean Smith told Scott in private that he should have won, but almost no one affirmed his claim.[71] There seemed to be a tacit understanding, though, that Scott's activism was to blame. A reader of the campus *Daily Tar Heel*, F. Wilton Avery, wrote a letter to the editor in praise of Scott as the ACC's best and noted that his activism likely cost him votes.[72] *Charlotte News* writer Bill Ballenger also wondered if Scott's work with the BSM had influenced voting, noting that Scott was "under pressure from black militant groups to quit basketball as a gesture against inequality in the system."[73] Similarly, a *Morning Herald* reporter asked Scott if the skewed voting had anything to do with his involvement in the BSM. Scott angrily replied, "That has nothing to do with that. . . . That's for all black students. This only concerns basketball."[74] But as Scott was well aware, the two were not so easy to separate. In using his clout to call attention to the BSM's work, Scott had made visible the links between sports and politics. For some white fans and media figures, that was clearly too much.[75] Indeed, a *New York Times* article noted that bar patrons in Hickory, North Carolina, watching the national semifinal game against Purdue, cheered for Scott early in the game but then later entertained the theory that Scott purposefully played poorly because he was "mad at the school" because of the ongoing protests led by the BSM.[76]

The one local press outlet to support Scott's activism was the student-run *Daily Tar Heel*. After Scott and Chamberlain met with Sitterson in February 1969, the newspaper published an editorial that praised the players for their decision to "use their positions as basketball stars as a club to force the Administration to act," even though their actions would likely "gall a lot of people." To the editors, it was "only proper" that black athletes use their "power" to help black causes, and they thought the two basketball players showed "maturity of intellect" and "courage of action."[77] Sports editor Owen Davis similarly praised the two, writing that he supported black athletes who decided to "take their stand." Although he guessed that the two would "be branded as troublemakers," Davis encouraged them to persevere, writing that "few achieve greatness by avoiding controversy." By calling attention to inequalities on campus, even those outside of sports, the two athletes were following their convictions and "should be respected by all for doing what they feel is right." Davis then described a scene from the team's recent trip to play against the University of Maryland. According to Davis, as the team's bus "passed by long streets of tenement row houses" that were populated "almost exclusively" with black residents, "Scott . . . peered out the bus window." A somber Davis wrote, "He can't pretend that what he saw is not real. The day of the dumb jock is fast fading." The *Daily Tar Heel* sports editor encouraged Scott to "follow his conscience."[78]

But that admonition was a challenging one for Scott and other relatively isolated black athletes. The following season, despite keeping a relatively low profile with regard to activism, Scott still lost out on the ACC Player of the Year award to Roche again, despite posting better scoring, rebounding, and assist numbers. While critics howled, and many noted the impacts of racism in the voting, the loss showed how activism and even forthright commentary on race could injure African Americans' possibilities in a deeply racist society.[79] And there was a personal cost: "I gave away my whole social life for college," Scott lamented in later years. Because "[white] people did not associate with blacks . . . and blacks did not socialize with whites," his "social life was very limited to what North Carolina had to offer."[80] Even with a supportive head coach, ravenous fans, and a relatively liberal campus community, Scott's activist efforts faced considerable obstacles and backlash. The years of 1968 and beyond may have been ones of revolt for black athletes, but for relatively isolated pioneers like Scott, the battles were not easy to fight or win.

Supporting the Wyoming 14: The Black Press and Challenges to White Leadership

If Scott's story shed light on the burdens borne by individual pioneers, the saga of the Wyoming 14 highlighted in stark contrast the uphill battle that black athletes, even in groups, faced when trying to challenge white leadership in the realm of athletics. Fundamentally, the protests centered on the school's contests against BYU and were part of the larger set of activism against Mormon religious beliefs and practices. But the discourse surrounding the protests, especially in the contrast between the coverage of events in the black press and its mainstream counterparts, revealed a significant schism when it came to power and authority in college sports.

The saga, which has been well documented by historian Lane Demas in his book *Integrating the Gridiron*, began in October 1969. Wyoming's football team had been very successful in the previous three seasons under head coach Lloyd Eaton, claiming the conference championship in each season and earning a top-ten finish in the Associated Press poll for the 1967 season. The 1969 season started in similar promising fashion, with the school winning their first six games. However, on Friday, October 17, 1969, the team's fortunes turned for the worse. That morning, fourteen black players on the team entered Eaton's office wearing black armbands. They intended to talk to the coach about the team's game the following day against BYU. The players hoped to support a campus Black Students Alliance (BSA) protest that was scheduled to take place outside the stadium. Eaton had caught wind of the planned protest earlier in the week and had warned the team that he had a no-protest rule for squad members. While the players hoped to negotiate with Eaton, the coach instead dismissed all fourteen from the team—using vehement (and according to some accounts) abusive language in the process. The stunned athletes, given no opportunity to state their claims or to even suggest the gestures they had in mind, emptied their lockers, returned to the student union to regroup, and then met with school administrators. After a series of separate marathon meetings with the players and coaches that lasted from Friday evening into the early hours of Saturday morning, the school's board of trustees upheld the coach's dismissal of the players.[81]

Eaton consistently framed the issue as one of discipline, arguing that as a coach it was paramount that he had control over his team. He told the press, "They came in together and they came wearing black armbands. . . . It was simply a matter of discipline. Black or white, it didn't matter to me. They broke the rule and I told them they were no longer members of the team."[82] His edict banning athlete protest, and another that prevented athletes from forming "groups or factions," affirmed his right to control the players on the team and to emphasize team unity over all else.[83] When later asked to explain why he had refused to listen to the players' grievances, he articulated a hard line: "They had already violated our coaching rule. There was no purpose in talking."[84] Having surveyed the landscape of black athlete activism in the years leading up to fall 1969, Eaton had clearly made his mind up to prevent any protests. Although he attempted, at times, to justify his stance on the grounds that athletes did not have time to demonstrate, that it would interfere with their education and their athletic careers, few gave much credence to the claim. In taking Eaton's side and upholding the dismissal of the fourteen players, Wyoming governor Stanley Hathaway said, "Demonstrators cannot be permitted to run a university."[85] Power and control were the real issues at stake.

Mainstream media coverage of the events often expressed sympathy for Eaton and his peers, seeing troubling signs in coaches' loss of power and control. Only two months before the Wyoming protests, *Sports Illustrated* had published a series on "The Desperate Coach," focusing on college coaches' loss of control and influence in the wake of student-athlete unrest. Although writer John Underwood did note the pressures faced by black athletes who had to perform on the field and also respond to the desires of "militants" for social protests, the article clearly expressed little sympathy: "Many black athletes read race into almost everything a coach says or does. Often mistaking discipline for discrimination, they have compiled an inventory of incidents that reinforces their belief that a lot of coaches are racists. These blacks challenge rules whenever they are contrary to their emerging cultural pride."[86] The broad-based support for Eaton in the Wyoming community—shown by the raucous cheers he received at the game following his dismissal of the players, and, according to the *New York Times*, the many letters and telegrams he received—indicates how many supported this line of thinking.[87] *New York Times* writer Anthony Ripley published a front-page story headlined "Irate Black Athletes Stir Campus Tension" in the wake of the Wyoming dismissal. In it, Ripley wrote about the "rising militancy" of black athletes on college campuses and expressed his belief that some black athletes were shooting themselves in the foot with their protests by making it so that white coaches would not recruit black players in the future.[88] One year later the *Times* published Neil Admur's article "Campus Crossfire: Coaches Trapped between Dissenting Athletes and Rigid Policies," in which he addressed the activism of black college athletes but focused on expressing sympathy for old, white coaches who were bewildered by their players' behaviors.[89] On the whole, many in the mainstream media sympathized with the plight of Eaton as he sought to retain control over his team.

The bugaboo of outside agitators—in the form of Black Power activists like the Black Panthers—surfaced in a number of white responses to the events. Ripley printed, without comment, WAC commissioner Hallock's comments that black players were the victims "of the power tactics of the extremists," as if they had been duped into protesting.[90] Demas argues that a wide range of people bought into this belief. Wyoming school officials warned residents that a group of two thousand Black Panthers was en route to lead protests and uprisings. Local residents cautioned readers of "outside influences" wreaking havoc on campus and in the community. Even the NCAA jumped on board, fanning the flames of white anxiety by publishing a story in the organization's official publication headlined "Militant Groups Doing Great Disservice to Black College Athletes." The story "claimed that the Black 14 were acting under the auspices of the Black Panther Party in Denver."[91] *Times* columnist Robert Lipsyte, one of the sportswriters most attuned to issues of racial inequity in sports, seemed to buy in to this narrative to some extent, writing that "the college athlete, particularly the black college athlete, is under increasing pressure from campus activists to involve himself in issues."[92] Although Lipsyte blamed on-campus groups, he still suggested that athletes were being pushed to engage in protests at the behest of others. While the Wyoming players dismissed the accusations out of hand, and there was no evidence of any outside groups leading the activism on campus, the circulation of this narrative showed how many whites refused to see beyond the supposedly level playing field of sports to recognize the realities of racism. And it also shows the deep anxieties many whites had about Black Power in general.

Still, there were some whites in the community and the mainstream media who thought that Eaton had gone too far. Campus faculty members, by and large, supported the athletes and criticized the school's actions. Wyoming's faculty senate voted 37–1 to rescind the suspension of the fourteen black football players until a hearing could be conducted.[93] Professors in the College of Arts and Sciences issued a resolution calling the players' treatment "a mockery of academic freedom." Some students, especially those from out of state, also joined in the protests on behalf of the athletes.[94] Even Lipsyte, who had expressed some concern about outside activists, expressed his skepticism that Eaton's "disciplinary hold on the squad was threatened" and his repression necessary.[95] Hallock, monitoring the situation as head of the WAC, called the situation "unfortunate," explaining that he did not "feel it was necessary for Lloyd to go as far as he did." In dismissing the players for a relatively minor event, from Hallock's perspective, Eaton had stirred up trouble across the conference and had encouraged more protest and unrest.[96] In this way, some mild critiques of Eaton did make their way into mainstream coverage, even if the majority of Wyoming whites rallied to the coach's side.

The black press, on the other hand, gave little credence to Eaton's perspective. Black newspapers across the country, including the *Chicago Defender*, the *Philadelphia Tribune*, and the *Baltimore Afro-American*, all reported on major developments in the saga, as did national publications such as *Jet* magazine.[97] These sources lambasted the school in particularly strong terms. One major theme in the black press was the violation of basic freedoms for the Wyoming

14. Although Eaton claimed to be interested in his players' education, *Defender* columnist A. S. "Doc" Young argued that Eaton had "[trampled] on the rights of the kids as students and American citizens," and disputed the idea that this was about "the discipline necessary to winning team sports."[98] For the relatively conservative Young, such criticism was especially sharp. Sheep Jackson of the *Cleveland Call and Post* also questioned the repression of the players' rights, linking the athletes' desire "to wear arm bands" to the many college students who had done so in protest of the Vietnam War.[99] In the *Afro-American*, Sam Lacy questioned Eaton's rights in restricting his players: "The athletes were wearing their own clothes, and . . . there should be no attempt on anyone's part to order a man to wear, or not to wear, clothing of his choice, especially since the incident did not occur" during any official football activity. He wondered, "How much does a college athlete have to sacrifice his principles" to play his sport?[100] In *Jet*, William Ashworth argued that the protests were fundamentally about "the right of black athletes, or any athletes, to protest symbolically."[101] One of the captions for the *Jet* story made an especially interesting assertion: that white protesters tended to focus on "principle" (such as signs quoting the Declaration of Independence) while those of black protesters tended to highlight "racial concern" (such as a sign asking "Is Being Black Being Wrong?").[102] While the mainstream press had danced around these issues, black publications forcefully condemned the infringements of the athletes' rights and highlighted the impacts of systemic racism.

An editorial by white journalist Roger Stanton in *Football News*, reprinted in the local Laramie newspaper, drew particular ire from Lacy and others. In the piece, Stanton criticized black athlete activism on campuses, including those at Wyoming. In response, Lacy supported the athletes, affirming their rights to protest and calling attention to the long-standing issues of discrimination faced by African Americans. Where Stanton criticized the "dissidents" for causing their teams to suffer, Lacy defended the protesters, writing that the players wanted "the same right to representation the colonials wanted at the Boston Tea Party."[103] When Stanton called for black players to "put the welfare of [their] team ahead of . . . petty grievances," Lacy ridiculed Stanton for believing that "the grievance over second-class citizenship and deprivation is 'petty.'"[104] Columnist Jim Ingram for the *Michigan Chronicle* also excoriated Stanton's column. After reading Stanton's piece, Ingram saw him as an example of "the ignorant, arrogant retinue of racist writers who has never taken the time to try and understand what we mean when we talk about racism." While Stanton argued that football provided a level playing field based on meritocracy, Ingram noted that black players did not have equal lives off the field, that they "can't even find decent housing because of . . . skin color."[105] For these writers, the myth of sports as a realm free from prejudice needed to be challenged; inequalities ran rampant throughout sports, inequalities that seriously curtailed blacks' rights and freedoms and that spoke to larger issues in American society.

Indeed, one of the key points raised by black writers was that Eaton had failed to recognize his black players as full human beings worthy of consideration and respect. Eaton said that he and the school's athletics department supported black athletes and were "trying to give them that chance to really do something for their people by getting [an] education." However, team captain Joe Williams indicated that Eaton had not allowed the athletes to express their position and had instead kicked them off the team without any conversation.[106] For writers like Jackson, this showed Eaton's failure to listen to his players: "He just doesn't understand the black players or their motivations or on the other hand he didn't want to understand."[107] Young agreed. He mocked Eaton for being "a few enlightenment years removed from awareness of the basics behind current events." He quoted defensive starter Tony McGee, who said, "We went in there to talk intelligently and to discuss the way we felt about the game." Instead of listening, Eaton "cussed at us and didn't even try to find out what we wanted to talk about." McGee said it was not right that they had to "face abuse" and that "this has to stop somewhere." Young agreed wholeheartedly, calling Eaton's actions "brutal, senseless callousness in face of legitimate demands for African-American rights."[108] As the season progressed, Wyoming lost its last four games, missing the contributions of the black players. *Michigan Chronicle*'s Jim Ingram saw this as the consequences of Eaton's inability to engage with his players as men: "He found out that black power is something that his team needed, but not at the price of black pride and manhood!"[109]

At stake, of course, was the issue of control. As college athletics desegregated across the country, coaching staffs remained almost entirely white. As a result, the collisions between older white coaches and younger black players were perhaps inevitable.[110] Young noted the racial issue in his commentary: he criticized the white Wyoming players for going on with the game against BYU, seeing in their actions a support of "the Neanderthalic" belief that "the coach is god."[111] Lacy similarly criticized the "dictatorship" of white coaches.[112] For Cal Jacox in the Norfolk, Virginia, *New Journal and Guide*, the protests at Wyoming reflected the imbalance of power at predominantly white schools: the athletes were fighting back against issues that "have been plaguing the Negro athlete on the major college campus for years."[113] While Stanton in his *Football News* column praised football for providing opportunities for black players, going back to Bobby Marshall's performance in 1905 at the University of Minnesota,

Protesters gather before a game after Coach Lloyd Eaton dismissed fourteen black players from his University of Wyoming football squad. Photo courtesy of the University of Wyoming, American Heritage Center, Irene L. Kuttenen, Schubert Black 14 Collection, Accession #10405, box 2, folder 7.

Lacy pushed back by noting that "there hasn't been a single black head coach in ANYTHING" in the world of integrated sports.[114] The disparity of coaching positions for black men, an issue largely neglected by mainstream publications, was a visible reflection of the relation of race to power and control.

One especially noteworthy example of black press coverage of the Wyoming 14 came through the television program *Black Journal*. A public television show that debuted in 1968, *Black Journal* concentrated on issues relevant to the African American community. In late November 1969 an episode of the weekly program featured a seventeen-minute segment on the Wyoming situation, highlighting many of the themes spotlighted by the black press. Political rights were clearly important to the program's producers. At the outset the narrator identified the Wyoming 14 as activists "in the struggle for racial justice," and the episode featured a significant amount of footage depicting black picketers outside the Wyoming stadium. In addition, the program featured interviews with white protesters, including one who asked, "What's more important, human rights or winning football? This is supposed to be the Equality State, not the football state." In this way the program showcased the lack of political rights that athletes had, but it also spotlighted the persistence of racism in the supposedly color-blind world of sports.[115]

Eaton's lack of understanding and compassion for his black players also surfaced a number of times in the segment, and the program affirmed the players' humanity and manliness. When one of the players recalled Eaton taunting the players that they should not have tested him by wearing their armbands, the player observed that Eaton seemed to think that he was "really God." Another noted that black athletes were expected to have "no social life." To Eaton and other whites at the school, the player lamented, "We're not human beings. We're not men." As the segment approached its conclusion, team captain Joe Williams vowed that he would be ready for the "next Coach Eaton" and that he would stand up for himself more directly than he had previously. According to Williams, the fight was worth it, no matter the outcome: "You are now a man. You're no longer a boy." "Dignity," one of the other athletes chimed in. "Pride," Williams added. Affirming their manliness and refusing to cower before the white authority in charge, the black players clearly inspired the program's hosts, Lou House and William Greaves. "Those are some dynamite cats, Bill," House observed.[116]

One further issue made its way into the episode: the nature of "amateur" college athletes. In introducing the story, Greaves used the word "fired" to describe the Wyoming 14. Of course, that terminology reflected an employer-employee relationship, a status that the NCAA had (and has) consistently sought to undermine through the terminology "student-athlete." But many in the media, and the black press in particular, refused to play along. After all, Lacy had used similar language when he pondered the injustices at Wyoming and the University of Washington, where head football coach Jim Owens kicked four black players off of his team because they did not "promise '100 percent commitment to the football team and its coaches.'" When an athlete "accepts an offer to go and work for a school," Lacy wondered, did he give up all his rights?[117] While Demas saw this as evidence of the media misidentifying the true nature of college athletes' positions, one might argue that these publications and programs were actually calling attention to the reality of big-time college sports.[118] As de facto employees, athletes ought to have certain rights contractually guaranteed and protected. The nebulous definition of the term "student-athlete" made that all but impossible.

In the end the Wyoming 14 faced considerable obstacles in their activist efforts. Almost immediately after their dismissal, NAACP lawyer William

Waterman filed a suit on behalf of the Wyoming players in federal court to have them reinstated, but the drawn-out process paid no dividends. U.S. District Court judge Ewing T. Kerr twice ruled against the players when the case came through his court, siding with the power of coaches to regulate athletes' behaviors.[119] While Eaton won the battle, he lost the war; failing to recruit more black players for his squad, Wyoming suffered through a 1–9 season in 1970 and the coach soon resigned. The players went different ways. Some, like Mel Hamilton, graduated from Wyoming. Others transferred to other schools to continue their education and playing careers. Two, Tony McGee and Joe Williams, went on to have successful playing careers in the National Football League.[120] Nearly all were scarred by the experience. Fifty years after their banishment, the surviving members were finally invited back to campus, where the university formally apologized and held a number of events in their honor. The surviving members walked with the current football team members to the game that weekend and received honorary jerseys in front of a packed house. It was a long time coming, an outcome nearly impossible to imagine when their lawsuit was rejected for the second time in the fall of 1971.[121]

Troy State and Beyond: Limited Power and NCAA Change

Activism among college athletes waned in the years after the Wyoming 14. By the time the courts definitively rejected the players' lawsuit, most campuses had settled into an uneasy peace. Even schools such as the University of Alabama—a football powerhouse whose head coach, Paul "Bear" Bryant, had come to represent authoritarian discipline and who had supported Eaton in fall 1969—saw significant changes.[122] Not only had black players joined the previously segregated varsity squad by fall 1971, but Bryant had allowed more student freedoms. Players grew their hair longer and even participated in on-campus activism. In fact, Wilbur Jackson, the first black player signed to a football scholarship at the school, regularly attended meetings of the campus Afro-American Association with Bryant's blessing.[123] That student organization had actually sued Bryant and the school only two years earlier for his failure to recruit black players for the team and had campaigned actively for a wide range of changes at the school.[124] Bryant's decision to allow Jackson and others to work with the group showed a significant difference from the intransigence of Eaton at Wyoming.

Indeed, the Wyoming 14 story was one of the last major stories of college athlete activism in the era. While small flare-ups emerged at schools across the country, they tended to be less expansive in nature and more easily resolved, such as a boycott by black basketball players at Cornell University over the issue of playing time in early 1972.[125] Scholars have offered two primary reasons for the gradual decline in protest. Some, such as sociologist Douglas Hartmann, have noted the loss of momentum in the civil rights and Black Power movements.[126] As Wiggins has argued, "It was nearly impossible for African American athletes to maintain the necessary energy and sense of purpose" for on-campus activism, especially because they faced "enormous pressure from coaches and others in the sport establishment to refrain from engaging in radical displays of racial protest."[127] Others, such as football-player-turned-professor Michael Oriard, have pointed to the NCAA's decision to adjust its policies on scholarships for student-athletes. At a little-discussed NCAA meeting in January 1973, the organization decided to change the terms of scholarships from four-year agreements to one-year grants. The switch had been years in the making: a number of schools had first tried to change the terms in 1969 as activism flared up on campuses across the country. However, pushback from administrators at historically black colleges and universities, who saw the move as a way to punish black athletes, killed the change. In 1973, though, with little discussion, the motion finally passed. Oriard notes that even if discussions of race and protest were not explicitly made by NCAA members in 1973, "they must have had the recent racial protests on their minds."[128]

A relatively small and mostly forgotten protest at Troy State University in Alabama suggests that the NCAA ruling might be the more compelling explanation. Troy State was an unlikely site of a significant protest. The school participated in the Gulf South Conference, a collection of smaller Division 2 colleges and universities that failed to generate the considerable media attention of their Division 1 brethren. In addition, the school had seemed to make good progress in terms of race and athletics as the 1970s dawned, earning some national acclaim in the black press in June 1971 when black track star James Batie was unanimously selected as team captain for the upcoming season.[129] The football team featured its first integrated squad that fall, with running back Cliff Dunham as its first black player.[130]

One year later, though, all was not well. At halftime of the team's September 30, 1972, game against Ouachita College, six black players left the team protesting what they believed to be unfair conditions and biased treatment from the coaches and athletic officials. In response, head coach Tom Jones kicked the players off the team and refused to allow them back on the squad. The Monday after the game, the players submitted a list of nine grievances to Jones. They included accusations of inadequate academic counseling, false pretenses in recruiting, an "unfair dress code," unequal distribution of work-study jobs, inadequate and unequal medical treatment, and "malicious slander of the black athletes." For those who had been paying attention, of course, these were familiar charges levied by black athletes at predominantly white schools across the country. However, Jones, who also served as the school's athletic director, dismissed the charges out of hand. Although he agreed to meet with the players, he made it clear that they would not be welcome back on the team, saying that the players had chosen to quit and that "there's no way you can trust them again" after their actions. The coach said he would talk to the players solely "to improve relations with any black athletes we might recruit in the future."[131] The football players were not alone in their protest at the school. According to a UPI story published in the school newspaper, officials believed that ten to twelve black athletes from the track team "planned" to quit their program and that up to thirty black athletes altogether might leave their teams. But, drawing a page out of the Wyoming playbook, the college was not sympathetic. According to the story, "The athletes who quit the teams were removed from scholarships and ordered out of the athletic section of a dormitory." Jones was characteristically blunt: "They didn't want to play so they quit, and other people have been shifted to fill their positions."[132] It was as if Lloyd Eaton had been channeled into a new person at a new school.

As at Wyoming, the players resisted the attempt to banish them from the team. On October 4 the Troy players held a press conference on the state capitol steps to outline their position. Dunham explained that, in his mind, he and the other players had not quit the team. Instead, the walkout was meant to "get the students and faculty to wake up" to the issues facing black students and black student-athletes at the school. He said that "a more radical" approach was necessary than simply issuing a list of grievances. He also explained that the three major issues were the "inadequate academic counsel" offered to blacks, the "unfulfilled promises to black athletes with regard to their scholarships," and the "improper utilization of players."[133] All of the other black varsity athletes at the school joined the protest and testified to their grievances. Track athlete Charles Allen described how a coach "tore up" his proposed course schedule and reregistered him in "music courses and such." Another athlete, George Echols, indicated that he had received a scholarship for less than one-sixth the amount he had been promised.[134] Although these protests were undoubtedly about race, they were also about the fundamental nature of college athletics: the exploitation of athletes for entertainment without adequate concern for their academic progress and without adequate remuneration.

Like the Wyoming 14, though, their efforts seem to have failed: the black players do not appear in the school's yearbook, for example, and the only stories circulating in the mainstream press in the weeks to follow lauded Jones's actions. In the *Birmingham News*, Alf Van Hoose effusively praised Jones for holding firm against the black players' demands, believing that Jones's actions entailed a "landmark stand."[135] On October 11 the newspaper printed another article celebrating that many had leapt to the coach's defense in his handling of the insurgency. Jones said, "My desk is covered with mail from all over the country." He also received telephone calls and telegrams and said it "was encouraging" to see that people "from all over the country" supported his actions. Jones said that the team's black athletes "were invited to appear before our athletic committee Wednesday to air their complaints," but he again asserted that they would not be able to rejoin the team.[136] Although Van Hoose cautioned his readers not to interpret his article as "applause for a coach jumping on black athletes," clearly race mattered. He cited Owens at Washington, Ben Schwartzwalder at Syracuse, and Eaton at Wyoming—all three of whom, of course, encountered black athlete protest—as coaches who would have been gratified by Jones's stand.[137] In this case the beleaguered white coach had reaffirmed his power, putting black athletes back in a subordinate position.

The timing of the Troy State uprising is suggestive: only three months later the NCAA made the pivot to one-year scholarship offers. While no records of the debates about the change exist, it's quite possible that this latest example of black student protest was a final straw for many college and university presidents. As historian Taylor Branch noted, the one-year scholarship rule meant, in effect, "that coaches get to decide each year whose scholarships to renew or cancel."[138] The rule gave formal backing to the punishment meted out by Jones. And it surely had a chilling effect on activism. Oriard calls the one-year scholarship limitation imposed in 1973 "a crucial event in the history of college football's fundamental contradiction" between a mission of academic uplift and a focus on revenue-generating athletic entertainment.[139] But it was also one more barrier against athlete activism. While protests did occur in later years—such as the boycott of practice in the spring of 1974 by black athletes at the University of New Mexico over the lack of black baseball players at the school—they were fewer and further between.[140]

The story of athlete activism on college campuses in the late 1960s and early 1970s is not monolithic—multiple issues and multiple outcomes emerged over time. Those looking for optimism might note the changes at Alabama or the support of Dean Smith at UNC. But the Troy State situation is a cautionary reminder of the ongoing realities of college sports. Although most historians agree that coaches were forced to adapt to the changing times and to listen to their players more than in the past, the fundamental imbalance of power persisted. As student-athletes, they lacked the formal protections of employees.

When the NCAA struck down requirements for four-year scholarships, they were still at the mercy of their coaches for the continuation of their education and their playing careers.

The sad case of Willie Muldrew showed the potentially devastating effects of this lack of athlete power. Muldrew was a black football player at Iowa State University. In the summer of 1968, he had been the spokesman for a group of black athletes at the school advocating for racial change. The group wanted the appointment of an official liaison to represent black students, more "expense money" for athletes, "an assurance that injured black players" be given adequate time to heal, and "the abolishment of an alleged 'quota' system" regarding the number of black athletes. In response, head coach Johnny Majors demoted Muldrew to the second team (despite his being an all-conference selection the previous year), and Muldrew quit the squad in protest. The school refused to honor the athletes' demands. Cut loose from Iowa State, Muldrew was not drafted by an NFL or AFL team, despite his accomplishments, and was tragically killed by an ex-girlfriend before he could join a team in the Canadian Football League.[141] Had Majors been more receptive, Muldrew's life might have taken a very different turn. His death—and the lack of power it revealed—showed how much work remained to be done.

* * *

Willie Muldrew's tragic death spoke to the complicated terrain in which black male athletes had to operate in sporting culture and the nation at large. As athletes across the country contested boundaries and pushed for change in numerous aspects of American life, the assertion and protection of black masculinity would emerge as one of the most important battlegrounds. As we will see in the next chapter, the historically hypermasculine sport of boxing, especially through the figure of Muhammad Ali, would provide one of the most compelling arenas in which to showcase alternative visions for black manhood.

CHAPTER 4

BLACK MEN / BLACK GLADIATORS

Redefining Black Manliness through Sports

On the evening of March 8, 1971, Bryant Gumbel, then a twenty-three-year-old journalist trying to make it into the world of television broadcasting, found himself weeping uncontrollably. The occasion was not the loss of a loved one or pet; nor was it a personal injury or distress. Instead, Gumbel cried because his idol, the larger-than-life boxer Muhammad Ali, had just lost a heavyweight boxing championship bout to fellow black fighter Joe Frazier. Gumbel was not alone in his distress. Other fans wandered around in a daze, uncertain how their favorite boxer had failed to come through. But there was more to Gumbel's tears, and the bitter reactions of those other fans, than just the sport. Bryant explained in later years that he was "certain that [he was] right to support Ali . . . to oppose the war, that the cause of Civil Rights was just, and when he lost, it was almost like, 'I can't be on the wrong side of those things.'"[1]

Clearly, the March 1971 fight between Ali and Frazier—the first of three bouts between the two men—had broader implications outside the ring that led to these extreme responses. Indeed, the bout was freighted with significance, evoking numerous issues, including patriotism and religious tensions. But racial politics lay at the heart of the impassioned responses to the fight, especially in debates over differing notions of black masculinity. Ali, the so-called people's champion, fought to reclaim the title he had lost as a result of his refusal to fight in Vietnam. His outspoken criticisms of white racism, defiance toward authority figures, and faith in the Nation of Islam made him a revered figure for activists, especially those aligned with Black Power. Meanwhile, by claiming the heavyweight championship while Ali was banished, cozying up to white politicians, and refusing to criticize the U.S. government, Frazier fit in with conservative opposition to the turbulence wrought by the 1960s. To Gumbel and others, Frazier, despite being black and having risen from poverty, represented a hope of the white establishment, a conservative force who did not speak to everyday African Americans' wants and desires. Ali's defeat marked a symbolic blow against a variety of deeply felt political causes.

Yet a closer look at the contemporary public discourse surrounding that fight—especially its buildup and the intense reactions that followed it—complicates traditional narratives in important ways. As the historical record reveals, there *were* African Americans who were interested in activism and civil rights who still favored Frazier, put off by Ali's antics, religious faith, and supposed bad attitude. Nor were reactions easily divided along age or gender lines; some young fans favored Ali, just as some women favored the more taciturn Frazier. Indeed, some in the black community appeared to favor neither fighter at all—finding value in the actions, beliefs, and statements of both fighters. That gap between Gumbel's polarizing assessment of the fight and the more complicated response in the wider discourse opens an important window into people's assessments of black manhood and the quest for civil rights in this era. What many responded to in the fight, implicitly or explicitly, were competing models of black manhood. Discussions of the two boxers before, during, and after the fight constituted a kind of forum on the best approach to racial equality—often divided between an "assimilationist" approach or a "Black Power" strategy. Yet they also forcefully spoke to the imbalance of power in the world of sports and beyond. By calling attention to ongoing inequities in boxing, especially in the financial arrangements for the fight, public voices spoke to a wide range of economic issues facing the black community, including the exploitation of talented black entertainers and the hopes—and dashed realities—of black capitalism. Debates about Ali and Frazier, then, were indelibly linked with efforts to earn black men the privileged position of male breadwinner in the American capitalist economy.

Black Manhood and American History

The two boxers' personal stories, which both entwined and diverged, help explain much of the American public's fascination with the fight. Muhammad Ali was born Cassius Clay in 1942 in Louisville, Kentucky. Introduced to boxing at the age of twelve, Ali used his astonishing agility to capture a gold medal at the 1960 Olympics in Rome. Turning pro upon his return from the games, Ali quickly ascended to the apex of the sport, claiming the heavyweight championship in February 1964. Soon after, Clay announced his conversion to the Nation of Islam and changed his name to Muhammad Ali, a controversial move that cost him many supporters, principally in the white community. Of particular note, Ali lost the patronage of the group of white businessmen from Louisville who had been his financial backers, and he eventually turned over his management to Nation of Islam official Herbert Muhammad. Ali retained his heavyweight crown until 1967 when, citing his religious beliefs, he refused induction into the U.S. Army. Immediately after his arrest for failing to serve in the military, Ali was stripped of his boxing licenses and championships. Although he appealed his conviction as a draft evader, Ali was unable to box and instead made a living by speaking at college campuses on topics related to civil rights, the Vietnam War, and his Muslim faith. Finally, in October 1970, while his case was still on appeal, Ali returned to the ring, as black Georgia state senator Leroy Johnson used his political clout to engineer a match against prominent white boxer Jerry Quarry. After winning that bout and then defeating Argentinean boxer Oscar Bonavena in December, Ali declared himself ready to reclaim his title.[2]

To earn a living while banned from boxing, Muhammad Ali spoke on college campuses. Here he visits Franklin & Marshall College in Lancaster, PA. Courtesy of Archives and Special Collections, Franklin & Marshall College.

Joe Frazier's path to the heavyweight championship mirrored Ali's to some extent but diverged in important ways. Born in 1944 in Beaufort, South Carolina, Frazier also took up boxing as a youth and worked his way up through the ranks. Moving to Philadelphia, Frazier made a name for himself as a brawling fighter in the style of Rocky Marciano. Four years after Ali, Frazier also won a gold medal in the Olympics, at the 1964 games in Tokyo, and turned pro thereafter. Initially encountering grinding poverty and long odds, forced to work in a slaughterhouse and a janitor as he pursued his career, Frazier soon signed with a multiracial group of Philadelphia-area investors who called themselves Cloverlay Inc. When Ali was banished from the sport in 1967, Frazier was one of the top contenders. By February 1970 he had claimed all of the heavyweight titles. Although Frazier did not serve in the military, because of a poor test result, he expressed his support for military service as an act of patriotism, an attitude that alienated him from many young people, black and white. Frazier also suffered from complaints that he was not a true champion because he had claimed the title while Ali was banished.[3]

The fighters announced in December 1970 that they had signed a contract to set up the long-awaited bout for March 8, 1971. Both fighters would earn $2.5 million from the match, an unprecedented purse and a sign of the intense interest the fight occasioned. After all, the previous year, Frazier had only earned approximately $300,000 for defeating Jimmy Ellis for the world heavyweight title.[4] The announcement set off a firestorm of pre-fight publicity as sports fans eagerly looked forward to the match-up of undefeated champions and marveled at the huge payout for the two fighters. However, right from the start, that discourse strayed far afield from boxing style and big-time payouts. Instead, observers used the fight to engage in discussions related to race and black manhood.

The Ali-Frazier match stirred up long-standing anxieties and hopes regarding black men's participation in public culture. For hundreds of years, sports and other forms of popular entertainment had played a vital role in America's racial caste system, simultaneously promoting and contesting black men's relegation to inferior roles. By the early twentieth century, as professional sports became increasingly popular in the United States, nervous white men, "obsessed with the connection between manhood and racial dominance," often looked to public spectacles such as athletics to affirm their beliefs in racial superiority.[5] The anxious, bitter responses to athletes like black boxer Jack Johnson showcased these anxieties. Johnson claimed the heavyweight championship in 1908, the first black boxer to do so, and violated social mores by marrying white women and flaunting his wealth. Immediately, whites set out to find a white challenger to defeat him. After Johnson won a series of lopsided victories over hapless white opponents, white newsmen and fans across the country urged former champion James Jeffries, who had retired undefeated in 1905, to come of out retirement. Heeding their calls, Jeffries agreed to fight Johnson in order to restore the heavyweight championship to the white race.[6] When Johnson quashed that hope by soundly defeating Jeffries on July 4, 1910, white men across the country responded with indiscriminate violence against African Americans. An editorial in the *Los Angeles Times* captured white anxieties about the fight's broader implications for manhood. Headlined "A Word to the Black Man," the text cautioned:

> Do not point your nose too high. Do not swell your chest too much. Do not boast too loudly. Do not be puffed up. Let not your ambition be inordinate or take a wrong direction. . . . Remember you have done nothing at all. You are just the same member of society you were last week. . . . You are on no higher plane, deserve no new consideration, and will get none. . . . No man will think a bit higher of you because your complexion is the same as that of the victor at Reno.[7]

Although the response to Johnson was an extreme case, it brought to light the extent to which people linked ideas of manliness with success in the sports world.

While white Americans anxiously sought to undermine black male sports achievements, black leaders saw sports as a way to claim access to positions restricted to white male citizens and to disprove stereotypes of black male inferiority. The stalwarts of muscular assimilation believed that sports success would force whites to see black males in a new light as they "began to show themselves in public in new ways" through their athletic achievements.[8] Sports stars who had followed Johnson, including collegiate stars Fritz Pollard, Paul Robeson, and Kenny Washington, and professionals such as boxer Joe Louis and baseball pioneer Jackie Robinson, carefully cultivated positive images of masculinity in order to gain access and change white perceptions.[9] Louis, in particular, crafted a public image meant to soothe white anxieties regarding black men's place in society when he claimed the heavyweight title in the mid-1930s. Refraining from boastful talk or intimidating behaviors in the ring, speaking with humility, and avoiding any public images with white women, Louis earned both black and white acclaim as he pummeled his opponents. Timing mattered; Louis claimed the heavyweight championship amid international turmoil, and his victory over German boxer Max Schmeling—held up by Adolf Hitler as proof of Aryan supremacy—united Americans and brought national pride during the long fight against Nazi fascism. As historian Anthony Edmonds has argued, Louis promoted a sense of racial pride for African Americans through his successes but eased white anxieties by not posing "a threat to the structure of racial custom and etiquette."[10] Louis and Johnson were important antecedents to Ali and Frazier, men who had navigated the arena of white public animosities toward black male achievement in very different ways.

Male athletes also battled a wide range of deeply ingrained stereotypes in mainstream public culture. The performance tradition of blackface minstrelsy, the first distinctly American form of popular entertainment, cast an especially long shadow that lasted well into the era of Ali and Frazier. Commencing in the first decades of the nineteenth century, black minstrelsy featured white male entertainers "blacking up" by applying the ashes of burnt cork to their skin. Dressed in outrageous costumes, misusing language, committing acts of violence, and following simple superstitions, the black characters who appeared on the minstrel stage depicted African Americans along a spectrum of childlike simpletons to frenzied psychopaths.[11] Later forms of popular entertainment would pick up on these stereotypes. Ragtime songs of the 1890s featured razor-toting violent drunks and watermelon-eating rural buffoons.[12] Hollywood films for the first half of the twentieth century traded almost exclusively in stereotypical roles for black characters. As film historian Donald Bogle notes, nearly every role for black males in a major Hollywood film fit one of three archetypes: the coon (a clownish simpleton or ignorant crook), the Tom (a docile, loyal, and subservient childlike man), or the brutal black buck (a lustful, frenzied savage).[13] These stereotypes made their way into newspaper, radio, and television news as well.

Of course, African Americans did not passively accept these demeaning representations. As noted earlier, sports provided one avenue to redefine black manliness and to reconceive images of black men. These alternative visions of black manhood, however, were not identical, and over the years, leaders proffered a number of different approaches. As historians Darlene Clark Higgins and Earnestine Jenkins have argued, "Black men's history and manhood has been a diverse experience, multi-faceted and complex."[14] In the late nineteenth and early twentieth centuries, for example, Booker T. Washington and W. E. B. Du Bois offered two contrasting visions for black political and economic advancement that necessitated two different approaches to manhood. While Washington was content to temporarily put aside social and political equality in order to bolster black employment, accepting roles in lower-tier jobs in the trades and industry, Du Bois insisted upon full equality, demanding that black men claim access to all rights afforded their white peers. A different dichotomy emerged in the 1960s, with Martin Luther King Jr. promoting racial integration and inclusion into the existing American democratic political and economic institutions and Malcolm X and other black nationalists arguing in favor of racial separatism and an overthrow of existing institutions. For many, these splits in political ideals dovetailed with notions of masculinity. According to feminist scholar Michele Wallace, for many black men in the 1960s, Malcolm X "was the supreme black patriarch," a tough, unerringly masculine man in contrast to the softer, feminine King.[15]

The early 1970s marked an especially potent moment for these discussions of black men in American civic and social culture. As historian Steve Estes has argued, during the civil rights movement, many male civil rights leaders used "masculinist strategies of racial uplift with the express hope of gaining economic autonomy, political power, and social status for black men."[16] The 1968 Memphis sanitation workers' strike, supported by Martin Luther King Jr. before his assassination in that city in April of that year, centered on redefining black manhood. As Estes notes, "These were working men, fighting for higher wages so that they could support their families and fulfill the traditional breadwinner role of men in a capitalist society."[17] Picketers in the strike "carried signs that read, in bold block letters, 'I *am* a man.'"[18] King himself frequently discussed the campaign for the Memphis workers, and his Poor People's Campaign more broadly, as an effort to bolster black manhood.[19] Black nationalists and Black Power advocates, although often at odds with King and his approaches, often operated from a similar set of assumptions. As sociologist Michael Kimmel notes, Malcolm X "spoke about reclaiming a manhood stolen from black men by white slavers and denied by two centuries of racist politics." Groups such as the Black Panthers "made black manhood a centerpiece of its appeal to young blacks."[20] However, as feminist scholar bell hooks has noted, Black Power advocates also tended to be more suspicious of the market, believing that "nothing about the capitalist system was legitimate."[21]

Despite the concerns of some Black Power leaders, much of the activism of the 1960s and 1970s supported traditional gender ideals that emphasized the man's power within the family, building on the ideal of the (white) male breadwinner.[22] Of particular importance in this context was sociologist Daniel Patrick Moynihan's 1965 report "The Negro Family." The publication suggested "that black women had emasculated black males by being matriarchs" and indicated that the failures of black families to have traditional, patriarchal gender roles were a key problem holding back the black community.[23] Moynihan and others believed that because black men had been denied access so long to the attributes of American manhood—namely, making enough money to support their families and being active political participants and community leaders—they should lay claim to the masculine prerogatives that their white male counterparts already had. In other words, as Estes has written, these men operated from the assumption "that men [were] more powerful than women, that they should have control over their own lives and authority over others." These were the fundamental assumptions of white manhood, so many black men took up these goals.[24] Indeed, Wallace argues that black women implicitly made a "bargain" with black men during the 1960s at the height of the civil rights movement—to "keep [their mouths] shut" as black men worked toward the "assertion of . . . manhood."[25] There would be a reckoning in terms of these patriarchal attitudes and assumptions, and the building storm surrounding the Ali-Frazier fight hinted at some of the challenges to these chauvinistic visions of manhood.

Pre-Fight Buildup and Alternative Masculinities

As the fight approached, these different models of masculinity were very much in the foreground of public discussion. In the mainstream media and the black press, writers contrasted the two boxers in terms of political meaning as much as, if not more than, in terms of fighting style. A cover story from *Ebony* magazine by Lacy Banks, for example, described the clash in these terms: "Ali is the people's champion. . . . He is greatly admired by militants, liberals and by philosophical and moral idealists." Banks quoted Ali as saying that he "wanted to be rough, tough, arrogant, the nigger the white folks didn't like," in the model of Jack Johnson. Meanwhile, Banks described Frazier as "the official champion," arguing that his core audience consists more likely of "conservative blacks" and even "Caucasians who see him, ironically, as some kind of 'Great White Hope.'" Frazier's history of working within the system—such as his willingness to enlist in Vietnam—contributed to these associations.[26] In *Sports Illustrated,* boxing writer Mark Kram noted how the public was framing the fight in similar ways: "The New Left," he wrote, "comes at Frazier with its spongy thinking and pushbutton passion and seeks to color him white, to denounce him as a capitalist dupe and a Fifth Columnist to the black cause." Hard-core conservatives, on the other hand, "just as blindly rancorous, see in Ali all that is unhealthy in this country, which in essence means all they will not accept from a black man."[27] For nearly everyone watching, the fight and the buildup to it were forums in which to debate the place of black Americans in society, and in particular the proper role for black men.

Ali gleefully embraced his role as a radical and cultural critic. In his entertaining press conferences, Ali depicted himself as "the one who could identify with the suffering of black people in the United States and all over the globe." In the process, Ali openly taunted Frazier as a tool of white supremacists: "'I know what's going to happen before the fight,' Ali said. 'That Joe Frazier, he's gonna get telephone calls and telegrams from folks in Georgia and Alabama and Mississippi saying, 'Joe Frazier, you be a white man tonight and stop that draft-dodging nigger.'"[28] Ali's insistence that he represented a bolder, more defiant manhood resonated with many, especially in the black community. In the *Baltimore Afro-American*, veteran sportswriter Sam Lacy lauded Ali's willingness to question authority, writing that Ali "was not overly impressed by the teachings in his home, that what Mister Charlie says is gospel and that there must be no question or rebuke."[29] In the *New York Amsterdam News*, writer Dick Edwards supported Ali as an icon of resistance, someone who "was hated by the Establishment because 'in the not too far distant past he would have been an uppity nigger.'"[30] According to Gumbel, Ali "seemed to think less of what the establishment thought of him than about the image he saw when he looked in the mirror." This attitude empowered "people who were young and black and interested in tweaking the establishment, and in cases shoving it up the tail of the establishment." Ali's victories made him "a heroic figure" for those hoping to envision a new America.[31] According to historian Jeffrey Sammons, Ali channeled "the disillusionment of many blacks with generations of unfulfilled dreams and broken promises" in the wake of the slow pace of change after *Brown v. Board of Education*.[32]

By a combination of design and accident, Frazier came to be associated with a more conservative, gradualist approach to change in American life. He had worked his way up from poverty to become heavyweight champion and saw in his own life story the values of discipline, hard work, and faith in the American system. Although he supported Ali's refusal to be drafted into Vietnam as a conscientious objector, Frazier also expressed his support for service in the increasingly unpopular war (a failed written test kept him out of service).[33] While Ali labeled Frazier an "Uncle Tom," Frazier also engaged in his own form of verbal intimidation, by continuing to refer to Ali as "Clay." By refusing to recognize Ali's new name and, by extension, his faith in the Nation of Islam, Frazier linked himself to critics of Black Power. As Gumbel recalled, "Only those who were bigots, rednecks, hardliners, continued to call him Clay, almost as an insult . . . and when Frazier chose to do that, to a lot of African-Americans, it was kind of like, 'Hey, who you siding with here? Take a look in the mirror.'"[34] Frazier also managed to alienate many of his black hometown Philadelphia fans by endorsing notorious white police commissioner Frank Rizzo, one of the most hated men in the black community for his department's extremely poor record of police brutality against African Americans. Frazier explained, "A lot of people feel differently about the commissioner. . . . And they might even get mad and call me a 'Tom,' but I think Rizzo would make a good mayor." These factors conspired to make it seem, in Banks's words, that Frazier's beliefs matched up well with "the wishes of WASPs."[35]

Much of the commentary in the mainstream press and in personal anecdotes indicates that many white Americans did support Frazier over Ali and that the issue of military service played a large part in determining fans' attitudes. Writer Budd Schulberg described a working-class white bartender at the Penn Plaza Club in New York in the hours before the fight, who crowed, "Well, how is Mr. Big Mouth? Oh is he gonna get *his* tonight! Fuggin' draft dodger. I wanna see Joe knock him cold." Schulberg writes, "Up and down the town, taxi drivers, bartenders, doormen, construction workers, New York's equivalent of the White Citizens Council, have been waiting for Frazier's star-spangled fist to shut up that big unpatriotic mouth once and for all."[36] *Life* writer Thomas Thompson wrote that when Ali "turned to the Muslims . . . refused the Army . . . [and] transformed himself from a Negro to an angry black man," many white fans "booed him because they felt they had been betrayed."[37] To that end, Robert W. Kelley of Seattle, Washington, wrote to *Life* magazine that he and "millions of *Life* readers wanted to see . . . Frazier's fist firmly implanted against Muhammad Ali's mouth."[38] That both Kelley and the unnamed bartender targeted Ali's mouth was surely not a coincidence; Ali's outspoken nature and critiques of mainstream society made him an especially contentious figure. *Time* magazine published letters from two women who complained about the prominent coverage of Ali, with Ruth M. Langstaff of Sacramento, California, indicating it was "an insult to all of the young American men who have bravely and not always willingly fought in our armed forces to have Cassius Clay's picture on the cover of TIME."[39] Frazier's willingness to serve in Vietnam—and, more generally, his willingness to work within the system inside and outside of sports—made him a more appealing boxer for many white Americans.

There was considerable irony in the rhetoric of Frazier as a "Great White Hope" and an "Uncle Tom." As Ali biographer Thomas Hauser has noted, in many ways Frazier's life was "more typical of black America than Ali." The "honest Bible-reading Baptist Joe" certainly embodied black Christianity's strong presence in American life, as did his working-class roots.[40] As black playwright and cultural critic Larry Neal observed, "Frazier is stomp-down blues, bacon, grits and Sunday church," symbolizing Southern black culture. And yet in the turbulence of the 1960s, that traditional identity had become less salient in popular culture. For Neal, Ali represented "body bebop," a defiance of traditional forms and norms that contested Frazier's conservatism.[41] While some black sportswriters such as Anthony "Doc" Young of the *Chicago Defender* looked askance at Ali because of his nontraditional religious faith (and seemingly supported Frazier because of his more traditional Baptist upbringing), many in the black community overlooked Ali's faith and celebrated his spirit of defiance.[42] As Gumbel observed in later years, "Frazier was more like your parents were. He just kind of went along. He did his job. He wasn't a proponent of the old order, but he didn't fight it, either." As a result, "fairly or unfairly, because he was opposing Ali, Joe Frazier became the symbol of our oppressors."[43]

The term "Uncle Tom"—often used by Ali in mocking Frazier—spoke pointedly to the importance of black manhood as people discussed the upcoming fight. On one occasion, Ali and Frazier staged a confrontation at Frazier's gym to drum up interest in the fight. Trading barbs and vowing to square off on the street right then and there, Ali went too far, telling Frazier not to "act like no Uncle Tom." Ali writes, "His eyes are blazing and I know suddenly now that the pretense is gone and this is no put-on. Joe has always been a little slow in making out whether or not I'm serious or putting on, knowing whether he's in on the joke or the joke is on him."[44] Although Ali claimed to be joking, to be using the phrase as a way to wind up tensions, Frazier's frustration was real. The term "Uncle Tom" had its origins in the minstrel stage versions (and later Hollywood films) of the Harriet Beecher Stowe novel *Uncle Tom's Cabin*. In these later versions, Stowe's heroic character—who in the novel embodied devout Christian faith, selfless love, and tremendous moral strength—became a passive rural simpleton, a devoted slave who lived to please white masters above all else.[45] To be an Uncle Tom was to be a dupe of the white establishment, overly docile and loyal to a fault—in other words, an Uncle Tom was not a real man. Ali continually used the phrase in connection with Frazier. And he did so in extreme ways: in one press conference, Ali imitated Frazier's speech, making him sound dumb, and pushed in his nose and tugged down his ears to mock Frazier's appearance.[46] Frazier did not take kindly, writing in his autobiography, "Let's face it: Clay was smooth, and quick, with the mouth. Me, I'm not much of a talker. But that doesn't make me ignorant, or a goddamn Uncle Tom. Or a disgrace to my race."[47]

However, Frazier acknowledged that Ali's words gained traction: "Repeat the lie often enough, and people begin to think it's so."[48] Ali continued to press this angle as the fight drew closer. Days before the event, Ali painted Frazier as a pawn of the white establishment. He argued that "nobody" wanted to talk to Frazier except, perhaps, President Nixon. Ali affirmed his belief that "98 percent of my people are for me. They identify with my struggle. Same one they're fightin' every day—in the streets and against the police. . . . Anybody who thinks Frazier can whup me is an Uncle Tom." Frazier bristled at the idea that

Ali represented black people more than he did; he pointed out "the hypocrisy of being labeled an Uncle Tom by a black man whose trainer was white," a reference to Ali's trainer Angelo Dundee in contrast to Frazier's all-black team.[49] But Ali's barbs seemed to stick: the magazine *Black Sports* featured a cover story with the title "Is Joe Frazier a White Champion in a Black Skin?" And Frazier found himself trying "to explain to [his son] Marvis what to do about classmates . . . who called his father a 'Tom.'"[50] The fight, then, became a referendum of sorts on each fighter's credentials as a black man: defiance versus acceptance, rebellion versus loyalty, and, most fundamentally, independence versus dependence.

Empowering "Black Gladiators": Debating the Fight's Financing and Promotion

The debates about manhood inevitably spilled out into one of the key aspects of the fight: the financing of its huge payout. The fighters' announcement in December 1971 that they had signed for the extraordinary purse of $2.5 million per boxer—more than eight times the payout of Frazier's previous title bout—naturally evoked considerable commentary.[51] Initially, coverage in both the mainstream and black press focused on the large payout and the character of the two white investors who had secured the deal: Jack Kent Cooke, an owner of several sports franchises and cable television ventures, and Jerry Perenchio, a booking agent for Hollywood entertainers such as singer Andy Williams. Story after story, especially in the mainstream press, lauded these men for their entrepreneurial savvy in snapping up the rights to the fight. Although some wondered if the two had spent too much money to make a profit, they admired the investors' courage and initiative. One article in *Newsweek* seemed quite pleased that the two polished businessmen did not fulfill the stereotype of "gruff, colorful men" who usually promoted boxing matches.[52] *Time* magazine and other mainstream publications such as the *Los Angeles Times* followed a similar angle, lauding Perenchio and Cooke for swooping in and getting the rights.[53] Only one note of discontent made its way into these accounts, and it was dismissed as a humorous aside. When Perenchio, at the press conference announcing the fight contract, targeted a "total gross box-office of $20 to $30 million" from the ancillary rights and the ticket sales from Madison Square Garden, Ali jokingly protested to Frazier, "They got us cheap. . . . Only five million out of 20 to 30. We've been taken."[54]

But writers in the black press saw a more sinister development in the terms of the fight's promotion and did not follow Ali in shrugging off the income gap between the white investors and the black boxers. Although impressed that Frazier and Ali would earn such large paychecks, writers Anthony "Doc" Young of the *Chicago Defender* and Claude Harrison of the *Philadelphia Tribune* held back any celebration of the two white promoters' ingenuity. In his first comments on the bout's financial arrangements, Young grumbled that the two boxers would not "participate in any of the ancillary rights—and this is where the 'real' money is to be made. They are, in essence, merely entertainers purchased for a night."[55] Young continued to press that angle in the days leading up to the fight, frustrated that black bodies would be exploited for white gain. Similarly, in Harrison's first column about the fight's promotion, he raised a number of important issues that linked economics and race. First, he was aggrieved to hear that tickets to view the fight in closed-circuit theaters could run from ten to twenty-five dollars, fees he declared "downright robbery." Harrison believed that anyone who spent more than ten dollars "has to have rocks in their head," and he quoted a number of local Philly boxing fans who agreed with him.[56] But at the end of the article, Harrison's critique took a more pointed turn as he lamented, "It's too bad Philadelphia didn't get the fight. Here at least some black faces would be in the crowd. No blacks are connected with the promotions at the Garden. They are ready to use black fighters but no front office officials."[57] Both of these black writers called attention to the exploitative nature of the fight's deal, as wealthy white investors stood to make millions on the backs of black boxers, with no black promoters holding high-level positions. Ticket prices, meanwhile, were so high that many poorer Americans would be unable to watch the fight, even on television. Black men would make money as entertainers, but they were still shut out of the halls of power.

These issues inspired two major civil rights organizations, the Congress of Racial Equality (CORE) and the Southern Christian Leadership Council (SCLC), to get involved in protesting the fight's promotional arrangements. CORE fired the first salvo, announcing plans in mid-January to boycott the fight and its closed-circuit broadcasts unless black groups were able to purchase television rights. After meeting with Perenchio, the group backed off, stating that an agreement had been reached for CORE to show the fight in selected cities across the country. Associate National Director Victor Solomon called the agreement "a major breakthrough for black people . . . in that blacks have been excluded of their fair share in this particular area." Although Perenchio attempted to distance himself from any activist intent, stating that his "favorite color is money—not white or black," CORE leaders clearly had bigger ideas as to the fight's significance. They hoped to use proceeds to "service black people," according to Solomon and, as such, took pride in their ability to buy in.[58] Solomon also explained that his group fought for the rights to the fight in several cities "because the white man will allow us to go into the arena and see the 'gladiators' battle but does not want any Blacks to reap financial benefits from the fight."[59] Although the negotiations were turbulent—at one point, CORE grumbled that their broadcast rights had been whittled from seven cities to just Harlem—eventually the group deemed the event a success. In addition to the broadcast in Harlem, CORE showed the fight in other locations, such as Baltimore and Washington, D.C., earning tens of thousands of dollars for community uplift programs.[60]

Although CORE succeeded in its efforts to prevent the exploitation of "black gladiators," SCLC struggled to accomplish similar goals. In early February the Philadelphia chapter of the group announced plans to boycott the closed-circuit broadcasts of the fight "if Chartwell Artists [Perenchio's company] doesn't give black businessmen an opportunity to operate closed-circuit TV showings of the fight." Joe Peters, the sports director of SCLC, explained his reasoning, using similar logic as CORE:

> We don't want Chartwell, which is giving all of its TV rights to its friends (Music Fair in Philadelphia and Concert West in Texas), to come into the black communities and take all the money and run back to its ivory tower. . . .
>
> I say, unless the black community gets an opportunity to make a bunch from this fight, don't support it.[61]

As had been the case with CORE, these activists saw the promotion as a clear-cut case of white businesses and promoters exploiting black male bodies for economic gain and doing nothing to help black Americans more generally.

SCLC followed through on its plans to protest the fight. The week of February 16, thirty pickets—twenty from the Consumer Education Protective Association and ten from SCLC—protested the high ticket prices for the fight outside the John Wanamaker Store in downtown Philadelphia, a department store selling tickets for the fight on behalf of local broadcast rights holder Music Fair Inc.[62] According to the story in the *Tribune*, Peters said that Music Fair and Chartwell "refused to allow blacks to bid for closed circuit outlets."[63] Phrases on picket signs included "Only the White Chauvinist Pigs Will Make Millions"; "Ali-Frazier, Yes! Chartwell, No!"; "Lower Ticket Prices"; and "Get-Rich Fight Promoters Exploit Black Community."[64] The protests continued into early March, and *Tribune* columnist Harrison speculated that they were one reason that "the $20 and $15 tickets didn't sell like hot cakes" in the weeks leading up to the fight.[65]

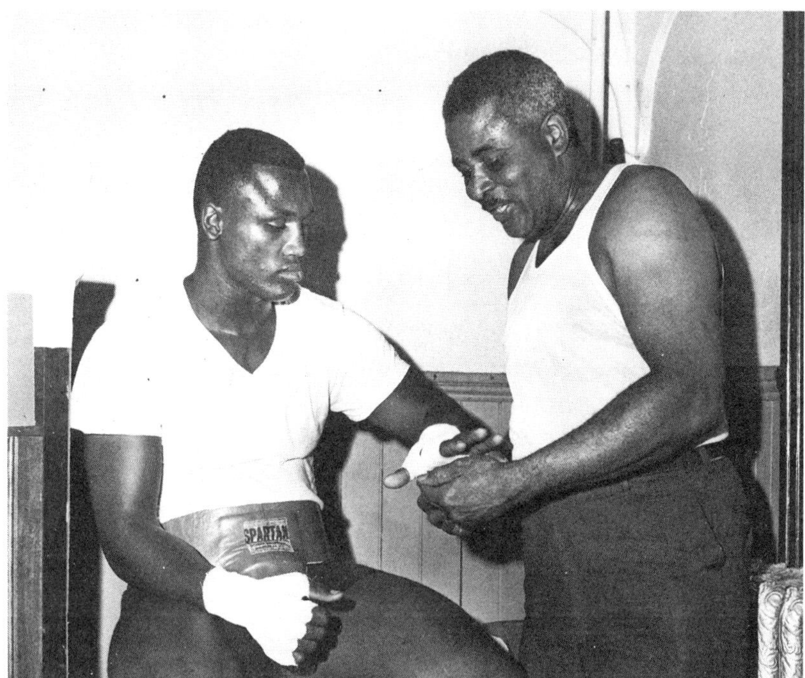

Joe Frazier with manager Yancey "Yank" Durham, who received criticism after pushing back against SCLC in Philadelphia. Courtesy of Special Collections Research Center, Temple University Libraries, Philadelphia, PA.

But as SCLC pressed its case, they met an unexpected obstacle: Frazier's manager, Yancey "Yank" Durham, who had brokered the fight deal on behalf of both fighters. When told of SCLC's protests, Durham reportedly told the group to "drop dead," a response that did not go over well with the leaders in SCLC. Durham defended himself, saying, "Before we signed with Chartwell . . . our doors were open to everyone, black or white, as long as the color of their money was green." He noted that several black groups had made offers but had been unable to come up with the money.[66] Durham rejected complaints that the fight would be inaccessible to the black community because of the high cost of tickets for closed-circuit showings and that black promoters should have been involved. Durham responded:

> What do I care how much money go here and how much go there. . . . I got two-and-a-half million dollars each for the fighters, and nobody has ever given me nothing. No white group has ever given me nothing. No black group has

> ever given me nothing, I worked for everything I got. I worked on the railroad; I worked as a stevedore; I worked with fighters. I had a number of fighters who were fighting, and this is the only fighter I ever had that be successful, so I ain't giving up nothing. I think it's right for the fighter I'm working with, and that's all I'm interested in."[67]

Working long, hard hours in and out of dingy gyms, scrambling to get by, Durham was clearly delighted to have finally struck gold with the Ali-Frazier fight. Thus, Durham defended himself by emphasizing his right as an individual to look out for his own best interests and that of his fighter, Frazier. It was an attitude that fit in well with the era of black capitalism and the concurrent efforts of Jim Brown and Billie Jean King.

Frazier pursued a similar course. Uninterested in helping SCLC's cause, he deflected questions about the promotion to Durham. And according to columnist Maurice Berube of *Commonweal*, a Catholic magazine with a liberal bent, CORE "was unsuccessful in its attempt to persuade Frazier to disavow the white racists who saw him as the means to defeat the Black Hope." Frazier explained, "I stand up for the black man, . . . but the most important thing, I stand up for Joe Frazier. That's where it all begins, each man standing up for himself and looking for his family.'"[68] Frazier repeated this message in a variety of forums, arguing that he was fighting not for his people, not for his country, but for his and his family's financial well-being.[69] In effect, Frazier used the opportunity of the fight to affirm his capability to serve as the traditional male breadwinner.

But that logic—privileging the individual over the group—did not fly with the SCLC's Peters and others in the black community. Although black leaders in the past had been content for athletes like boxer Joe Louis to eschew overt political stands on behalf of the community, believing that the athletes' public success alone benefited African Americans, times had changed. "From what Durham is saying he is taking an 'I have got mine, you get yours' policy about the issue,'" Peters said. "It's time for every black man with any power to let the world know where he stands."[70] Peters kept up his criticism of Durham as the fight drew near: "Unless Durham crawls into a hole and stays there he will live to regret telling us to 'drop dead.' . . . He is going to need black fans to make a buck after Frazier quits. Durham must realize that boxing in Philadelphia would not be worth two cents without the support of the blacks." For Peters, Durham's individualistic rhetoric rang hollow because it failed to recognize the importance of the black community in his own rise to prominence. Boxing manager Joe Gramby, a longtime trainer in Philadelphia, agreed with Peters's criticism, saying Durham was "as wrong as can be" in telling the SCLC to drop dead.

Gramby mused, "How can he be against SCLC[?] Is his memory so clouded by his present position in life that he has forgotten how hard we fought to get equal rights right here in Philadelphia?"[71] At heart was an issue of manhood: while Frazier's and Durham's focus on individual uplift fit well with the climate of black capitalism and with the American economy more generally, it did not speak to Black Power's emphasis on community empowerment.

Peters and the *Philadelphia Tribune*'s Harrison did not limit their criticisms to Frazier and Durham; they also chastised Ali for failing to support black promoters and institutions. In fact, right after the fight deal had been signed, Harrison wondered whether Ali would support Leroy Johnson, the man most responsible for engineering Ali's return to the ring by setting up his first bout against Quarry in Atlanta. Harrison wrote, "If Ali has the guts he claims to have he will tell the promoters that Sen. Johnson is in for a piece of the action or there will be no fight."[72] Johnson had gone out on a limb in arranging for Ali's boxing license for that fight, and Harrison felt it only fair that Ali reward the man who had made his ring return possible. Peters picked up on that issue once the SCLC launched their protests, chastising Ali for not ensuring that Johnson and his partner, Jesse Hill, had opportunities to secure the broadcast rights. According to the article, "Peters said it was time for Ali to stop talking about what he wants to do for his black brothers and start doing something."[73] For all of Ali's bravado and boasting that he was the "people's champion" and that he represented the struggles of black people, his lack of attention to the inequity of the fight's promotion was striking. Although he supposedly "said he was deeply sympathetic with his people's position" with regard to the CORE boycott, Ali seemed mostly unconcerned with the financial issues—other than his own $2.5 million.[74] In his autobiography, published in 1975, Ali wrote, with admiration, about his manager Herbert Muhammad's strategy for landing fight deals, particularly the March 1971 bout."The first bidder that comes in with the cold cash and puts it in a Muhammad Ali bank account, that's the one we deal with," Muhammad said. "We got higher bids than five million, but Jack Kent Cooke and Jerry Perenchio put the money up in your name and Frazier's name."[75] Making no comment at all on any of the controversy that emerged regarding the fight's promotion, Ali emphasized a similar message to Frazier—an individualistic outlook on financial success.

The fight's promotional saga spoke to the limitations of black capitalism and the emphasis on black entrepreneurship, echoing the frustrations of Jim Brown and Billie Jean King. The newly formed journal *Black Enterprise* (which did not cover the fight), noted how the lack of preexisting capital had crippled the black business community (and the black community in general). In its

February 1971 issue, one month before the fight, black Massachusetts senator Edward W. Brooke wrote an editorial about the needs for changes in the economic sector to benefit African Americans. Brooke cautioned that "pride in being black" and government "rhetoric" were "not enough." Instead, he called on skilled African Americans to "put their talents to work for the development of our black communities"—a clear message of black self-uplift. However, Brooke also called for outside intervention as well, arguing that "an infusion of capital is a must if black businesses are to survive."[76] As cultural critic Mike Marqusee noted in his biography of Ali, "The chief obstacle to black entrepreneurship—in sports or elsewhere—has never been a shortage of entrepreneurial skills, but of capital."[77]

And it was ultimately capital that separated the winners of the promotional rights to the bout—Cooke and Perenchio—from the losers. Cooke's ready supply of capital—the result of his many successful business ventures—enabled the two to secure the fight. In the end, Cooke estimated a total profit of $1.5 million from the fight to be split between him and Perenchio. Cooke said he was "terribly happy" with the fight returns, even though he made less than the fighters. "I went into this to have fun," he said. "I'm rather well off and I don't need the money."[78] For the various groups who saw this as economic exploitation, that attitude must have been galling. *Jet* and *Ebony* publisher Robert E. Johnson ruefully observed that the fight "was for the primary enrichment of two white businessmen: Jack Kent Cooke and Jerry Perenchio."[79] From his vantage point with the BEU, Jim Brown grumbled that Cooke represented "the establishment that a lot of people are fighting so hard." Cooke got the fight, Brown argued, because he "bought everybody out." He saw it as a sign of the power of "the big buck."[80] In fact, the only charitable contribution made by the two white promoters came when Perenchio donated two thousand dollars for four scholarships for "young men and women from the lowest economic backgrounds."[81] If capitalism was to pull black Americans upward into the American middle class, a broader distribution of wealth than that was surely necessary.

One segment of the media that tackled these issues was the radical left-wing press. Michael Stewart, writing in *Workers' Power*, a labor magazine out of Detroit, called the fight "the biggest rip-off I've ever witnessed," citing the high ticket prices for closed-circuit viewing and for live viewing, the attempts to sell commercials during the broadcast for four hundred thousand dollars a minute, and the appearance of the boxers in commercials for the shampoo Vitalis. And he offered an incisive critique of the fight's promotional arrangements, linking issues of class and race together:

> The amount of money involved limited the promotional rights to only the very rich, thus confirming the old adage that the rich get richer and the poor . . . well, they pay $15 for a ticket. More than this, the promotional setup discriminated against the very people without whom this fight could never have taken place, the black people of this country.
>
> There were reports that several black organizations had tried to get the local promotional rights. The idea of course, was to try to route some of the profits to be made off these fine black athletes towards programs to help the black community, to the fight against racism, for black liberation. Unfortunately, very few, if any, black groups in this country have the kind of money to enable them to put up the two-thirds in advance.
>
> Of course, the two promoters, Cooke and Perenchio, claimed that they weren't discriminating, they were just using 'good business sense.' The fact is, however, that here, as elsewhere, this kind of 'good business sense' discriminates against blacks and other oppressed minorities. It is no mistake that black groups, and blacks in general, do not have the kind of money or connections necessary to promote these fights.[82]

Although Stewart did not call out black capitalism specifically, he likely had those policies in mind as he offered his critique.

Faith in black entrepreneurship was misguided to Stewart because blacks were facing a stacked deck—white investors had the stronger hand thanks to accumulated capital and connections established during centuries of discrimination. Although not using the term, Stewart's ideas resonated with the idea of systemic racism, with Carmichael's argument that "the ordering and structuring" of the U.S. economy worked to relegate African Americans to lives of "dependence and oppression."[83] The corrective Stewart saw was for Ali and Frazier to use their clout to alter the promotional arrangements for the (seemingly inevitable) rematch. Stewart argued that the two fighters "should demand that black organizations be given the distribution rights, at least for their local areas, and that tickets be priced low enough so that everyone who wants to, can attend."[84] In effect, he called for a modest form of affirmative action—giving black groups first priority in promoting the fight in heavily black areas.

An article in *Wildcat*, an alternative left-wing press operating out of San Francisco, went even further. The author was disgusted that Ali and Frazier would probably "clear" only about four hundred thousand dollars from the fight after taxes, whereas "the promoters, who didn't suffer any pain or work up any sweat . . . are getting upwards of $25 million!" That accounting oversimplified things considerably but nonetheless reflected activists' sense of the power dynamics at work. Frazier and Ali, according to the author, "are selling their labor just like in any other gig, and, just like any other workers, they don't own the means of production, in this case their own bodies. The promoters are capitalists who take theirs off the top because they control the capital."[85] Like the left-wing social critics who saw American labor unions as too focused on wages and benefits—instead of social transformation—the *Wildcat* saw Ali's limited control over his own person as a sign of the larger imbalances in society.[86]

That observation—about the ownership of the fighters' bodies—was especially astute. As Ali prepared for the fight, two documentary crews squabbled over the rights to film his workouts. One group, led by journalist Richard Durham, was associated with the Nation of Islam, and the other worked for Perenchio. As the two filmmakers fought for access to the fighter, Perenchio himself got involved. During one squabble, according to Ali's longtime fight doctor, Ferdie Pacheco, Durham yelled at Perenchio, "This ain't no plantation deal! You don't get the house, the field hands, and all the cotton for no two and a half million!" Perenchio responded by "pointing a manicured fingernail at Ali's sweaty chest" while saying, "We got a contract for this," explicitly affirming his ownership of Ali's body.[87] For the *Wildcat* columnist, this aspect of the fight, and the exploitation of poor people to participate in the brutal sport, rendered the whole bout an outrage. Ali's earlier efforts with Main Bout (and his later support for black promoter Don King) appear to have been his efforts to contest this arrangement. For the *Wildcat*, however, the answer was not a more even distribution of the promotional proceeds. Instead, the author called for revolution, insisting that "when all the people like us around the world get together, we're going to have the real, genuine Fight of the Century, and the smart money will be on the People."[88] Neither black capitalism nor affirmative action would be enough to dismantle the inequities wrought by the market and system racism.

* * *

Certainly, not all of the pre-fight rhetoric engaged directly with these issues of black masculinity and economic exploitation. There certainly was interest in the fight purely as a boxing event. Stories in *Sports Illustrated*, the *Amsterdam News*, and the *Afro-American* analyzed the fighters' styles and discussed the relative merits of the two fighters without focusing on racial tensions or political meanings. And there was plenty to discuss in this regard, including the high payout, the very different sizes and styles of the boxers (the tall and quick Ali versus the short and brawny Frazier), the impacts of Ali's lengthy absence from the ring, and the different personalities of the fighters (the loquacious Ali and the taciturn Frazier).[89]

Readings of the two fighters were not monolithic—if Ali's fans skewed African American, young, and liberal, and Frazier's tended toward white, old, and conservative, those boundaries could be porous. African American high school student Gary Bell, for example, favored Frazier because Ali was "always bragging."[90] Meanwhile, white writer Budd Schulberg noted that his own sixteen-year-old son was an Ali fan: "I dig the way he dances around those old fighters. . . . And the way he rhymes and picks the round. . . . He knows he's 'the greatest,' so why not say it?"[91] While some older black journalists like Doc Young clearly favored Frazier because of his modesty and Christian faith, other veteran sportswriters such as Sam Lacy admired Ali for his defiance.[92] No matter one's personal leanings, the interest was intense—so much so that bomb sweepers came through Madison Square Garden before the bout, and security officials kept a sharp lookout for snipers.[93] According to John Condon, one of two publicists for the fight for Madison Square Garden, journalists requested more press passes than for any previous event in the arena's history.[94]

Finally, after all the hype and hoopla, the fight night arrived. Tickets for the bout had sold out almost immediately. Celebrities packed the stands, with famed actor Burt Lancaster part of the broadcast team and noted singer Frank Sinatra taking ringside photographs for *Life* magazine. African American fans attended in droves, donning a stunning array of fashions that inspired countless follow-up articles and photos in *Ebony* and *Jet*.[95] In the *Defender*, interest was so intense that the newspaper featured a reader's poll regarding who would win the fight, with readers picking Ali by more than a two-to-one margin.[96] Ali entered the ring first, resplendent in red robes with white trim. Applause, and a small scattering of jeers, greeted his entrance. Frazier followed soon after, in light green robes trimmed with gold. The mixed roar of the crowd continued. After the introductions and rules, the two men stepped into the center of the ring and began their fight.

In the early rounds, Ali danced away from Frazier, landing blows to Frazier's face and head consistently. By the middle rounds, though, Frazier found his form, plowing his way through Ali's defenses to land punishing blows to Ali's midsection. Although Ali played to the crowd, shaking his head as if the punches did not hurt him, they clearly had some effect. Back and forth the fight played out—Ali punching to the head, Frazier landing shots in the body. It was an evenly matched and thrilling fight. In the eleventh round, however, Frazier finally caught up to Ali and punished him, landing a crushing left hook that wobbled Ali considerably. As the round ended, Ali barely escaped to his corner, saved by his own guile and the bell. But he responded, landing some hard punches to Frazier in the fourteenth and penultimate round that seemed to swing the momentum his way. Finally, though, in the fifteenth and final round, Frazier came through, catching Ali with a devastating left hook to the jaw that sent the challenger tumbling to the canvas. Although Ali picked himself up, the knockdown ensured that the fight would go to Frazier. Soon after, the ring announcer made the verdict clear: Joe Frazier had retained the heavyweight championship with a unanimous decision.

Aftermath: Ongoing Debates about "the Brotherhood"

But if the bout was over, the larger fights surrounding the contest only gained in intensity afterward. Central to the discussions that emerged in the fight's wake were the competing definitions of black manhood that had circulated before the bout. Stories about the fight in both *Ebony* and *Jet* were diplomatic, covering the event itself and praising both fighters for their efforts. In *Ebony*, Banks devoted his analysis to the fashions worn by black fans at the fight, contrasting the flamboyant attire of Ali fans with the more buttoned-down conservative looks of Frazier fans. The fight was such big news that Robert Johnson, the publisher of *Jet* and *Ebony*, felt inclined to pen his own story in its aftermath, which he did in the following issue of *Jet*. He minced no words regarding his loyalties, calling Ali "one of the few Black heroes still alive" and labeling Frazier "the unheralded, white-created champion." But Johnson's gripe was largely with the promotional financing of the fight, which netted considerable millions for its two white promoters.[97] In *Jet* the news of the fight's outcome earned front-page status, with a cover photo of Frazier in his boxing robe with the bold headline "Joe Frazier Proves He Is the Greatest."[98]

Many *Jet* readers disagreed with that assessment and in doing so affirmed their own visions of black masculinity—favoring the Black Power defiance of Ali to the conservative, modest deportment of Frazier. Thomas Mitchell Jr. of Chicago wrote in to say that Ali had only lost because of the "government" and the "Pentagon," a reference to Ali's refusal to be drafted and his long layoff. But Mitchell was not discouraged, writing that Ali "is a Black MAN, which is ever so much more important than being a Black boxing champion. He represents the new spirit in Blacks." Mitchell believed that Frazier would never be as "respected" as Ali because he was not a "winner" in the same way.[99] Meanwhile, Pleasant Williams of Belle Glade, Florida, argued that Ali "is a leader, a true leader, a good one. Any man who turns down $10 million to avoid being an Uncle Tom, but striving for his people, is nothing but a man, and I mean a man."[100] One black listener who called in to New York radio station WMCA after the fight expressed similar sentiments. She observed, "It is just sad because this man

Ali is so large. There hasn't been a man this large in our image."[101] Even Black Panther Party supreme commander Huey P. Newton indicated that Ali was "still our champ" in an open letter to the boxer. Newton said, "Ali is still the champ 'not because you are the master boxer (and you are, of course), but because you are the heavyweight champ who has refused to compromise Black manhood.'"[102] For these fans, then, Ali earned acclaim because of his defiance as a black man. In his refusal to be drafted, his outspoken confidence, and his unwillingness to back down from the white power structure, Ali modeled a hardened and proud masculinity that contested pervasive stereotypes. He represented Black Power's focus on racial pride, self-determination, and criticisms of established white power.

Ali's defeat disappointed his many fans, but it did not diminish his status as an avatar of black manhood. A self-identified "young black woman," Deborah Altman of Beaver Falls, Pennsylvania, acknowledged she was "hurt" by Ali's loss and "cried bitter tears at *our* loss" but that "through those tears I was able to see victory." Ali's ability to get back in the ring and fight showed that black people "won the right to stand up to all injustice and say 'no we won't go to Vietnam and murder innocent people for racist America and then return home to racism and genocide.'" Further, Ali earned for his people "the right to practice our own religious and political beliefs." Even though Ali lost the fight, Altman believed that Ali "won the greatest victory . . . a little piece of freedom we didn't have before. And pride, precious pride."[103] Ali's symbolic power in this regard stretched across the globe. A. Sivanandan, a Sri Lankan émigré to England and noted Black Power advocate, was disappointed by Ali's defeat but nonetheless felt emboldened by the boxer's strength:

> Tonight the black world weeps that their king has passed away. But tomorrow and tomorrow and tomorrow . . . every black man will become his own king—for that is the legacy that Muhammad Ali leaves. . . . The civil rights movement had only served to cordon off the black athlete in a Bantustan of sport. It was left to Malcolm X and the Black Power movement to threaten the total release of the negro. Muhammad Ali is the epitome of that release. And it is this that bugs white society. He is not just a prizefighter, he is not even one man. He is many men—and all of them black.[104]

These responses show the potency of Ali as a model of Black Power's many components—from Pan-African unity, to racial pride, to defiance of established norms and more.

But those responses were not the only ones. Although pro-Ali letters and reactions tended to be more prominent, a significant percentage of African

American fans thought Ali got the comeuppance he deserved. In criticizing Ali and implicitly or explicitly supporting Frazier, these readers celebrated an alternate vision of black manhood. Seattle reader Ritzy Gail Wright believed that "both heavyweight fighters . . . fought well" in their bout, but she thought that Ali had been put in his place. Although he claimed to be "Super Bad," like the lyrics of a James Brown song, she believed the more appropriate song was "Your Good Thing Has Come to an End."[105] One issue later, a reader wrote in to complain that *Jet* featured only pro-Ali, anti-Frazier letters. Reader Barbara Gray of Hopkinsville, Kentucky, was distressed that readers set out to "tear down" Frazier, "whose strenuous training has profited him a championship reign through his own blood and sweat efforts." Clearly, Gray admired Frazier's work ethic and felt aggrieved that other readers did not support him.[106] Similarly, Da Gretta N. Johnson of Greensboro, North Carolina, accused readers of being "so Black crazy" that they failed to "distinguish between sense and nonsense," encouraging readers to accept Frazier's win and give him the credit he deserved. And she let slip her own distaste for Ali, who she believed had "[caused] many embarrassments because of his loud mouth."[107] Doc Young contrasted Frazier's work ethic and "hard-shelled determination" with Ali's decision to "mash his religion . . . on sport" and his "undisciplined" habits.[108] Even thirteen-year-old *Philadelphia Tribune* reader Doris Bradley found value in Frazier's more subdued manner. In a poem called "The Fight," Bradley contrasted the "cool" Frazier with Ali, whose "loud" antics showed that he "was really the fool."[109] For these African American fight viewers, Frazier modeled a different kind of black manhood, one based on hard work, personal modesty, and, though it was often left unsaid, Christian faith.

One event in the immediate aftermath of the fight called special attention to these issues. In the wake of his victory over Ali, Frazier's home state of South Carolina invited him to address the state legislature on April 8, 1971. Frazier accepted the honor. In his speech he acknowledged that although "a proud and happy man," he was also "somewhat sad" that he was "one of the very few black citizen guests" to have been invited to speak at the state house. He noted that "there must have been more black men or black women also deserving of this honor." Frazier then called attention to the black representatives in the crowd, noting the progress their presence indicated. He emphasized that his story showed the value of hard work, the ability of Americans to pull themselves up in society. But he concluded with a call for more work on behalf of racial integration: "We must save our people, and when I say 'our people,' I mean white and black. We need to quit thinking who's living next door, who's driving a big car, who's my little daughter going to play with, who is she going to sit next to

Frazier's decision to accept an invitation to speak at the South Carolina State House led to considerable criticism from many African Americans. Courtesy of Richland Library, Columbia, SC.

in school. We don't have time for that."[110] For Frazier, his victory provided proof of the possibilities of uplift but also called attention to the work yet to do. His rhetoric, though, fully embraced the integrationist vision of civil rights leaders like Martin Luther King Jr. and pushed back against the black nationalism of many groups such as the Black Panthers and the Nation of Islam.

For many, Frazier's appearance at the South Carolina legislature marked a betrayal of his race. As Ali biographer Hauser noted, Frazier "was invited and accepted as the man who defeated Muhammad Ali."[111] Frazier's victory over the draft-dodging, Muslim, Black Power advocate earned him his acclaim from the mostly white politicians. In this way he stood in for the values of many white Americans, including those opposed to racial justice. An editorial in the *SOBU* newsletter, the publication of the Student Organization for Black Unity, criticized Frazier in just these ways, believing he was being used as a political puppet to make things look better than they really were.[112] The hope of muscular assimilation had been that sports would open doors for African Americans by changing white perceptions inside and outside the sporting realm. In many ways, Frazier continued to pursue that strategy, hoping that his modesty, work ethic, and boxing skill would convince whites to open up their hearts and minds. However, the doubts about muscular assimilation that had gained steam in the mid-1960s only grew in the early 1970s. For those suspicious of sports' capacity to instigate larger social changes, they saw Frazier's performance in front of the legislature as affirmation of the existing status quo. In *Soul* magazine Michael Guarino saw Frazier fans as those who "cherished illusions and watered down tastes."[113] These critiques of Frazier fit in with broader concerns of Frazier as, in the words of *New York Amsterdam News* reader Eloise Valentine, "a yes, boss, man."[114] Instead of challenging white America and demanding recognition and a full seat at the table, these critics saw Frazier as accepting dominant norms and politely asking for recognition under white terms.

Those critiques resonated with ongoing debates about the fight's financing and promotion. Indeed, commentary and developments continued in the weeks, and even years, following the bout, much of which centered on black men's role in the economy. In the aftermath of the fight, Roy Innis, the national director of CORE, expressed his desire to be actively involved in promoting the anticipated rematch: "We want a major hunk of the promotion the next time and are willing to bid two or three million dollars. The fighters are black. Blacks should be in at the top, too."[115] In *Jet* noted black journalist Chuck Stone argued vociferously that black promoters needed to be involved in any major bout involving black fighters.[116] One of the lessons of the Ali-Frazier fight for many in the African American community was that the exploitation of black gladiators for white profit could no longer continue. Black promoters and managers needed more of a presence in the fight game to enable African Americans to reap the full benefits of their athletic stardom and to take on the positions of power in sport and the economy that were dominated by white men. Although this position certainly criticized the existing system, it was a different and less pointed criticism than that offered by the radical press. These black critics accepted capitalist entrepreneurship but simply wanted black Americans to get more moneymaking opportunities, a strategy that had a long history in the black community with proponents over time including Frederick Douglass, Booker T. Washington, Marcus Garvey, the Urban League, the Nation of Islam, and CORE.[117] It was a strategy that dovetailed with the Poor People's Campaign and the emphasis on the black male breadwinner.

And it was a strategy whose days were numbered. By 1971 second-wave feminism had been making major strides in American life, with the legal and political efforts led by NOW and the cultural revolution sought by groups in women's liberation. The expectation that black women would put aside calls for gender equity in order to support black men's efforts for patriarchal authority would soon be put to the test, and the rhetoric surrounding the fight hinted at the discontent bubbling up. The January 1971 issue of *Ebony* featured

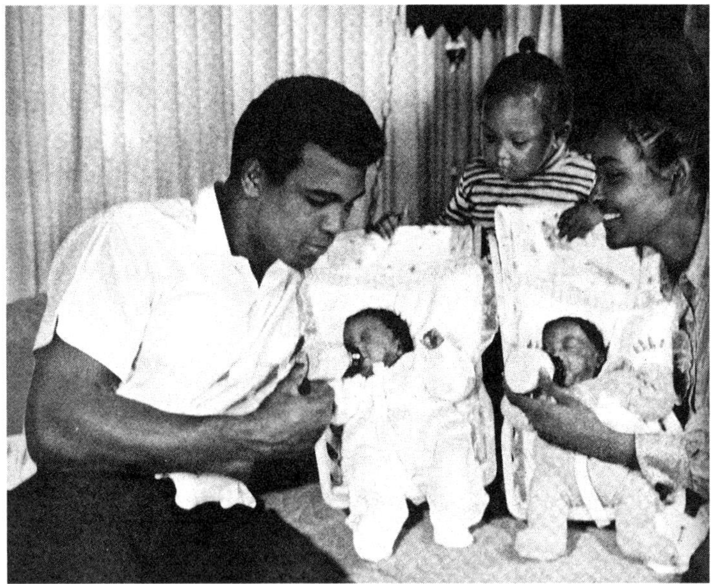

Ali, shown here with his second wife and three of his children, espoused patriarchal views that limited women's place to the home. Credit: Johnson Publishing Company Archive. Courtesy Ford Foundation, J. Paul Getty Trust, John D. and Catherine T. MacArthur Foundation, Andrew W. Mellon Foundation, and Smithsonian Institution.

a front-cover story about "The Quiet Family Life of Muhammad Ali." The story depicted peaceful domestic scenes: Ali and his wife, Belinda (also known as Khalilah), doting on their infant twins while older daughter Maryum looks on in the background. Other scenes show Maryum and Ali preparing to rake leaves and Ali playing with his children. The article refers to him as "the gentle king of" his "household."[118] In a 1972 story in *Ebony*, Ali even criticized women's liberation, calling it "just another trick of the white people to keep black women from joining the black man in his struggle to be free." He dismissed the movement's relevance: "Personally . . . I don't think black women are paying any attention to Women's Lib: so it's not even worth worrying about. In our Islamic faith, the woman's No. 1 place is in the home, raising her children and taking care of her husband and family, having dinner ready when he comes home, the way it should be."[119] At least one reader was miffed. Mrs. Grace Piro, of Landover, Maryland, criticized the magazine for emphasizing "the fact that Muslim men don't stoop to washing dishes or running the vacuum cleaner." She believed that this encouraged Muslim men to "look for loopholes in the Koran" that put extra burdens on women.[120] That discontent portended the rise of black feminism as the 1970s progressed.

In the end, the first Ali-Frazier fight marked an especially powerful moment to consider alternate models of black masculinity. Coming in the aftermath of civil rights and Black Power, and in the midst of the Vietnam War, black capitalism, and second-wave feminism, the bout channeled numerous debates about the place of black men—especially black athletes—in American society. Although many attempted to paint Muhammad Ali as *the* representative of black America, no brushstroke could have been broad enough to encompass the countless hopes, beliefs, and circumstances of African Americans. Instead, Frazier and Ali offered models for two different ways for black America to progress. One was to work within the system, to put faith in work ethic and modest deportment as a means of changing white perspectives on blacks' capabilities and qualities, and in doing so to open up new realms of society to black participation. The other was to defiantly challenge white American norms and inequalities, to boldly assert blacks' capabilities and make no pretense of playing along with whites in power. The heightened response to both men across racial lines suggests that these models resonated with broader social concerns in a time of upheaval. That both rested on traditional patriarchal assumptions of the male breadwinner in a capitalist society only spoke to the limits of social change in this era. Even as observers debated the relative merits of Frazier and Ali, more often than not they clung to dominant gender and economic norms. Patriarchy and systemic racism clung on tenaciously.

Of course, the rhetorical debate between Ali and Frazier and the strategies for change they embodied were not parts of a zero-sum game. Some saw value in both approaches and called for unity. The group promoting the "Fight of the Champions" commissioned black Pulitzer Prize–winning poet Gwendolyn Brooks to write a commemorative poem. Titled "Black Steel," and included in the official program, Brooks's poem was a celebration of the fight and fighters, but its main message was one of caution: "When the last bell's business dulls away," Brooks wrote to the two fighters, "know that the echo's message is black love." After the violence of the bout, Brooks enjoined the boxers to "pick up the pieces of the Brotherhood," an apparent nod to the racial divisions that had emerged in the pre-fight buildup. The survival of "black love" after "the Challenge and the Blood," Brooks implied, was the fight's most important legacy. Here, then, Brooks celebrated the two fighters (the "Uttermost of Warriors") and their historic bout as an affirmation of black pride, seeing the fight as a moment to affirm community connections. She hoped that community rifts would heal in the fight's wake.[121]

Others picked up on this call for unity. Rutha Frazier of Chicago called on readers to stop "putting another Black man down" in their reactions to the fight.[122] Noted sociologist and black athlete activist Harry Edwards agreed that the fight had taken on larger issues but urged listeners at a workshop in Washington State University to see the bigger picture. "I hope your man fought a good fight last night," he said, "because both of mine did."[123] And that would be the challenge for African Americans. Could they recognize the validity of both models of masculinity and find a way to come together over their differences? Or would their divisions continue to hinder their efforts at ongoing social change? Perhaps Muhammad Ali himself recognized the importance of those efforts. In a humble and heartfelt interview, which many in the media seemed to miss, in which he acknowledged his defeat, Ali said, "Anyway, Frazier is a nice fella. He's got a family, nice kids. He's another brother."[124]

* * *

Muhammad Ali's sense of brotherhood with Joe Frazier spoke to wider currents of racial connection and cultural affinity. Even as Ali and Frazier powerfully represented black manhood to a national audience, a new basketball league was offering viewers a glimpse of dynamic African American culture nearly every day. That is where we turn our attention next.

CHAPTER 5

THE ABA AND THE ORIGINS OF HIP-HOP AMERICA

On January 27, 1976, nearly twenty thousand fans, basketball players, and coaches in Denver, Colorado, buzzed with excitement. Julius Erving, the six-foot, seven-inch superstar small forward for the New York Nets, and the best player in the struggling American Basketball Association, was measuring his steps from the foul line at one end of the court to the three-point line at the other. The occasion was the first-ever slam dunk contest in professional basketball history, an event created to drum up fan interest at the annual All-Star game and to help bring additional attention to the league. As Erving reached the three-point line and turned toward the far basket, the crowd held its breath. Then, in his long, loping strides, his large Afro framing his handsome face, Erving ran toward the basket, the league's red-white-and-blue ball cradled in his hand. As the crowd noise built, Erving reached the foul line and—impossibly—took off, fifteen feet from the basket, elevating high in the air and throwing down a slam dunk. Bedlam ensued: the crowd roared, the television announcers expressed their amazement, and fellow players watching from the sidelines jumped up and down in celebration. It was a signature moment that encapsulated much of what made the ABA an exceptional basketball league—the innovative risk-taking, the joyful camaraderie, and, perhaps most significantly, the celebration of personal style—from hair to dunk choices and everything in between.[1]

While many have noted the stylistic innovations of the ABA and its deep roots in a broader black aesthetic rooted in improvisation and rhythmic complexity, few have pondered the political implications of this style during the Black Power era. Although most historians have seen the years of the early to mid-1970s as a time when black athletes began to retreat from social activism as Black Power waned, the ABA complicates that narrative. By exploring the style of the ABA—in terms of play and fashion—we can see how black athletes did not entirely withdraw from political activism as the 1970s progressed. Instead, they channeled their energies into challenging mainstream cultural norms through their play and their public personas. In doing so, they participated—and in some ways led—a broader revolt against white conventions that profoundly impacted American culture and politics. Indeed, the players in the ABA constituted one of the first mainstream outlets for hip-hop culture; long before 1979's "Rapper's Delight" brought the music of this new cultural form to the masses, ABA players gave voice to the urban discontent at the heart of hip-hop. Although their victories were not complete—and a backlash emerged—nonetheless, the ABA brought about a profound shift in cultural values and norms that has had lasting implications.

Basketball Origins, Urban Hoops, and the Rise of the ABA

The sport of basketball originated at a YMCA in Springfield, Massachusetts, in 1891, and quickly became one of the most popular sports for urban Americans. By the 1920s, teams comprised of white immigrant urbanites, such as the Original Celtics (from New York) and the South Philadelphia Hebrew Association, and African American clubs such as the New York Renaissance and the Harlem Globetrotters (who originated in Chicago), competed against one another in well-attended contests across the country, bringing the sport to wider audiences.[2] As basketball took root in urban settings in the Northeast, mid-Atlantic, and upper Midwest, black Americans brought a distinct aesthetic to the game that would have profound repercussions for the sport—and that would eventually emerge most visibly with the ABA.

Numerous commentators and scholars have identified a distinct black cultural style, one emphasizing polyrhythms and improvisation, that manifested in numerous outlets, including visual art, clothing style, quilts, music, storytelling, and preaching. In an anthology devoted to the black cultural aesthetic, scholar Gena Caponi-Tabery argues that these wide-ranging cultural expressions "articulate and transmit the ideas, values, and beliefs that connect African Americans."[3] Several key features define this aesthetic:

> (1) rhythmic and metric complexity; (2) individual improvisation and stylization; (3) dialogic interaction or call-and-response; (4) active engagement of the whole person and the whole community; (5) social commentary or competition through indirection and satire; (6) development of a group consciousness or sensibility—the invisible conductor.[4]

These trends have surfaced in numerous forms. Historians Graham White and Shane White, for example, note that the fashion choices and music styles of nineteenth-century slaves were inherently linked by an underlying "African American aesthetic." The use of contrasting colors in quilts and clothes coincided with black music forms in that both "were linked by an underlying rhythm that was alien to Euro-American cultural forms." Indeed, the color and fabric choices of clothes and quilts, like many features of black music, created a sense of "unpredictability and movement."[5] Others have pointed to the influence of this aesthetic in visual art, religious preaching, and poetry.[6]

This distinct style entered mainstream culture especially through music and sports, and many saw the two in similar terms. Cultural critic Nelson George noted a connection between the various forms of improvisations on the basketball court, from the slam dunk, to the no-look pass, to the head fake, with other improvisational moments and trends in African American culture, from blues, to jazz, to religious sermons and hip-hop.[7] An oft-quoted 1970 *Time* magazine essay by black writer Ralph Ellison also spoke to this connection: "Without the presence of Negro American style, our jokes, tall tales, even our sports would be lacking in the sudden turns, shocks and swift changes of pace (all jazz-shaped) that serve to remind us that the world is ever unexplored, and that while a complete mastery of life is mere illusion, the real secret of the game is to make life swing."[8] In baseball, by far the most popular team sport in the United States through the 1940s, many have noted the distinct playing style brought to the game by African American players. Often called "tricky baseball," the style featured an emphasis on speed and individual virtuosity on the base paths, along with a willingness to engage in verbal putdowns of opponents—traits that echoed the improvisation of jazz and the verbal bravado of the blues.[9] Similarly, Caponi-Tabery has noted the numerous connections between jazz and basketball, with both being "ensemble pieces depending on fundamental knowledge of the art but also on the ability to improvise in the moment."[10]

A number of pioneering black coaches and players brought this improvisation and rhythmic complexity into basketball. Although most note that this black style developed on playgrounds, particularly in urban areas, black college coaches such as John McLendon and Clarence "Big House" Gaines and early black professional teams such as the Rens and the Globetrotters helped to promote a faster-paced version of the game to a broader national audience.[11] McLendon, who studied under James Naismith at the University of Kansas, was especially important in bringing a fast-break style into institutionalized basketball. First at North Carolina College, then at Tennessee A&I University, where he won three consecutive NAIA championships (an integrated national championship tournament for smaller colleges and universities), and finally with the semi-pro Cleveland Pipers, McLendon coached a frenetic style of play that proved remarkably successful.[12] Gaines followed McLendon's lead, employing the fast break at Winston-Salem State University after seeing how effective it was for McLendon. Caponi-Tabery points out that the fast break needed players who could improvise in order to be successful. As she notes, "Basketball depends on fluid interaction among a group of players whose roles are interchangeable, any one of whom may score at any moment, and any one of whom may showcase a personal style or 'trademark' in the process of scoring."[13] The emphasis on improvisation and personal virtuosity thus fit well with the black aesthetic.

However, historian Pamela Grundy notes that McLendon's coaching style was far from free-form. It featured complex plays and required players to make quick decisions based on careful preparation. As Gaines once said, players needed to "adjust and adapt to the defense," even as they rushed down the court.[14] These traits had practical (and even political) implications. According to Grundy, black coaches' efforts to instill discipline and quick-thinking skills into their players buttressed broader cultural forms that spoke to survival in a white-dominated world: "Athletic discipline thus became a part of a broader cultural array of warnings and strategies that ranged from the tales of tricksters who devised inventive schemes to avert direct confrontations, to the fast-paced exchange of insults in the verbal dozens, which encouraged participants to develop both verbal eloquence and cool self-control."[15] Players employing McLendon's fast break sped up the game, but they also learned to think on their feet, a vital skill in an often hostile world.

Black professional teams also played their part in changing the game and bringing a black style to the sport. The Rens, led by black businessman Bob Douglas, emerged as the most dominant professional team of the 1930s. Douglas, who immigrated to the United States from Jamaica in 1901, first discovered basketball in 1905 and became hooked on the sport. By 1923, he had arranged with the owner of the Harlem Renaissance Casino, a multiuse entertainment facility, to play games on Sunday evenings. Naming his new team the Renaissance to appease the casino owner, Douglas put together an impressive squad that began to dominate New York basketball. Soon after, the team began to travel across the country (including the South, which had been traditionally ignored by traveling teams) and took the basketball world by storm. At one point the team won more than eighty-eight consecutive games against white and black clubs and professional teams alike.[16] According to historian Ben Green, the Rens players became known for their "ball-handling exhibitions and spectacular passing," both elements of the dynamic black style of play.[17] In 1939 the Rens won the first World Professional Basketball Tournament, held in Chicago, against an all-white team from Wisconsin. These exploits brought national attention to black basketball and black players' skills.[18]

The other team that generated national attention and brought even more of the black aesthetic into the sport was the Harlem Globetrotters. The Globetrotters started out as a Chicago team called the Savoy Big Five, after the Savoy Ballroom that served as the team's home court. Originally run by Dick Hudson, an African American and former football star, white entrepreneur Abe Saperstein assumed control of the squad in late 1926. Changing the team's name to the Harlem Globetrotters in order to capitalize on Harlem's reputation for black innovation and to link his team to the Rens, Saperstein, a booking agent, used his connections in the entertainment industry to get more (and relatively more lucrative) performances for the squad. Under Saperstein's management, the all-black team combined winning basketball with on-court showmanship. Although the team played competitive basketball in barnstorming contests, à la the Rens, they quickly became known for their on-court entertainment exploits. In order to entertain fans and drum up ticket sales, the players employed a "*black* style of ball played on the courts of Bronzeville," the black section of South Chicago. As Green writes, "It was a game of speed, quick passes, and ball-handling wizardry."[19] Globetrotter Marques Haynes, who joined the team in 1947, brought special acclaim as a result of his ball-handling skills. Haynes was a wizard with the basketball, dribbling in unconventional ways and creating a playful quality to what had been a humdrum aspect of the game. George writes that Haynes "popularized show-time dribbling as a manifestation of Black style," bringing more attention to black basketball in the process.[20]

While the Rens and Globetrotters earned considerable success as barnstorming teams, they lacked the permanence of a league-based professional squad. Although professional basketball leagues had come and gone throughout the early decades of the twentieth century, the sport achieved some stability in 1949 with the formation of the National Basketball Association (NBA), which merged two rival leagues—the Basketball Association of America (BAA) and the National Basketball League (NBL).[21] One year later the league began to integrate its previously all-white teams. First, the Boston Celtics selected Chuck Cooper, a recent graduate of Duquesne University, with the first pick of the second round of the NBA draft, making him the first black player drafted into the league. Later in that same draft, the Washington Capitols selected Earl Lloyd of the historically black West Virginia State University, and he would be the first African American to play in an NBA game when he took the court on October 31, 1950. Finally, in the spring of 1950, the New York Knicks signed Nat "Sweetwater" Clifton, then a player with the Globetrotters, to a professional contract, making him the first black player to sign with an NBA team. Although none of the three would become stars in the league, they opened the door for other black players in ensuing years.[22] By the mid-1960s, African American stars dominated the league, earning the majority of slots on All-Star teams and claiming the league's Most Valuable Player award with increasing regularity.[23]

But even as the NBA achieved solid financial stability, a new league emerged to contest its dominance in the sport: the American Basketball Association. Primarily the brainchild of California entrepreneur Dennis Murphy, who saw opportunities for expansion in the realm of professional basketball, the ABA began operations in 1967 with eleven teams and with former professional basketball star George Mikan as its first commissioner.[24] League owners planned from the outset to force a merger with the established NBA. The year before, the young American Football League (AFL) and the more established National Football League (NFL) had announced merger plans to head off economic competition between the leagues, and some ABA owners hoped to follow suit. In fact, Murphy had originally intended to start an AFL franchise, but the AFL-NFL merger took place before he could. Turning his attention to basketball, he thought, "What the hell, the AFL had worked, hadn't it? They got a merger. Maybe we could force a merger with the NBA." Indiana Pacers owner Dick Tinkham had a similar mindset. Noting that the entry fee for an expansion franchise in the NBA was $1.5 million, he leaped at the chance to start an ABA team for only a $5,000 entrance fee. If the two eventually merged, he would stand to make out well.[25]

Although hopes for an eventual merger motivated many of the league's owners, they also set out to differentiate their teams from those in the NBA. The league embraced a number of stylistic innovations in order to drum up fan interest, most notably a tricolored ball in red, white, and blue instead of the usual brown, and the three-point shot, which planners copied from the defunct American Basketball League. As the league struggled to compete with the NBA, team owners pushed boundaries in a host of other ways, bringing in players who had been blackballed from the NBA (such as Connie Hawkins and Roger Brown, both tarnished by loose associations with gamblers), allowing players who had not yet graduated college to enter into their league under a "hardship rule" and using lucrative contract offers to poach NBA stars such as Rick Barry. One limitation that continued to vex ABA owners was the lack of a national television contract. As a result, they were desperate to increase ticket sales to bring in revenue. The Miami Floridians employed bikini-clad "ball girls" to help out on the sideline to entice male spectators; some teams hosted cow-milking contests and similar events at halftime; others offered giveaways of board games to lucky fans in random drawings.[26] In addition, the lack of a television contract prompted the ABA to be more creative with promotional strategies, and they began to market personalities and superstars in more effective ways as a result.[27] With the need to attract attention, journalist Franz Lidz writes, "ABA players let every kind of freak flag fly—from Afros on their black players to handlebar mustaches on their white ones."[28]

One last contextual factor shaped the ABA and its players in important ways. As the 1970s got under way, outspoken athlete activism became less common. Amid a declining economy and white backlash toward the Black Power movement, athletes on the whole became more cautious about getting involved in controversial issues.[29] The stances taken by Brown, King, and Ashe in the early 1970s spoke to this gradual retreat from the visible, vocal activism of Harry Edwards and others, embracing liberal capitalist arguments instead of calling for broad, sweeping changes. Even Muhammad Ali showed subtle change in approach and rhetoric in this era. Whereas in 1964 he had stated his independence through his religious choice and name change, and he had visibly defied the United States in his refusal to serve in Vietnam, by the early 1970s Ali was more cautious. As noted in chapter 4, when Ali fought Joe Frazier for the heavyweight championship in 1971, he did not insist on black promotion of the fight, nor did he recreate Main Bout Inc. Certainly, Ali retained his verbal wit and spoke for African American empowerment, saying that he fought for "black people in the United States and all over the globe" in his fight against the "Great White Hope" Joe Frazier (because of Frazier's relatively conservative politics). But Ali did not participate in the same degree of economic and political activism that had marked his early career.[30]

Still, if overt political activism geared toward particular institutional aims declined in the early 1970s, numerous activists—including Ali—nonetheless profoundly influenced the nation. As historian William L. Van Deburg has argued, one of the major achievements of the Black Power movement of the late 1960s and early 1970s was to effect cultural transformation in the United States. Although Black Power groups—and other African American organizations and leaders—had their differences regarding the economy, their faith in American democracy, and other key issues, nearly all of them hoped to reimagine the place of black Americans in the broader culture as one way to dismantle systemic racism. In order to break the bonds of oppression and discrimination, "black Americans had to be awakened [and] unified" so that they could "establish their own values." This was fundamentally a cultural war against white normative "cultural hegemony."[31] In this climate, a wide range of black social practices spoke to an increased sense of pride and group empowerment. In the Black Arts Movement, "there came to be a considerable interest in establishing, or at least theorizing, a black aesthetic by which black art and culture could be evaluated and taught and through which new art could be created in a manner that promoted black self-determination." To create a new aesthetic was to affirm African Americans' identity and heritage and also to fight back against cultural domination and oppression.[32] With this social background, soul food restaurants flourished, music artists embraced black pride, and Blaxploitation films targeted African American audiences with strong black male leads who put white authority figures in their proper place.[33] With Black Power emerging just as the ABA was getting started, and with desperation to find fans and revenue to compete with the NBA, the league allowed for experimentation and innovation and thus would potentially be more open to new forms of expressive culture—even those that brought in the ideals and values of Black Power.

Playing "with the Chains Taken Off": The ABA and the Rising Stature of Black Basketball

By 1971 the upstart ABA had collected an impressive range of talent: guards and forwards such as Charlie Scott, Julius Erving, Billy Cunningham, and George McGinnis dazzled fans with their skills.[34] And it had become clear that the style of basketball played in the new league was quite different. Because the league lacked elite centers on par with the NBA, teams in the ABA often adopted a fast-paced style well-suited to smaller, athletic players. As former player Bob Bass observed, "The ABA . . . was a wide open league, a league that ran the fast break and didn't have a lot of big men clogging the middle. . . . The accent was on speed and finesse."[35] The controversial three-point shot also changed the game: with shooters camped out behind the arc awaiting opportunities to take long-distance shots, there was more space close to the basket for players to drive for layups and dunks. San Antonio star George Gervin observed, "That's what the fans really admired about the ABA, you know, was our fast-paced style. You had a chance to really show your skills and make some great moves and stuff because you stayed in the flow of the game."[36] Open to renegade players, adopting new rules, and embracing nonconformist fashion trends, the ABA constituted a rebellion against traditional culture.

Although there were pragmatic and rule-based reasons for the ABA's nontraditional style of basketball, the ABA's fast-paced and wide-open style also reflected a mainstream embrace of the black style of basketball. Indeed, the ABA built on the achievements of McLendon, Gaines, and the early traveling teams by offering more opportunities for black players—and the exhibition of black style—at the professional level. Countless former players, coaches, and journalists noted the more open style of play in the ABA. Billy Cunningham, who starred in both the NBA and the ABA, and later earned a championship as an NBA coach, observed that "the ABA players and coaches forced a faster pace of the game, they pushed the ball up the court, they created a more exciting brand of basketball."[37] Not only was the game faster, but it also offered more opportunities for improvisation and innovation. Guard Charlie Scott, who starred in both leagues after graduating from UNC, noted, "[In the NBA,] you don't do what is not fundamentally sound. People would try things in the ABA that you would not try in the NBA because you had the freedom to do that." In the ABA, "creativity was really basketball."[38] Player agent Ron Grinker made similar observations and in doing so highlighted the black cultural aesthetic that underlay the ABA style of play. Instead of the NBA's focus on "fundamental basketball" with set plays, "the ABA was Julius Erving, it was glitzy, get the ball out and let's run and jump and play above the rim and we'll make things up as we go along. The NBA was a symphony, it was scripted; the ABA was jazz. People weren't sure exactly what they did even after they did it. They felt something and they tried it."[39] Former broadcaster Van Vance also picked up on the connection between the ABA's style and certain music forms. The ABA had players who "were able to ad-lib . . . like a jazz musician, OK? . . . They played it freestyle."[40]

No one embodied that improvisational style more adeptly than the ABA's brightest star: Julius Erving. Erving entered the league in 1971, taking advantage of the ABA's willingness to sign players before college graduation by leaving the University of Massachusetts after his junior year. Signed to the Virginia Squires, Erving quickly developed a reputation as the most dynamic player in the league. Making shots from difficult angles, rising above the other players on the court, and moving with grace and agility, Erving impressed nearly everyone. Some teammates, dazzled by his antics, "stopped dead and watched" a particularly memorable shot on replay during a game. Opponents such as David Thompson and Bobby Jones (later to be a teammate) marveled at his exploits,

Julius Erving's acrobatic dunks came to represent the ABA's on-court innovations and flair. Credit: Johnson Publishing Company Archive. Courtesy Ford Foundation, J. Paul Getty Trust, John D. and Catherine T. MacArthur Foundation, Andrew W. Mellon Foundation, and Smithsonian Institution.

with Jones admitting, "I enjoy watching him, because each time he goes to the basket, I may be seeing something I'll never see again."[41] Others agreed, and most celebrated Erving because of his on-court flair and his ability to improvise on the fly. Zelmo Beatty reminisced that "no one could run and dunk and swoop down on the basket with the style of a young Julius Erving."[42] Johnny Kerr, an executive with the Squires, recalled that "a young Julius Erving was like Thomas Edison. He was inventing something new every night."[43] As Erving's career progressed, he began to draw national attention, especially after his trade to the New York Nets in 1973. Journalists praised his "airborne acrobatics," and Erving himself believed that his "freedom of motion," his ability to "drive, float and change direction in the air better than most of the other players," made him stand out.[44] These attributes—his improvisational style and above-the-rim game—were taken to represent the league as a whole. As ABA executive Carl Scheer recalled, "The spirit of the ABA was the spirit of Julius Erving. On the court, he expressed it in his style of play."[45] In this way, the improvisational moves that "Dr. J" employed, and that came out of the black basketball tradition, firmly linked the ABA to the African American cultural aesthetic.

Improvisation was only one aspect of the black aesthetic to influence the ABA's brand of basketball. Many noted a rhythmic quality to the up-tempo style of play, echoing the "rhythmic and metric complexity" identified as one of the black aesthetic's defining features. In a 1975 article for *Esquire*, white writer Jeff Greenfield identified rhythm as one of black basketball's defining qualities, by which he meant "an instinctive quality," a more "free-form" style of play.[46] Charles Scott concurred, believing African Americans' success in basketball stemmed from the game's rhythmic qualities and an African American cultural affinity for rhythm. "Basketball is a lot of rhythm," he explained, and "once my rhythm gets started . . . it's almost impossible to stop me."[47] *New Pittsburgh Courier* writer John Henry Johnson agreed, noting numerous examples of the game's rhythmic qualities: "He gets a pass on a pick and swishes through a jump shot in one beautiful sweeping motion. Other times it takes a pass fake, a dribble or a split-second pause before the jump and the shot."[48] Successful players could negotiate the changing speeds and shifting circumstances on the court, reading the events like musicians finding opportunities to riff.

Not only did on-court playing style speak to a black aesthetic, but on- and off-court fashion choices did likewise. Fashion was an especially important aspect of Black Power. Historian Jeffrey O. G. Ogbar deems it "the most immediate and obvious marker of Black Power's influence."[49] As Ogbar notes, "generations" of African Americans had been inundated with messages in various cultural forms indicating that blacks "were ugly. Vicious stereotypes depicted black men and women as grotesque in movies, cartoons, advertisements . . . tourist postcards, and popular sayings."[50] Changing one's fashion, according to historian Tanisha Ford, enabled more people to get involved in activism. While not everyone could, or did, get involved in mass demonstrations and protests, many more could, and did, make fashion choices that reflected their political beliefs. By the 1970s, "soul sisters and soul brothers expressed their black consciousness and cool through dress."[51] By donning "denim overalls, platform shoes, beaded jewelry, and dashikis and other garments with African prints," they made an important political statement. These fashion choices enabled "a symbolic baptism in freedom's waters through which they could be reborn, liberated from the cultural and social bondage of their slave or colonial pasts."[52]

The ABA's black players appeared to embrace fashion's liberating possibilities wholeheartedly. Photographs and video footage of ABA stars show them in a wide range of flamboyant attire. "There was some serious flavor in the ABA," Erving observed. Scott agreed: "We all did what we wanted to do. Everybody had beards and mustaches and bell-bottom pants and loud-colored shirts and big Afros." These fashion choices gave players "their own identity."[53] Cunningham

Flashy fashion choices by Erving and other ABA players also contributed to the league's rebellious reputation. Credit: Johnson Publishing Company Archive. Courtesy Ford Foundation, J. Paul Getty Trust, John D. and Catherine T. MacArthur Foundation, Andrew W. Mellon Foundation, and Smithsonian Institution.

agreed, noting that players "were expressing themselves more openly. You saw the afros, you saw the sideburns." In a cultural climate of experimentation and rejection of traditional norms, according to former player Steve "Snapper" Jones, "everybody was trying to do their own thing, so this expression carried over to sports."[54] Both white and black players (and coaches) appeared to share in the stylistic freedom. White players let their hair grow long, and coach Larry Brown wore overalls on the sidelines instead of the traditional suit; permed hair and checkered coats for coaches were common.[55] However, black players in the ABA, and to a lesser extent the NBA, appeared to embrace nontraditional fashions to a greater extent than did their white peers. A March 1970 *Ebony* story about the NBA's New York Knicks noted that star Walt Frazier's "super-cool demeanor" also matched up with his fashion choices, which tended to be "the 'new look' personified." With "colorful shirts, wide-brimmed hats, latest-cut suits and broad-toed shoes" and his "extra-long sideburns," Frazier cultivated an image of a "staunch individualist."[56] While Frazier earned notoriety because of his stylized appearance, such attire was the norm in the ABA. In *Ebony* magazine's 1975 feature on Erving, for example, photographs depict him leaving a game in a stylish fedora, talking with a reporter while wearing a two-tone blazer, and donning an oversized newsboy hat and mixed-stripe V-neck sweater.[57] ABA star guard Larry Jones earned the moniker the "Mad Hatter" because of his large collection of idiosyncratic hats.[58] By embracing the fashion revolution, a key component of Black Power, these players expressed their affinity for that movement and affirmed their racial pride even if they did not necessarily engage in outspoken activism.

Hair offered another way to engage in personal protest, rejecting mainstream norms that labeled "kinky hair . . . 'nappy' and unmanageable, while curly or wavy texture was known as 'good hair.'" As the Afro grew in popularity, it became a "[bold] statement of black pride, a metaphorical exclamation point, affirming the beauty of black people and their hair."[59] Blacks and whites alike knew the political implications of the hairstyle: when the Jackson Five adopted the hairstyle, white journalists asked if the then-teenage act supported Black Power.[60] Similarly, as Lew Alcindor (who later changed his name to Kareem Abdul-Jabbar) rose to stardom with the UCLA Bruins, an article in *Ebony* noted that he "proudly sports a 'natural' hair style, most popular among Negro militants, and stoutly professes his pride in being black."[61] Athletes who adopted the hairstyle, then, or copied the fashion sense of the Black Panthers or other Black Power groups, deliberately challenged mainstream cultural norms. Indeed, the facial hair choices of Boston Celtics star Bill Russell attracted critics, as his "goatee, a hip, bebop-inspired look, was viewed by some Beantowners as evidence of subversion."[62] The intense response of Oregon State football coach Dee Andros to black player Fred Milton's facial hair, as discussed in chapter 3, was another example of the political meanings many ascribed to personal style.

The Afro for black players was a particularly important stylistic element in the league, a reflection of how Black Power fashion influenced the ABA. Photographs of players in the early 1970s reveal how widespread the hairstyle was, and the players were undoubtedly aware of the political implications. As Nelson George writes, "The wearing of an Afro hairstyle . . . could be perceived as a break with acceptable athletic protocol."[63] Nonetheless, ABA players embraced the haircut. In fact, not only did many black players wear their hair in that style, but there was also an unofficial competition to have the largest one possible. Snapper Jones recalled, "The bigger the Afro, and actually the more militant you could look, the better it was." To him, the Afro in motion during the game "kind of accentuated nastiness." Darnell Hillman of the Indiana Pacers earned attention for the impressive size of his Afro, and he secretly offered tips to Erving on how to best groom the impressive hairdo.[64] At an ABA reunion in 1997, Hillman was honored by his fellow alums with a prize for the "best Afro." Erving recalled that Hillman "walked to the front of the room with a Denzel Washington strut. . . . Of course, he has a corporate haircut now."[65] Long past the age of Black Power, Hillman had let go of the hairstyle that had been his calling card, but the award spoke to the centrality of the Afro to the league.

In addition to the Afro, black players' on-court style in the ABA played a key role in conveying political messages. Indeed, the emphasis on individual expression added political meanings to how the ABA's black players played the game. For African Americans longing to showcase their innovations within a mainstream culture that had largely ignored, or derided, their contributions, the ABA offered considerable possibilities. Erving described his experience in the ABA as being akin to having "the chains taken off" so that he could play a more open style: "I developed my own style of play which is . . . at times sort of a playground style." Veteran broadcaster Bob Costas noted the wild fashions but argued that "the real flair was on the court." Erving saw the ABA as a place to engage in "a little experimentation" while "encouraging an individual to excel in a team sport."[66] Just as Black Power promoted black identity and pride, and as it affirmed the creative contributions of African Americans, the ABA's distinct style—on and off the court—achieved similar aims. Erving's reference to being free from "chains" speaks to the idea that individual style meant liberation from mainstream (white) oppression. In embracing a free-form style of play, along with the hairstyle and fashions of Black Power, the players in the ABA articulated an affirmation of a liberated black identity, what Douglas Hartmann has referred to as "the politics of oppositional style."[67]

Perhaps the feature of the ABA that best encapsulated these varied elements of the black aesthetic was the slam dunk. Although the dunk had been a part of basketball for decades, in the ABA the shot took on greater prominence and became more celebrated for its artistic values. According to player Dan Issel, "The dunk was a bigger play in the ABA. . . . It was a statement of your manhood and your talent." Just as Black Power called for an affirmation of black manhood, slam dunks offered an avenue for displaying fierce pride and strength. Meanwhile, because of the attention paid to dunking, a team's pregame warm-ups, which often featured dunks, "became a show" in the upstart league.[68] Fans would arrive early to watch Erving perform "an assortment of driving dunk shots" for the crowd.[69] And there was no doubt that the attention paid to the dunk came from the influence of black style. An isolated moment on the court, the dunk called attention to the skill and artistry of the dunker. It often required improvisation to navigate the defenders around the basket. In throwing down a dunk over a defender, a player not only scored but also engaged in intimidation, showing off strength and skill. One story in *Jet* noted that Dr. J had "turned the 'slam dunk' into an art form,"[70] and he was not alone. In the ABA, Nelson George writes, the dunk became "an integral part of professional basketball's tapestry."[71] While many believe that the dunk "may have originated on the playgrounds of African American communities," it was in the ABA that it received more attention than ever before.[72] By the time Erving lined up for this free-throw-line dunk at the 1976 All-Star game, the league had become synonymous with high-flying slam dunks.

Hip-Hop America and Basketball: Embrace and Resistance

Erving's reference to the "playground" origins of his style, and the speculation about the dunk's origins, also shed light on another meaning embodied in the style of the ABA's black players. As cultural critic William Rhoden has argued, "The gestures that make up black style—the chest bumps, the high fives, shakes and shimmies" constitute "a specialized form of black expression, a consequence of being 'outside of,' or 'other.'"[73] That sentiment had special resonance in the wake of white flight from the cities and the terrible legacies of urban renewal. As African Americans found themselves increasingly isolated in declining urban cores, basketball became an outlet for self-expression. According to George, the sport provided a way to levy "one's personal stamp on any given contest . . . to tell your story." In the urban parks and playgrounds, the game "was faster, louder, more stop-and-go, and . . . defiant of established standards of performance."[74] Although Erving did not speak directly about urban isolation and the failures of urban renewal, he celebrated playground basketball because of its lack of "constraints" and its "beautiful" emphasis on personal "reputation."[75] The dunks thrown down by Erving and others—linked by many to the ABA—were a way to express, in George's words, "a humanity otherwise suppressed by white authority."[76]

In fact, African American playground basketball, especially at famed locations such as New York's Rucker Park, provided a key link between the lived realities of urban minorities in the wake of white flight and the world of professional basketball. Many have pointed to the Rucker Tournament, a city-run summer league for youth, as an especially important moment in the development of black basketball. The tournament was the brainchild of Holcombe Rucker, a returning World War II veteran. Frustrated by the racism he encountered during and after the war, and able to land only a relatively low-level position with New York's parks department upon his return to the United States, he decided to start the tournament in 1946 as a way to keep youths occupied during the summer months. At first restricted to high school students, the tournament expanded over time as it became more and more popular, adding college and professional divisions to the competition in 1953 and 1954, respectively. The best players in New York and elsewhere began to flock to the tournament, finding high-quality competition and enthusiastic crowds. Initially located at 130th Street and 7th Avenue, the tournament moved to its more familiar location at 155th Street and 7th Avenue in the mid-1960s.[77]

As a particularly visible embodiment of the playground style that was developing in urban parks across the country, Rucker served to show off black basketball and to elevate the game. As Vincent Mallozzi has written, the tournament involved "kids who perfected their moves on playground courts throughout the city, bringing to the blacktop the grit, muscle, and determination it took to survive on the mean streets where they were raised." Combining "hard-nosed basketball . . . [with] high-flying, artistic moves to the basket," the players brought "the true identity of the city game" to dazzled spectators, black and white.[78] Erving, who became one of the biggest draws at the tournament in the early 1970s, waxed poetic about playground basketball: "Nothing can compare to the playgrounds. . . . You have no constraints, no formality, no distractions."[79] Erving's assessment of the relative freedom of the playground game corresponds to Mallozzi's analysis of the game as "a mostly black, free-flowing, loosey-goosey, wide-open, one-on-one, run-and-gun, behind-your-back, between-your-legs, shake-and-bake, in-your-face makeover of James Naismith's original game." Donnie Walsh, a white college star and NBA guard, agreed with the greater freedom offered at the tournament, describing his playing at Rucker as being akin to "the thrills of playing in jam sessions with great musicians of the thirties and forties. That's the kind of feeling you had playing up there." Freed from the constraints of more formal settings, Rucker games featured lively crowds who would enthusiastically celebrate big moments with gusto—games had to be paused sometimes to let the crowds celebrate an especially big dunk or block.[80] In this way the tournament anticipated the free-form, celebratory style of play offered by the ABA.

Both in the moment and in looking back, numerous commentators and participants ascribed larger meanings to the playground contests of the 1950s, 1960s, and 1970s. Nelson George writes that "Rucker was . . . a place where philosophy and aesthetics were discussed via body language." New York–raised basketball star Kareem Abdul-Jabbar recalled that "the Black schoolyard game demanded all the flash, guile and individual reckless brilliance each man would need in the world facing him."[81] Former Knicks player Dean Meminger, an African American, argued that players growing up in the ghetto saw every game as "a test of manhood" and brought that attitude to the court.[82] Many noted that the playground style offered an opportunity to boost one's self-image in a world where seemingly few other options existed. Richard "Pee Wee" Kirkland talked about the esteem that came from playing at Rucker and other playground sites: "We knew about the NBA and college, that they could all of a sudden be an option for us, but in the ghetto the street ball players, not the pros, had all the respect."[83] Writer David Wolf, who wrote *Foul*, the biography of playground legend and ABA and NBA star Connie Hawkins, wrote that the basketball court provided "for many young men in the slums, the only place they can feel true pride in what they do, where they can move free of inhibitions and where they can, by being spectacular, rise for a moment against the drabness and an anonymity of their lives."[84] The way to succeed in this playground game, Greenfield argued, was through "the *unexpected*; to develop a shot that is simply and fundamentally different from the usual methods of putting the ball in the basket." Coming up with new ways to score "stamp[s] uniqueness on young men who may feel it nowhere else."[85]

Although some of that analysis was overgeneralized and more than a little over-romanticized, the broader patterns identified—the need for an outlet for self-expression, the demand for recognition and respect, and the innovation that came out of these circumstances—spoke to larger trends in American urban cultural life in the postwar years. In fact, while many compared the style of play cultivated on playgrounds and in the ABA to the improvisations of jazz, a better comparison might have been made to emerging hip-hop culture. Terry Pluto, author of the definitive oral history of the league, made that point in a documentary about the St. Louis Spirits, one of the league's most colorful teams, observing that "the ABA probably was early rap music, we just didn't know what it was."[86]

Pluto's offhand comment was astute; the parallels between hip-hop's emergence in the early 1970s and the ABA's ascendance in the same time frame speak to shared social and cultural forces at work. Most historians of hip-hop locate the genre's origins in the South Bronx of the 1970s. Like most urban centers in the United States, New York City suffered from the effects of white flight as middle-class white families moved to the suburbs, taking advantage of Federal Housing Administration loans and the GI Bill's mortgage benefits for returning veterans. As whites moved out to racially exclusive suburbs, taking capital with them, poorer people of color were left behind. City infrastructure crumbled because of the dwindling tax base, and city planners tried numerous methods to boost their cities' appeal. Urban renewal policies of the 1950s and 1960s sought to make cities more accessible by car, which required highway construction into and through urban centers. In New York, construction of the Cross-Bronx Expressway, the brainchild of longtime New York planner Robert Moses, decimated homes and businesses for the mixed-race residents of the South Bronx. In their places, monolithic housing projects emerged, accentuating the flight of whites out of the city and leaving behind a seemingly forgotten and increasingly impoverished black and Latinx underclass.[87]

The bleak economic circumstances and the arrival of Afro-Caribbean immigrants (especially from Jamaica) provided the backdrop for the four elements of hip-hop culture: graffiti, b-boying (or break dancing), DJ-ing, and rapping (or MC-ing). As many cultural analysts have noted, all four centered on affirming identity and building community in the face of public neglect and social isolation. The graffiti that emerged with hip-hop was not the mural artwork or political sloganeering of the previous thousands of years of human history; instead, it was artistic tagging that celebrated individual identity through clever representations of artists' names and assumed identities. Break dancing encouraged individual virtuosity and created community through spontaneous dance-offs on street corners and at other public locations. The genre's music elements—DJ-ing and rapping, which both borrowed heavily from Jamaican reggae house party traditions—required improvisation, showing the practitioner's skills in looping beats or coming up with rhymes on the fly. Rappers, too, could not only affirm their individuality but also call out recognition for their local community, proudly identifying their neighborhoods as they crafted clever rhymes.[88] As Michael Eric Dyson has noted, hip-hop provided a way for its musicians and performers to provide a voice "for less visible or vocal peers." The practitioners of hip-hop culture "represent lives swallowed by too little love or opportunity."[89] Although hip-hop would not receive widespread media attention until 1979, with the release of the hit single "Rapper's Delight," the cultural elements for all of its practices were already in place by the early 1970s.[90]

Indeed, is it any wonder that the ABA's rise coincided with the dawn of hip-hop? The graffiti artists who were starting to engage in artistic tagging that celebrated individual identity in the late 1960s; and DJ Cool Herc, who hosted the first hip-hop house party in the summer of 1973; and Dr. J and his majestic dunks of the early and mid-1970s, were connected by not only the time period but also the urban setting of neglect. As scholar Tricia Rose argues in her seminal work, *Black Noise*, hip-hop marked an attempt "to negotiate the experiences of marginalization, brutally truncated opportunity, and oppression" characteristic of declining and increasingly segregated urban spaces.[91] The parallels with basketball—especially the playground style and the ABA's embrace of that style—are clear, although most historians and scholars have missed this vital connection. In promoting an improvisational game, one that encouraged players to create on the fly, and in celebrating individual accomplishment and calling attention to individual prowess through thundering dunks, the ABA brand of basketball picked up on the same impulses as hip-hop culture. When Jeff Greenfield identified the black style of play in 1975 as "the basketball of electric self-expression," he unknowingly linked this brand of basketball to nascent hip-hop culture.[92] As George notes, "Basketball courts[,] where dreams of public glory, mad loot, and innovative, idiosyncratic style are dearly held,"[93] picked up on and influenced the music, dance, and art of hip-hop America. Through their various artistic expressions, these artists, musicians, and athletes all offered, in the words of hip-hop historian Jeff Chang, "a strike against their generation's invisibility."[94]

Responses to these expressions of style, these affirmations of black identity, varied. On the one hand, many whites and blacks alike enjoyed the flair brought to the game via the ABA and other black athletes. In a 1967 article in *Esquire*, for example, white writer George Frazier praised the style brought to sports by athletes such as Satchel Paige, Muhammad Ali, and Jim Brown, noting they seemed "so blithe, so self-possessed, so casual."[95] Black NBA star Walt Frazier argued that the ABA attracted fans to basketball because of "the transition to a speed, showtime style game."[96] A 1974 story in the *New York Times* about the Nets referred to the team playing "Showtime Basketball," anticipating the moniker of the popular 1980s Los Angeles Lakers, who played an up-tempo style reminiscent of the ABA.[97] In *Newsweek*, writer Pete Axthelm praised Erving's combination of flair and hard work, arguing that his aerial acrobatics worked "to transform his sport into graceful ballet, breath-taking drama or science-fiction fantasy—depending upon his mood of the moment and the needs of his team."[98] White star player Rick Barry described Erving as "the most exciting basketball player I've ever seen." Fans agreed with Barry, as Erving's drawing power in the ABA and in his later NBA career spoke to the considerable popularity of the innovative style he embodied.[99]

The embrace of Erving and other ABA stars had long-lasting and wide-reaching effects. Veteran broadcaster Bob Costas believed that one of the biggest contributions made by Erving and the ABA "was to legitimize flamboyance, [to prove] that flamboyance and selfishness were not synonymous." By watching Erving and the other stars of the ABA, fans learned "that you could flash style and still be a team player, that you could entertain and still play the game in a way that deserved respect."[100] Few would argue with George's assessment of black basketball's popularity among broad segments of the population, black and white: "The flash and funk of the late 1960s and 1970s had helped transform the sport. Pro teams dotted the national landscape, many with Black coaches and a majority of Black players. At large colleges everywhere white alumni embraced the school's Black stars, marveling at their huge Afros and tomahawk dunks."[101] In 1976 the two leagues agreed to a merger by which four of the ABA's remaining franchises—the New York Nets, the Indiana Pacers, the San Antonio Spurs, and the Denver Nuggets—entered the NBA. A special draft was held for the other ABA players to be selected by NBA teams.[102] After the two leagues merged, the ABA's style continued to influence the game. Michael Jordan's later superstardom in the 1980s and 1990s drew on this appreciation of "black culture's . . . spontaneity and improvisation, its brash experiments with performance, its fascination with those who exceed limits."[103]

And yet, even as stars like Erving (and later Jordan) won white admiration for their grace and innovation, a backlash against black success on the court also took place, as whites often fell back on demeaning stereotypes to denigrate black achievements. Some of the media coverage of Erving and other ABA stars reflected that tendency, and these trends would be exacerbated in later years as hip-hop culture made its way more fully into the mainstream. At the most basic level, many white Americans lamented the dominance of black athletes in the sport and the attendant lack of white stars. As historian Adam Criblez notes, by the end of the 1970s, after the ABA-NBA merger, the NBA's rosters were 70 percent black. Coming in the wake of the political turmoil of civil rights and Black Power, many whites found this destabilizing.[104] Even within the ABA, there was resistance to black players' increasing prominence. Adolph Rupp, the longtime University of Kentucky men's basketball coach, apparently held these concerns. Rupp, who served briefly as the figurehead president of the ABA's Memphis Tams, said, according to one account in 1972, "The trouble with the ABA is that there are too many nigger boys in it now."[105] Rupp was surely not alone in that opinion, and black writers of the time noticed these attitudes. John Henry Johnson, writing for the *New Pittsburgh Courier* in March 1973, observed that the increasing number of black pro basketball players was impressive but denied that the league had "liberal employment policies." He argued that "if talent was the only yardstick," teams would keep more black players, but that "for economic reasons"—the desires of white fans—teams had to "keep three or four whites" on each team.[106] Clearly, there was resistance to black-dominated sports.

As the 1970s progressed, overt political activism proved less and less acceptable to many in the sports world, especially if it embraced Black Power's more aggressive tone. The case of Warren Jabali provided a key litmus test in this regard. Jabali was an all-star performer in the ABA, starting his professional career with the ABA's Oakland Oaks in the 1968–1969 season, winning a championship with the club that year, and being named an all-star in 1970, 1972, 1973, and 1974. He converted to Islam in 1971, changing his last name from Armstrong to Jabali, and became known as an outspoken player. At the start of the 1974–1975 season, he found himself unemployed, a fact noted by some in the black and mainstream press. In the *New Pittsburgh Courier*, writer Ulish Carter indicated that Jabali was not being hired because he "is the type of man who speaks his mind and is not afraid to challenge the establishment in regards to race and other important issues of today."[107] Jabali agreed, claiming that he had been "blackballed" because he participated in a "boycott of the All-Star luncheon" the previous year.[108] Although his former team, the Denver Nuggets, denied the charge, it was clear that Jabali's outspoken personality was being held against him. For Carter, the issue was power: "As long as the coaches and other men in decision making positions in the ABA are lily white, a Black player doesn't stand a chance if he stands up as a Black man."[109] Carter's point spoke to a central problem with the ABA: as much as the league embraced black players and the style they brought to the game, the league's ownership and management remained almost entirely white.[110] Resistance to political activism was too difficult to overcome in this scenario, a sign of the limits to black advancement in sport and society.

The ABA's style of play led to more subtle forms of backlash as well. Many whites disparaged the league as one that promoted selfish play and that neglected the hard work required to play good defense. While black players embodied selfishness according to this line of thinking, white players became the icons of a team-first mentality.[111] The familiar stereotypes of the unthinking, naturally athletic black athletes were contrasted with the cerebral, team-oriented white ones.[112] These had lasting impacts in media coverage, with the use of contemporary phrases such as "playground ball," "street ball," and "hotdogging" continuing to be applied primarily to black players and the black improvisational style.[113] Former college basketball star and writer John Edgar Wideman poignantly described how whites used complaints about the black style of play to implicitly criticize African Americans on the whole: "When I was coming up, if a coach yelled 'playground move' at you it meant there was something wrong with it, which also meant in a funny way there was something wrong with the playground, and since the playground was a black world, there was something wrong with you, a black player out there doing something your way rather than their way."[114] That underlying criticism surfaced time and again in responses to the ABA and later manifestations of black style.

Even star players were not immune. Journalist Bill Simmons argues that there were racial undertones to how many white fans perceived black stars, especially those who came out of the ABA. When Portland defeated the Philadelphia 76ers for the NBA championship in 1977, most white fans celebrated the outcome. Portland was led by white center Bill Walton, while Philadelphia's stars were George McGinnis and Erving, both black players who came up through the ABA. Many white fans, according to Simmons, viewed the 76ers "as a disorganized schoolyard team, a product of the ABA and its 'look at me' culture, just a bunch of high-priced blacks who didn't care about making each other better."[115] Mainstream media coverage of the era reflected those beliefs; for example, a March 1975 *Baltimore Sun* story by Alan Goldstein contrasted the defense-first approach of the NBA in comparison to the "high-scoring" ABA. The people interviewed, such as Chicago Bulls coach Dick Motta, clearly believed that the ABA was illegitimate because of its lack of focus on defense. Goldstein concluded the article by noting that "Motta, and other coaches like him, obviously would prefer watching a Jerry Sloan dive over a press table to save a ball from going out-of-bounds to watching an acrobatic shot by Julius (Dr. J) Erving." The two examples are classics of the racial codes attached to basketball players: the white Sloan linked to effort and selflessness, and Dr. J to athletic grace and personal glory.[116]

Most scholars of black style—and indeed the players themselves—have argued that these critics missed the point. The individual panache brought to the game was meant to entertain the crowd, but it was also meant to boost their teams' chances of winning. Although George acknowledges that some of the ABA players "did themselves and the game a disservice with their attitude," which was too focused on individual accomplishment and not enough on team success, he also argues that the backlash was too severe.[117] Indeed, historian Joel Dinerstein argues that people who saw end-zone celebrations in football and slam dunks in basketball as emphasizing the individual over the team, as an act of selfishness, neglected to consider the shared qualities of these acts: "In African American culture . . . the individual achievement *reflects back on the community*; in other words, African Americans often find ways to share the moment of scoring with a real or perceived audience."[118] Wideman echoes this observation in his description of an incident of pickup basketball, when a player named Sekou threw down a marvelously difficult slam dunk over two defenders: "It wasn't about turning people into chumps or making anybody feel bad. It was Sekou's glory. Glory reflected instantly on all of us because he was one of us out there in the game and he'd suddenly lifted the game to a higher plane. We were all larger and better."[119] Black players saw themselves as performers meant to inspire the audience in a shared exchange. Erving, for one, knew of audience expectations: "When it's my turn to solo" through a dunk or improvised play, he observed, "I'm not about to play the same old riff."[120] As Caponi-Tabery argues, the "showmanship" that came along with the dunk and other moves also led to increased revenue for the sport. And these moves—though criticized frequently and consistently—have become well established as normal and "winning" aspects of the game.[121]

Although the ABA officially ceased to exist in 1976 when it merged with the NBA, the stylistic innovations it encouraged did not disappear. As scholar David Leviatin notes, one of longtime NBA commissioner David Stern's great achievements was to harness black basketball style and make it more appealing to the mainstream (white) public. Stern, who became the NBA's executive vice president in 1978 and its commissioner in 1984, took the elements brought in by the ABA—"its wide-open, above-the-rim, fast-paced style"—and skillfully marketed the game in a way that brought in new fans.[122] In the 1980s and 1990s, basketball stars such as Charles Barkley and Allen Iverson would follow in the ABA's stylistic footsteps, bringing a hip-hop style and cultural politics further into the mainstream.[123] Although the direct political engagement of athletes such as Ali, Jim Brown, Billie Jean King, and Harry Edwards would become less and less common as the 1970s progressed and the 1980s dawned, nonetheless the transformations ushered in by the ABA and by hip-hop continued to spread throughout American and global cultures. Jordan's ascendance in the 1980s as a global icon spoke to this embrace of black style, as he was especially known and celebrated for his acrobatic moves in the air and his innovative shotmaking. Signing endorsement deals with some of the largest companies in the world, starring in Hollywood films, and appearing on the front cover of numerous mainstream media publications, Jordan spoke to the rise of black style in the global market.[124] Tensions certainly remained. Writing in 1990, Wideman pointed out the contradictions of Jordan's success as an icon: he was a black man who was celebrated and loved even at the same time that another black man, convicted felon Willie Horton, served to demonize black people and swing a presidential election.[125] But Jordan's superstardom spoke to a wider embrace of black style than ever before.

The 1990s, meanwhile, saw increased public discourse about "'street' or 'blacktop' basketball." The style of play, which was "fast-paced, inventive, expressive, in-your-face basketball," became increasingly prominent in media coverage and advertisements, although few noted the style's long historical roots.[126] And although Jordan famously refrained from getting involved in controversial politics, the growing spread of hip-hop culture inevitably forced people to come to terms with the underlying factors that had led to the genre. In sports, teams such as the University of Miami football team gleefully taunted opponents, wore flashy attire, and demanded attention. Cultural critic William Rhoden defended the Miami players and others from criticisms that their style was too obnoxious and too unsportsmanlike in its promotion of self. White fans and coaches were willing to use black athletic ability, according to Rhoden, but didn't want to deal with the real challenges that black athletes had to go through in their daily lives. Black athletes, such as the Miami football players, came to school "with their own baggage, baggage that a history of living in a white supremacist country had helped to pack." Their trash talking, their style of play "developed in response to quotas and denial of black humanity."[127] As Allen Iverson and others embraced their urban identity fully in the late 1990s and early 2000s, there at least came a possibility that people would see more of the deprivations suffered in the wake of white flight and would recognize the cultural barriers that existed for African Americans to achieve success and respect.[128] By the time of the Black Lives Matter movement, black athletes were sufficiently well positioned culturally and financially to speak out on police brutality and other issues.[129] The rise of black style in mainstream basketball, first through the ABA, had created an opening in which later black politics could find firmer footing for expression.

Style and Substance

The ABA, then, was more than a curious footnote in the history of professional basketball. Freed from the constraints of the more traditional NBA, and open to experimentation in order to drum up fan interest, the ABA provided a fertile ground for black basketball players to cultivate their style. Coming in the aftermath of the mainstream civil rights movement and during the heyday and waning years of Black Power, the ABA embodied the cultural rebellion and resistance of the era. In celebrating individual brilliance through slam dunks and no-look passes; in embracing an improvisational style through a high-paced, open-form game; and in wearing their hair in Afros, the black players of the ABA brought a black aesthetic to the mainstream and promoted black pride. If the players shied away from the overt activism of Muhammad Ali of the late 1960s, they nonetheless engaged in personal politics that had lasting implications. In particular, through their performances on the court, hip-hop culture made its first significant entry point into the American consciousness. In addition, new possibilities for black sports superstars—and stars in other realms of entertainment—emerged. The ABA players acted, as Ralph Ellison had noted of black Americans in general, to levy "pressure upon the nation to live up to its ideals." They "[gave] creative tension to [the] struggle for justice and for the elimination of those factors, social and psychological, which make for slums and shaky suburban communities."[130] The creative vision they brought to sports like basketball was a part of the process by which black Americans forced whites to recognize their presence and to think about new possibilities for the shape of the future. The style of the ABA was, perhaps, its most impressive substance.

CONCLUSION

Activism Unfinished

As the ABA commenced its third season in October 1969, change was brewing in the "national pastime"—baseball. That fall, St. Louis Cardinals outfielder Curt Flood received the bad news that he had been traded to the perennially mismanaged Philadelphia Phillies. An All-Star with the Cardinals, one of Major League Baseball's most successful franchises, Flood lamented the turn of events. He had been a member of the Cardinals for the previous twelve seasons. Thirty-one years old and nearing the end of his playing career, he had no desire to start over again with a struggling franchise. But what could he do? MLB's player contracts all contained the so-called reserve clause, language that affirmed team control over a player even when his contract expired. Flood had little power; he either had to report to the Phillies or retire from the game. But the activist spirit of the 1960s was alive and well: Flood decided to stand his ground. In December 1969 Flood wrote to MLB commissioner Bowie Kuhn and announced his refusal to accept the trade. "After twelve years in the Major Leagues," Flood wrote, "I do not feel that I am a piece of property to be bought and sold irrespective of my wishes." Affirming his desire to play baseball in the upcoming season, Flood asked to be released from his obligation to the Phillies so that he could sign with a team of his choice. It was a momentous rejection of the imbalanced power structures in MLB—structures that put the fate of hundreds of players in the hands of two dozen or so wealthy owners.[1]

Flood's campaign for free agency required careful negotiation with the racial politics of post–civil rights America. Marvin Miller, the executive director of the Major League Baseball Players Association, had been actively searching for ways to challenge the reserve clause, but to gain the support of the majority-white MLBPA, Flood had to couch his demands in color-blind terms. When Flood compared himself to a "well-paid slave" in an interview with Howard Cosell, he earned considerable scorn and rebuke in the popular press.[2] Questioned by Dodgers player Tom Haller as to whether "black militants" had motivated him, Flood demurred, explaining that while his racial identity made him "more sensitive to injustice," this issue was about being "a ballplayer, a major league ballplayer," not specifically a black athlete.[3] Only then did the MLBPA feel comfortable supporting his efforts. As scholar Abraham Iqbal Khan has argued, Flood faced a rhetorical dilemma: even though black athletes did gain power and increasing voice in the 1960s and 1970s, there were still limits to what they could do or say in the face of well-established systems and norms. For Flood to gain any support, he had to subsume his racial identity in the market economy. This strategy, according to Khan, marked "liberalism's insidious

St. Louis Cardinals outfielder Curt Flood protested his trade to the Philadelphia Phillies in 1970, leading to increased challenges of MLB's reserve clause. Credit: Johnson Publishing Company Archive. Courtesy Ford Foundation, J. Paul Getty Trust, John D. and Catherine T. MacArthur Foundation, Andrew W. Mellon Foundation, and Smithsonian Institution.

conservatism," its tenacity in reaffirming existing institutions.[4] Even as many black players supported Flood, recognizing, as scholar Gerald Early notes, the "paternalism" inherent in professional sports, other black stars shied away, concerned about "retribution from the owners" and the bad public relations of complaining about relatively high salaries.[5]

Flood's lawsuit failed when the U.S. Supreme Court ruled against him, but his efforts inspired others to challenge the system. By the end of 1975 the reserve clause was essentially dead and free agency had arrived in baseball. Although the payoff for professional athletes would be significant, the limited framework in which Flood operated spoke to the narrow outcomes of the change. Flood sought greater freedoms for players, but he did not advocate creating a new league owned by his peers. Players would make more money, but there would be no revolution in the ownership structure of professional sports.[6]

The Curt Flood story offers a window into the tangled legacy of the activism of the late 1960s and early 1970s. There is no question that this era helped usher in new kinds of athletic possibilities: from the racial integration of college teams in the South, as in the case of Scott, to the opening up of new sporting opportunities for women at the amateur and professional levels. Working in concert with one another, athletes also saw that they could flex political muscles—the successes in initiating Black Studies programs, hiring black coaches, opening up women's opportunities in distance running, and creating athlete-based advocacy programs like the BEU, all pointed to the power athletes might exercise beyond merely creating opportunities for themselves. The growing prominence of athletes as celebrities made it possible for athletes to challenge long-held stereotypes and affect patterns of cultural representation, too. King's performance in the Battle of the Sexes, the high-flying dunks of the ABA, and Ali's and Frazier's starring roles as black men spoke to the possibilities of shifting public attitudes toward women athletes, urban African Americans, and black men in general.

American athletes' activism paid dividends internationally, too. Of particular importance to black activists from the 1960s through the 1980s was the place of apartheid South Africa. One of the issues driving Edwards's proposed boycott of the 1968 Olympics was the presence of South Africa and Rhodesia, as both nations relegated black people to second-class citizenship. One of the real successes of the OPHR was banning these two countries from the 1968 games. Ongoing activism kept the pressure on the IOC to maintain the ban against South Africa and Rhodesia until their apartheid policies were dismantled.[7] Tennis player Arthur Ashe also led a campaign to challenge apartheid in South Africa by advocating for the right to play in tournaments in the nation. He finally gained entrance in 1973. For the next two decades, Ashe continued to call attention to the nation's policies, getting arrested in 1985 for protesting outside the South African Embassy in Washington, D.C., and encouraging prominent athletes to boycott events in the country.[8] The black press, in particular, followed this activism closely over the years, calling attention to athletes' responsibilities to help others in the Black Diaspora.[9] Although certainly not the only factor, sports activism played a role in shaping international opposition to apartheid, leading to a new biracial government in the mid-1990s.

And yet real limits remained. The arrival of free agency in baseball and the ABA's merger into the NBA in 1976 marked important endpoints to a time of heightened athlete activism. In the years following these events, the pace and prominence of athlete protests declined at nearly all levels and in nearly all sports. The critiques of both athletics-specific practices and broader social trends largely vanished from popular sports discourse. Discerning how and why that was the case, and where that activist spirit went, requires an assessment of the pivotal issues left unaddressed by this era's social movements in sports.

* * *

While international sports activism in the 1960s and 1970s showed key signs of success, the globalization of domestic sports leagues in ensuing decades brought a number of challenges that have yet to be resolved. Latino and Afro-Latino baseball players had a long history in professional sports in the United States—in both MLB and the Negro Leagues. In the years following Robinson's debut in 1947, MLB players such as Minnie Miñoso and Vic Power navigated tricky terrain as both racial and ethnic pioneers. Often facing a language barrier that led to press misquotations and mockery, encountering racial discrimination, and missing family and friends in the Caribbean and elsewhere, these players shouldered remarkably challenging burdens.[10] The defiance of superstar outfielder Roberto Clemente, who insisted on fairer treatment by the press, was an important wake-up call for many white Americans, but obstacles remained well into the 1980s and 1990s.[11] With the arrival of free agency to MLB in 1976, demand for Latino players escalated as owners sought cheaper options to fill out their teams. These players often received low pay in poor conditions in their home countries and in the minor leagues and then faced discrimination, biased media treatment, and hostility from teammates and opposing players even once making it into MLB.[12] Well into the twenty-first century, home run celebrations by Latinx players led to bench-clearing brawls, events motivated at least in part by white racism.[13]

By the 1980s and 1990s, other sports saw increasing foreign presence as well, with players from across the globe taking up starring roles in the NFL, NBA, and MLB, and with prominent NCAA teams.[14] Here, too, the story was a mixed bag, and the NBA was often the locus for key issues regarding race, ethnicity, and nationality. While many foreign players experienced enthusiastic support, such as China's Yao Ming, stereotypes persisted. Other players mocked Yao's language, referred to him with demeaning terms such as "Chinaman," and the Miami Heat hosted an offensive "fortune cookie night" when Yao's Rockets came to play.[15] Even Asian Americans like Jeremy Lin faced demeaning stereotypes and outright hostility because of their ancestry.[16] While globalization has altered the makeup of teams and transformed sports in many ways, white normative hegemony has continued to cast a long shadow over the sports world.

In addition to the changes wrought by globalization, economic imbalances remained one of the most confounding aspects of American society—inside and outside sports. That Curt Flood found himself writing to a white male commissioner asking to prevent one white male team owner from trading him to another white male team owner reveals the inequalities in financial power and control in the world of sports and beyond. Many of the activist campaigns and movements of the 1960s and 1970s had economic underpinnings: Billie Jean King's work to improve women's pay, Jim Brown's founding of the BEU, Muhammad Ali's efforts with Main Bout Inc., college athletes like Charlie Scott who sought better conditions for minority employees, and hip-hop's call for recognition of urban neglect. Nearly all failed to change the wealth gaps that existed between men and women, and between whites and blacks. Brown's efforts faltered because Nixon's fall from grace ended his political support and because his hopes for the capitalist market depended on African Americans facing fair competition in the business world; Brown made few accommodations for the uphill climb African Americans faced in the American economy. King's efforts to raise women athletes' pay helped but did little to transform the broader culture surrounding women's athletics or to ameliorate the paucity of media coverage and commercial endorsements available to women athletes. These troubles were especially acute for black women athletes, whose intersectional status made them even more neglected in the capitalist marketplace. The post-athletic struggles of tennis pioneer Althea Gibson and Olympic sprinter Wilma Rudolph, who both experienced financial woes and mental health challenges after the ends of their athletic careers in the 1960s, speak to this reality.[17] Meanwhile, the fact that Virginia Slims founder Gladys Heldman lost her leadership role when the tour merged with the USLTA meant that white men retained control, even of women's sports. And while ABA players made their upstart basketball league a haven for personal expression and some increased earnings, they too played for white owners—both before and after the merger with the NBA.[18]

The Ali-Frazier fight similarly evoked the missed opportunities regarding minority financial empowerment in the sports world. Much of the discourse in the aftermath of the fight centered on more equitable distribution of resources for African Americans, exemplified by the emergence of the first major black fight promoter, Don King. However, even that victory was fraught with complications. King, in prison in Cleveland for manslaughter at the time of the Ali-Frazier bout, was inspired by the fight's popularity and revenue potential. He later told Ali, "They let us see your first 'Fight of the Century' against Frazier in '71, and it was then that I decided not to return to gambling, but to go into show business."[19] Using his garrulous personality and his connections to organized crime figures (and their finances), King quickly ascended in the fight promotion scene, bringing about major bouts (and record multimillion-dollar purses) for Ali in Kinshasa, Zaire, in 1974 and in the Philippines in 1975. King used his blackness to great effect, connecting himself to Black Power and ideals of economic self-uplift.[20] Initially, black press figures celebrated King's arrival. "Until King," *Black Enterprise* writer Diane Weathers observed, "there had never been any Blacks who had major roles, behind the scenes, in the closed-door rooms where the deals are made and the power lies."[21] King's ability to step in and claim some of this power and money was a heartening sign of progress.

Yet King's story also spotlighted capitalism's limitations as a means of uplift, fulfilling the warnings of earlier leaders such as W. E. B. Du Bois about the pitfalls of relying on the marketplace. In the 1940s Du Bois had cautioned against putting too much faith in capitalism, worrying, according to historian Manning Marable, that "Black entrepreneurs as a group had absolutely no ethics or morality regarding their own people."[22] As his career progressed, King became notorious for stealing from his fighters, black and white, depriving them of deserved income and padding his own finances at their expense. King embodied capitalism's focus on *individual* attainment of wealth. As heavyweight champion Larry Holmes ruefully observed in later years, "Don looks black, lives white, and thinks green."[23] Prominent Nation of Islam minister and Ali confidant Jeremiah Shabazz was even more direct: "He spouts a mixture of Americanism and black nationalism, and says whatever he has to say to win fighters over. But after they're used up, they mean nothing to him and he discards them like they were firewood."[24] The hope had been that King's entrance into the world of prizefight promotion would lead to a more equitable distribution of revenues for African

Americans, whereby black promoters would earn money that they would then funnel back into their community. But King belied that faith, acquiring as much money for himself as he could, giving scant amounts to help black causes, and pursuing his own self-uplift with little thought to others.[25] Although observers such as Shabazz, Holmes, and others were disgusted by King's behavior, they should not have been surprised: King took capitalism's emphasis on the individual to its extreme. His endorsement of Donald Trump as president fits this broader pattern.[26]

Don King's failures to provide economic uplift to the black community were echoed over and over again in the years that followed; black socks like those of Tommie Smith and John Carlos could easily have been donned again, with the same meaning, in any of the Olympic Games that followed. The wealth gap remains large; according to the U.S. Federal Reserve in 2019, African American families' wealth, on average, was "less than 15 percent that of White families."[27] And that rate of disparity has been long-standing: the 1962 Survey of Consumer Finances revealed an almost identical racial wealth divide.[28] Racial and gender disparity in sports ownership and management has persisted as well. Not until 2002 did any of the three major professional sports leagues—Major League Baseball, the National Football League, and the National Basketball Association—have a racial minority as a principal owner of a team. By the spring of 2018, whites constituted more than 93 percent of the majority owners in those three organizations.[29] Front-office positions, too, remain almost exclusively white in all of the major pro leagues, and white men occupy head coaching positions at extremely disproportionate levels to the number of white players, especially in college and professional football and in baseball.[30] In his autobiography, *I Never Had It Made*, published in 1972 just before his death that same year, Jackie Robinson lamented the lack of black managers and executives in baseball. The "sickness of baseball," according to Robinson, was that "baseball moguls and their top advisers" believe that black athletes "are lacking in the gray matter that it supposedly takes to serve as managers, officials, and executives in policy-making positions."[31] The faith that Billie Jean King, Jim Brown, and others evinced in the capitalist market, without addressing the ownership and leadership imbalances in the worlds of sports and business, limited the capacity to create broader change and equity.

Such faith was not limited to the world of sports; indeed, both the Republican New Right in the 1970s and neoliberal Democrats in the 1990s put faith in the market's possibilities to create equality. The economic policies of Ronald Reagan prioritized governmental deregulation and tax cuts, arguing that removing interference from the market would encourage economic growth and thus lead to better standards of living for all Americans. Neoliberal Democrats such as Bill Clinton argued for the necessity of some forms of regulation and the taxation of the wealthy and corporations but nonetheless favored economic development by removing barriers to global trade. Both saw an expanded economy as the solution to social inequalities, believing that market growth would extend across racial lines.[32] However, the ongoing wealth gap and the persistence of race-based ghettos in the United States are visible signs of the lack of change from both approaches, no matter how ideologically different they might appear at first glance.[33] That such inequities continued to impact sports leadership is no surprise.

Power relations in amateur athletics also remained relatively unchanged after the unrest of the late 1960s and early 1970s. Athletes initiated considerable change on campus, increasing the number of black athletes and generating heightened media coverage of black athletic accomplishment. In many ways their efforts were more far-reaching than those of professional athletes. While many of their calls for change did relate to sports—most notably regarding playing time, racial abuse, and medical aid—they also pursued issues outside sports and even outside campus life. In linking their causes to the demand for Black Studies programs, African American head coaches, black students' educational and social needs, and aid to minority university employees, black college athletes branched out in impressive ways. They helped bring about new academic disciplines and courses and generated employment opportunities inside and outside of sports.

But the power structures in college sports remained largely unchanged. The NCAA's model of the "student-athlete" remained the norm for decades, keeping school and NCAA administrators in control of athletics and revenues. Academic injustices abounded. In the 1980s the academic shortcomings of high-profile athletes such as NFL star Dexter Manley, who attended Oklahoma State University for four years but was functionally illiterate, and Chris Washburn, who starred for North Carolina State University for two years despite scoring less than 500 on his SAT exam, caused significant criticism of the NCAA's failure to deliver on the education athletes had been promised.[34] Even the NCAA's attempts to install higher academic standards drew criticism. When the organization passed Proposition 42 in 1989, which required a minimum SAT score and grade point average for scholarships, Georgetown University head coach John Thompson protested bitterly, walking off the court before a game in 1989 to challenge the policy change. The new rule, Thompson argued, would disproportionately deny African Americans access to higher education. According to Thompson, the larger problems were the systemic issues that subjected many poor black people to subpar educational experiences—and college was one opportunity to address those challenges.[35] Although the NCAA eventually backed down from Proposition 42, it did little to address the wider concerns raised by Thompson and others, leaving the NCAA to mirror, and frequently exacerbate, America's racial inequalities. Academic malfeasance would continue into the twenty-first century: a series of scandals at Florida State University, UNC, and the University of Missouri revealed how numerous schools kept athletes eligible for competition without providing the education promised by the scholarships provided.[36] And numerous studies showed that African American male athletes, especially in the "revenue sports" of men's basketball and football, continued to graduate at much lower rates than their peers.[37]

Meanwhile, as television contracts brought escalating contracts for (predominantly white, male) coaches, athletes saw little changes to their material benefits or their rights. Former UCLA basketball star Ed O'Bannon grew frustrated that he and other athletes did not profit from television replays of games featuring them, or even from video games that employed their likenesses. His successful 2009 lawsuit against the NCAA was a watershed moment in student-athletes' fight to control their own destinies, one whose implications have yet to be fully realized.[38] Other legal challenges to the NCAA's absolute authority over its student-athletes emerged, augmented in popular culture by veteran journalist Taylor Branch's exposé on the NCAA's repressive policies, published in *The Atlantic* in October 2011.[39] In early 2014 Northwestern University's starting quarterback, Kain Colter, announced his intent to unionize the school's football players. Although the National Labor Relations Board refused to certify the union, it marked one more assault against the NCAA's control over its athletes.[40] However, when former U.S. secretary of state Condoleeza Rice chaired a commission to explore the status of college basketball in the light of revelations of illicit payments to recruits and academic misconduct at prominent colleges and universities, the group did nothing to challenge the amateur status of college athletes. While empowering athletes to have more access to professional advice, it did nothing to grant the student athletes rights akin to employees—they remained subordinate to the NCAA's will.[41] The "student-athlete" construct remained a barrier to equity.

Another group who still lack power—and pay—is women athletes. Perhaps more than in any other arena, women's sports would seem to be a success story. Billie Jean King's efforts with the Virginia Slims Tour improved circumstances for women tennis players and laid the cultural framework for megastars like Serena Williams. Meanwhile, the efforts of Gibb and Switzer coupled with Title IX opened up countless opportunities for women in athletics. Yet serious barriers remained for women in terms of pay and media coverage. The U.S. Women's National Soccer Team remains the most visible representation of the pay imbalance between men's and women's sports. Despite the team's global success in winning four FIFA World Cup titles and four Olympic gold medals—more than any other nation—the players on the team received less pay than their male counterparts, who have never reached the final of any major international competition. The team filed multiple complaints and lawsuits over the years, and finally attained equal pay with the men's team in an agreement reached in spring 2022. Still, the bitter resistance of the United States Soccer Federation to pay equality speaks to the ongoing barriers for women athletes. They are certainly not the only example, as the average salary for players in the Women's National Basketball Association in 2020 was less than 2 percent of the $7 million NBA players earn on average. Similar disparities exist in other sports, including hockey. Even tennis has not fully achieved gender equity in terms of pay, despite King's efforts and activism in later years by Serena Williams and others. Although all of the so-called Grand Slam tennis events have equalized pay between men and women, smaller tournaments continue to pay men more for their titles.[42] Title IX, meanwhile, has improved funding for women's sports markedly, but spending for men's athletics programs in high school and higher education continues to exceed women's athletics, especially at the Division 1 level.[43]

Disparities in media coverage play a significant part in the ongoing pay imbalances and contribute to women's ongoing objectification. The paucity of television coverage for women's sports has been an issue for decades, one that continues into the present day. Not only have women's sports been neglected, but major networks often prioritize coverage of male sports *not in season* over current women's teams and leagues.[44] In 2002 sociologist Michael Messner argued that "sport's center is still, by and large, a space that is actively constructed by and for men," referring to the dominant media visibility and flow of money to men's athletics.[45] Few would dispute that contention today. As leading sports historians such as Susan Cahn and Jaime Schultz have noted, even when networks do cover women's sports, they often continue to depict women as objects of male heterosexual desire. This trend is especially visible in the heightened attention given to women's beach volleyball, in which competitors usually don two-piece bathing suits. The women's fitness industry—emerging in women's magazines in the late 1970s—has gained market power in recent decades. But despite a push for body positivity, much of the rhetoric continues to be focused on exercising for weight loss and sexual desirability.[46] The activism for women's increasing access to sports, in the form of distance running and the campaign for Title IX, did open new doors. But deeply embedded gender norms were not easy to eradicate, and liberal feminism made little headway against the power of dominant media institutions that continued to circulate notions of male supremacy and female objectification.

Black women continue to face particular challenges in sports as a result of their race and gender. Many mainstream feminists neglected the issues and circumstances of African American women, a trend visible in the relative absence of black women from the campaign for distance running. The rise to prominence of Venus and Serena Williams in the 1990s certainly showcased new possibilities for black women in a predominantly white sport, but the sisters faced significant media scrutiny and fan animosity. When Serena Williams wore a short, form-fitting "catsuit" at the 2002 U.S. Open, criticism abounded. Some claimed the outfit was too revealing and sexually suggestive, others criticized the suit for showing off her "mannish" and muscular build, and still others fell back on demeaning animalistic descriptions and caricatures. Although there were those who rose to her defense and celebrated her curves, the discourse revealed, as Schultz noted, the continued impacts of "the hegemonic racialized order in women's tennis."[47] The Williams sisters are not alone. Usually facing intersectional pressures related to some combination of race, gender, sexuality, religion, and class, many African American women athletes face extra media scrutiny and criticism. Highly publicized incidents featuring the Rutgers University women's basketball team (referred to as "nappy-headed hos" by radio host Don Imus), Olympic gymnast Gabby Douglas (criticized for her supposedly unkempt hair), and gymnast Simone Biles (who a rival Italian gymnast suggested got better scores because of her race) reveal the ongoing pressures heaped upon black women athletes.[48] The failure of women's activism in the 1960s and 1970s to draw from black feminism, to recognize these intersectional pressures, limited the breadth of its changes.

The struggles women face in mainstream sports are also a reflection of the tenacity of patriarchy. As much as Ali and Frazier represented two different models of manhood, both affirmed a patriarchal masculinity that limited women's significance and prioritized the male breadwinner. The multiple cases of domestic violence associated with Jim Brown, Muhammad Ali's demeaning comments about women's liberation, Joe Frazier's insistence on his role as primary caretaker, and Joe Namath's famed (and celebrated) womanizing spoke to the persistence of gender norms that put men in positions of power. As Cahn argues, these imbalances have been difficult to address. Sports, she argues, are an integral part of "the social hierarchies that have historically granted men greater authority" in society.[49] At times that authority has spilled out into "hypermasculine" beliefs and behaviors. Perpetrators of sexual assault on college campuses have been disproportionately represented on sports teams.[50] Dominance on sports teams has often been linked to dominance of women more generally, particularly with regard to sexual conquests.[51] The scandal at Baylor University in 2016, when it came to light that football and athletic department officials had ignored reports of sexual assault by football players against women at the school, was a disheartening but by no means singular example of how big-time men's sports could breed tolerance for hypermasculinity and sexual violence.[52]

The persistence of patriarchy and violence against women also echoed another issue left largely unaddressed in the 1960s and 1970s: the wide-ranging homophobia of American society. As noted in chapter 1, Billie Jean King remained closeted throughout her playing career, a reflection of the homophobic culture in the United States. Even in the early 1990s, Penn State University women's basketball coach Rene Portland had an official team policy banning gay women from her squad.[53] However, as more queer women athletes acknowledged their sexual identities, including basketball star Sheryl Swoopes in 2005, explicit barriers to gay women athletes began to crumble.[54] For gay male athletes, coming out of the closet in the 1960s and 1970s was almost unthinkable, given the hypermasculine associations with most sports.[55] The publication of David Kopay's memoir in 1977 marked an important first step in breaking through, as Kopay came out of the closet five years after retiring from the NFL.[56] Still, it would not be until 2013 that a male athlete in a major U.S. team sport came out of the closet while actively playing: Robbie Rogers in Major League Soccer and Jason Collins in the NBA.[57] Progress has certainly been made, with Carl Nassib coming out in June 2021, making him the first NFL player to do so while still playing.[58] Of the three major professional leagues, by early 2022 only the MLB had not featured an openly gay player on an active roster.

One related issue emerged just as the activist era was drawing to a close, and its lack of definite resolution has also lingered into contemporary times. In 1976 tennis player Renée Richards attempted to play in the U.S. Open and was denied entry. Although she had earned a place in the tournament, officials rejected her application because she had transitioned from male to female one year prior. Born Richard Raskind, the forty-one-year-old had long felt trapped in a man's body. After undergoing gender reassignment surgery, she began to play tennis competitively, winning a tournament in La Jolla, California, in early 1976. When news media caught wind of her story, controversy ensued. Some women's players supported her, while others argued that her biology gave her an unfair advantage. At one tournament in New Jersey, twenty-five players withdrew in protest of her entrance into the field.[59] Even Billie Jean King hesitated to welcome Richards into the women's tennis fold. In August 1976 King indicated that she was still uncertain because Richards had "male hormones" and had the benefits of playing men's competitive tennis for many years prior.[60] Eventually, King and most of the other players on the tour came around; by April 1977, King was publicly supporting Richards's case and even filed an affidavit on her behalf with the federal court judge overseeing her lawsuit. When the judge ruled in Richards's favor, she joined the tour and competed in a number of events in ensuing years.[61] Still, the mixed response to Richards from men and women alike foretold the thorny debates regarding transgender athletes that would continue in the decades to come.[62]

A different kind of ambivalence continued to impact African Americans inside and outside of sports. The transformation in public attitudes toward Muhammad Ali and the enthusiastic embrace of the black style of basketball spoke to a growing widespread acceptance of black culture in American life. However, that embrace did not necessarily undermine systemic racism—black bodies still remained disproportionately underfed, brutalized, and isolated. Black cultural critics have long observed this disconnect. In 1992 bell hooks cautioned that mass culture's interest in "the Other" was "embedded in the . . . deep structure of white supremacy." As much as white people might flock to black film stars, desire intimate relations with minority people, or listen to black music, their primary interest was in finding "more intense, more satisfying . . . ways of doing and feeling" and not in genuine human connection.[63] A number of intellectuals and scholars, including Patricia Collins and Abby Ferber, have linked this tendency to sports, seeing the commodification of black bodies for white pleasure as a manifestation of a supposedly color-blind nation that ignores the lived realities of African Americans.[64] As Todd Boyd has argued, many white fans loved the performances of black athletes like Allen Iverson, celebrating his Most Valuable Player award for the 2000–2001 NBA season, but also criticized his language, hairstyle, clothing choices, and manners. In doing so, they gave little thought to the harsh realities of his early life in urban poverty and the racism he encountered via the criminal justice system. In criticizing Iverson's distinct style—including his many tattoos and his cornrows—these critics affirmed dominant norms rooted in middle-class white America, perpetuating systemic racism's denial of black lives and bodies.[65]

The qualified embrace of black culture also meant that the decades after 1976 saw tremendous financial success for minority athletes, especially in the realm of commercial endorsements. However, those opportunities often came with a political price. Although athlete salaries skyrocketed after labor unions successfully negotiated with owners, limitations remained for socially conscious black athletes. Even as African American stars like basketball player Michael Jordan and golfer Tiger Woods earned huge endorsement deals and received global fame, they refrained from getting involved in controversial political issues for most of their careers, leery of alienating white fans and sponsors. The career of O. J. Simpson is especially revealing. By 1969, Simpson—on his way to NFL stardom—began to cash in on athletic celebrity in unprecedented ways, earning massive endorsement deals from companies such as Hertz Rent-a-Car, General Motors, and others. As historians, scholars, and cultural critics such as Arthur Ashe, Leola Johnson, David Roediger, and William Rhoden have noted, Simpson appeared to transcend traditional limitations in the public representations of black men to build a financially lucrative career as a commercial pitchman and Hollywood actor.[66]

And yet, as impressive as these gains were for professional black athletes, they fell far short of the sweeping, community-centered goals espoused by Brown and others during the peak of athlete activism between 1964 and 1976. In effect, these athletes followed the Booker T. Washington model of working hard within the system and gaining material rewards as a result. However, the individual business successes attained by O. J. Simpson, Michael Jordan, and other star black athletes not only accepted the U.S. capitalist economy, but they also made no significant inroads into correcting the wider wealth inequalities facing the black community. As professional athletes enjoyed new power to negotiate contracts and encountered new opportunities to earn money on Madison Avenue, the dreams of collective control over local resources were forgotten. By the 1980s Jordan's and Simpson's achievements on Madison Avenue and in Hollywood showcased the muted political voice that often accompanied athletes' financial success. Both athletes attained their mainstream success apparently because they willingly gave up any kind of controversial political or social activism. Their individual wealth came with a deemphasis of racial identity and a carefully crafted image that avoided controversial politics.[67]

If Simpson or Jordan ever appeared without shoes during their heyday, it was likely to sell a brand of socks and not, as Smith and Carlos had done, to raise awareness of black poverty. In the 2020 documentary *The Last Dance*, Jordan praised Ali for his activism but defended his apolitical stance, saying, "I never thought of myself as an activist. I thought of myself as a basketball player. I wasn't a politician when I was playing my sport. . . . I was focused on my craft. Was that selfish? Probably. But . . . that's where my energy was."[68] Some of Jordan's own teammates criticized his apathy. Craig Hodges, a backup shooting guard who played with Jordan on the Chicago Bulls team in the late

1980s and early 1990s, publicly chided his star teammate on more than one occasion for failing to get involved. The tipping point was Jordan's refusal to boycott a game, or even publicly address police violence, during the 1992 NBA finals when the Rodney King riots broke out. After game two of the series, Hodges accused Jordan in a *New York Times* article of "bailing out" by refusing to comment on the violence and unrest.[69] After the Bulls claimed the championship, Hodges continued to push for change: he attended the team's celebration at the White House in a dashiki and brought President George H. W. Bush an eight-page letter detailing the issues facing the African American community. This political engagement had consequences: when the season ended, Hodges found himself out of a job with the Bulls, and no other NBA teams would even offer him a tryout, much less sign him.[70] The experiences of Mahmoud Abdul-Rauf, traded away from his team after protesting the "Star-Spangled Banner" only four years later, further showed the consequences for black athletes who spoke out.[71]

That silence and political impotence of athletes like Jordan frustrated many, including former athletes such as Jim Brown and cultural critics such as William Rhoden.[72] Rhoden's 2006 book, *Forty Million Dollar Slaves*, argued that the figure of the black athlete had become "a spectacle that exists at the pleasure of its white owners." According to Rhoden, black sports stars lacked access to "true power" in sports and thus surrendered their ability to effect change for the black community.[73] Many activists, as seen through the struggles over the Ali-Frazier fight promotion and even Brown's work with the BEU, had hoped that the quest for black equality could be best realized through a reformation, or even revolution, of the capitalist system. But as those hopes failed or fizzled into disappointments such as Don King, the movement lost power to effect wide-scale political and economic change. As prominent black athletes shied away from contesting the uneven power dynamics in sports, the exploitation of black bodies for the benefit of a select few wealthy whites continued.

By the 1990s, much of the activism of the 1960s and 1970s had been forgotten. The individual financial successes of star athletes and the growth of sports as entertainment obscured the ongoing inequalities inside and outside the playing fields and courts. Meanwhile, "color-blind" rhetoric came to dominate discourse and policy in the 1980s, making race-based campaigns for justice seem to many like a vestige of an earlier time.[74] As historian Jacquelyn Hall argued in her 2005 essay "The Long Civil Rights Movement," conservative co-option of the civil rights movement's legacies and meanings led to a neutered understanding of the struggle for black equality. Many legislators, journalists, and educators pigeonholed the movement as being solely about ending public discrimination and gaining voting rights, presenting the Civil Rights Act of 1964 and the Voting Rights Act of 1965 as complete solutions to the issues facing African Americans. As a result, they elided the quests for equal public representation, access to leadership positions, just policing, and, most crucially, economic reparations, all of which had been central to the black struggle for decades.[75] Similarly, as enforcement of Title IX began the process of leveling the gendered playing field, increased opportunities for women and girls in the amateur realm took attention away from ongoing inequalities in terms of media coverage, sexualization, and pay. If minority athletes and women athletes could play, and get either scholarships or compensation for doing so, what was there to complain about? Why would anyone look back to the BEU or to Wyomia Tyus or to Warren Jabali?

Still, by the time the second decade of the twenty-first century arrived, frustrations with ongoing inequalities exploded into mainstream American culture, including the world of sports. We return, then, to where we started: LeBron James and Laura Ingraham. When Ingraham spoke out against James for criticizing Donald Trump and for his participation in calling attention to issues of police brutality, she harkened back to the politics of the 1980s and 1990s. Her demand to "shut up and dribble" sought to disconnect sports from the world of politics, to keep black athletes in a subordinate position in American civic life. James's response, and his refusal to limit his voice, marked another flicker in the rekindled flame of activism from an earlier era. But it was also something new. Although much of the activism in the 1960s and 1970s centered on issues in the world of sports and then extended—sometimes haltingly—into broader social concerns, the activism of the second decade of the twenty-first century more often *started with* issues in the broader community. The kneeling by Colin Kaepernick and Megan Rapinoe, the T-shirts with the names of victims of police brutality worn by members of the WNBA's Minnesota Lynx (and the similarly emblazoned masks worn by tennis star Naomi Osaka), and the use of social media to speak out on systemic racism by James and others—none of it was meant to benefit athletes directly. When the members of the WNBA's Atlanta Dream actively campaigned against owner Kelly Loeffler's attempts to win a seat in the U.S. Senate, they protested her national politics, not her team management. They sought to change power at the highest levels.[76]

Of course, recent sports activism *has* engaged with issues connected to athletics—most notably, in the campaigns for equal pay in women's soccer and elsewhere. But the groundwork laid in the 1960s and 1970s—and perhaps the lessons learned from the retrenchment of the 1980s and the painful legacies of unresolved issues—has opened up new possibilities for athletes to extend their fight into new arenas of life. When NCAA athletes campaigned

Maya Moore, a member of the WNBA's Minnesota Lynx, who have played pivotal roles in extending athlete activism outside the realm of sports. Photo by Lorie Shaull.

directly to fans that they were #NotNCAAProperty, they built on the work of athletes before them but went beyond it, too, challenging the institutional structures that limited the ability to earn fair compensation and arguing for their own empowerment.[77] As men's basketball players in the NBA team up with women's players in the WNBA to challenge systemic racism and to promote women's athletics, they push sports activism beyond the somewhat limited silos of the 1960s and 1970s.[78]

The growing understanding of intersectionality—that is, the overlapping vectors of oppression based on multiple identities—has undoubtedly played a hand. Black feminists such as the Combahee River Collective in the 1970s and Kimberlé Crenshaw in the 1980s transformed intellectual approaches to oppression by refusing to limit their analysis to one category or another. By recognizing that identities such as race, gender, class, sexuality, and nationality can impact one's position in society, and that they can overlap or diverge, these scholars encouraged a more wide-ranging and nuanced analysis of the forces at work in people's lives.[79] They also, implicitly or explicitly, encouraged solidarity by recognizing how a dominant hegemony rooted in white, middle-class, heteronormative, Protestant Christian values limited the possibilities for a wide range of people who did not fit neatly into mainstream culture.

A broadened understanding of the forces at work in American life might well explain why NBA star Stephen Curry tweeted his support for Oregon women's basketball player Sedona Prince in March 2021. When Prince called attention on TikTok to the rampant inequalities faced by women's teams in the 2021 NCAA March Madness basketball tournament, Curry accused the NCAA of "trippin'."[80] The problems faced by women's college basketball players do not directly affect Curry, but they are part of larger systemic issues that continue to impact minorities inside and outside of sports. His support, and that of other male athletes across the color line, shows that understanding. That awareness also helps explain why athletes like LeBron James have sought increased empowerment in the worlds of sports agencies and media institutions. James has worked with his agent, Rich Paul, to use his leverage as a star to have greater control over his career—to dictate the terms of where he will play and for whom he will play. In the process, he has helped to wrest control from white owners and general managers to mostly black players, something that has inspired athletes across racial and gender lines.[81] He also helped start the HBO talk show *The Shop: Uninterrupted*. On it, he and black entrepreneur Maverick Carter have discussed political issues that have cut across entertainment forms, gender lines, and amateur and professional divides. On one episode, for example, Carter met with Rapinoe, women's professional basketball player Sue Bird, and NFL player

LeBron James has been at the forefront of players pushing for more power in basketball and beyond—even when it has led to negative pushback. Photo by Erik Drost.

Malcolm Jenkins (among others) to discuss a wide range of interconnected issues related to race, gender, and sexuality facing athletes and entertainers.[82]

New media forms have made these alliances and critiques more possible and potent. By making use of social media to champion issues and to promote political stands, athletes engage more directly with fans than ever before, steering clear of biased media coverage and undermining attempts to silence their voices. Completing the revolution will entail a considerable transformation in American society: an economy that does not allow one race and gender to dominate affairs; mainstream media that reframe women's accomplishments in non-sexualized and demeaning ways; institutions inside and outside sport that empower minorities with leadership positions in proportion to their participation; a national culture that recognizes the worth of all its citizens, no matter their race, gender, sexuality, and religion; all this and more. Sports alone will not create this change. But maybe, just maybe, if athletes continue to compete outside the ring, court, and field for a more equitable society, the nation might get closer to these ideals than it ever has before.

NOTES

Prologue

1. Robert Lipsyte, "Clay Discusses His Future, Liston, and Black Muslims," *New York Times*, Feb. 27, 1964. For more on reactions to Ali and his relationship with Malcolm X, see Johnny Smith and Randy Roberts, *Blood Brothers: The Fatal Friendship between Muhammad Ali and Malcolm X* (New York: Basic Books, 2016).

2. See Anthony O. Edmonds, "Joe Louis, Boxing, and American Culture," in *Out of the Shadows: A Biographical History of African American Athletes*, ed. David K. Wiggins (Fayetteville: University of Arkansas Press, 2008).

Introduction

1. Chris Barnewall, "LeBron Responds to News Pundit: 'I Will Not Shut Up and Dribble. . . . I Owe It to the Youth,'" CBS Sports, Feb. 19, 2018, https://www.cbssports.com/nba/news/lebron-responds-to-news-pundit-i-will-not-shut-up-and-dribble-i-owe-it-to-the-youth/.

2. See Christina Cauterucci, "The WNBA's Black Lives Matter Protest Has Set a New Standard for Sports Activism," Slate.com, July 25, 2016, https://slate.com/human-interest/2016/07/the-wnbas-black-lives-matter-protest-has-set-new-standard-for-sports-activism.html/; Megan Garber, "They Took a Knee," The Atlantic.com, Sept. 24, 2017, https://www.theatlantic.com/entertainment/archive/2017/09/why-the-nfl-is-protesting/540927/; "Heat Don Hoodies after Teen's Death," ESPN.com, March 23, 2012, https://www.espn.com/nba/truehoop/miamiheat/story/_/id/7728618/miami

-heat-don-hoodies-response-death-teen-trayvon-martin/; Norah O'Donnell, "Team USA Members on Historic Fight for Equal Pay in Women's Soccer," CBS, Nov. 20, 2016, https://www.cbsnews.com/news/60-minutes-women-soccer-team-usa-gender-discrimination-equal-pay-2019-07-10/; Ricky O'Donnell, "Derrick Rose Explains Why He Wore 'I Can't Breathe' Shirt," SBNation.com, Dec. 8, 2014, https://www.sbnation.com/nba/2014/12/8/7356267/derrick-rose-chicago-bulls-eric-garner/; and Rohan Nadkarni and Alex Nieves, "Why Missouri's Football Team Joined a Protest against School Administration," SportsIllustrated.com, Nov. 9, 2015, https://www.si.com/college/2015/11/09/missouri-football-protest-racism-tim-wolfe/.

3. Jason Diamos, "Abdul-Rauf Vows Not to Back Down from N.B.A.," *New York Times*, March 14, 1996.

4. Jesse Washington, "Still No Anthem, Still No Regrets for Mahmoud Abdul-Rauf," *The Undefeated*, Sept. 1, 2016, https://theundefeated.com/features/abdul-rauf-doesnt-regret-sitting-out-national-anthem/.

5. For a history of American women's sports, see Susan Cahn, *Coming on Strong: Gender and Sexuality in Women's Sport*, 2nd ed. (Urbana: University of Illinois Press, 2015); and Allen Guttmann, *Women's Sports: A History* (New York: Columbia University Press, 1991). See also Jon Sterngass, "Cheating, Gender Roles, and the Nineteenth-Century Croquet Craze," *Journal of Sport History* 25 (1998): 398–418. For more on the Carlisle Indian football team, see David Wallace Adams, "More Than a Game: The Carlisle Indians Take to the Gridiron, 1893–1917," *Western Historical Quarterly* 32, no. 1 (2001): 25–53; and John Bloom, *To Show What an Indian Can Do: Sports at Native American Boarding Schools* (Minneapolis: University of Minnesota Press, 2005). For more on nineteenth-century black boxers, see Jeffrey T. Sammons, *Beyond the Ring: The Role of Boxing in American Society* (Urbana: University of Illinois Press, 1990). For more on Lewis, see Gregory Bond, "The Strange Career of William Henry Lewis," in *Out of the Shadows: A Biographical History of African American Athletes*, ed. David K. Wiggins, 38–57 (Fayetteville: University of Arkansas Press, 2006).

6. See Patrick B. Miller, "To 'Bring the Race along Rapidly': Sport, Student Culture, and Educational Mission at Historically Black Colleges during the Interwar Years," in *Sporting World of the Modern South*, ed. Patrick B. Miller, 129–52 (Urbana: University of Illinois Press, 2002). See also Cahn, *Coming on Strong*, 110–39; Pamela Grundy, *Learning to Win: Sports, Education, and Social Change in Twentieth-Century North Carolina* (Chapel Hill: University of North Carolina Press, 2001), 158–89; and Rita Liberti, "'We Were Ladies, We Just Played Like Boys': African American Women and Competitive Basketball at Bennett College, 1928–42," in Miller, *Sporting World of the Modern South*, 153–74.

7. See, for example, Gena Caponi-Tabery, *Jump for Joy: Jazz, Basketball, and Black Culture in 1930s America* (Amherst: University of Massachusetts Press, 2008), 35–50; Allen Guttmann, *The Olympics: A History of the Modern Games*, 2nd ed. (Urbana: University of Illinois Press, 2002); David K. Wiggins, "The 1936 Olympic Games in Berlin," *Glory Bound: Black Athletes in a White America* (Syracuse, NY: Syracuse University Press, 1997),

61–79; and Wayne Wilson, "Wilma Rudolph: The Making of an Olympic Icon," 207–221, in Wiggins, *Out of the Shadows*.

8. For more on baseball's Negro leagues, see Leslie Heaphy, *The Negro Leagues, 1869–1960* (Jefferson, NC: McFarland, 2003); Kadir Nelson, *We Are the Ship: The Story of Negro League Baseball* (New York: Little, Brown, 2008); Robert Peterson, *Only the Ball Was White: A History of Legendary Black Players and All-Black Professional Teams*, rprt. ed. (New York: Oxford University Press, 1992); and Jules Tygiel, "The Negro Leagues," *OAH Magazine of History* 7, no. 1 (1992): 24–27. For more on the Globetrotters and Renaissance, see Ben Green, *Spinning the Globe: The Rise, Fall, and Return to Greatness of the Harlem Globetrotters* (New York: Amistad, 2005); Damion L. Thomas, *Globetrotting: African American Athletes and Cold War Politics* (Urbana: University of Illinois Press, 2012); and Ron Thomas, *They Cleared the Lane: The NBA's Black Pioneers* (Lincoln: University of Nebraska Press, 2002). See also chapter 5.

9. For more on "muscular assimilation," see Miller, "To 'Bring the Race along Rapidly,'" 129–52.

10. See Gail Bederman, *Manliness and Civilization: A Cultural History of Gender and Race in the United States, 1880–1917* (Chicago: University of Chicago Press, 1995), 42; Al-Tony Gilmore, *Bad Nigger! The National Impact of Jack Johnson* (Port Washington, NY: Kennikat Press, 1975); Thomas R. Hietala, *The Fight of the Century: Jack Johnson, Joe Louis, and the Struggle for Racial Equality* (Armonk, NY: M. E. Sharpe, 2002); Randy Roberts, *Papa Jack: Jack Johnson and the Era of White Hopes* (New York: Free Press, 1983); and Geoffrey C. Ward, *Unforgivable Blackness: The Rise and Fall of Jack Johnson* (New York: Knopf, 2004).

11. For a brief summary of Louis's importance, see Edmonds, "Joe Louis, Boxing, and American Culture."

12. See, for example, Jules Tygiel, *Baseball's Great Experiment: Jackie Robinson and His Legacy*, 25th Anniversary Edition (New York: Oxford University Press, 2008).

13. For more on Ali, see Muhammad Ali, with Richard Durham, *The Greatest: My Own Story* (New York: Random House, 1975); Gerald Lyn Early, *The Muhammad Ali Reader* (Hopewell, NJ: Ecco Press, 1998); Anthony O. Edmonds, *Muhammad Ali: A Biography* (Westport, CT: Greenwood Press, 2006); Elliot J. Gorn, ed., *Muhammad Ali: The People's Champ* (Urbana: University of Illinois Press, 1995); Thomas Hauser, *Muhammad Ali: His Life and Times* (New York: Simon and Schuster, 1991); Mike Marqusee, *Redemption Song: Muhammad Ali and the Spirit of the Sixties* (New York: Verso, 2000); and David Remnick, *King of the World: Muhammad Ali and the Rise of an American Hero* (New York: Random House, 1998). For an excellent biography of Russell, see Aram Goudsouzian, *King of the Court: Bill Russell and the Basketball Revolution* (Berkeley: University of California Press, 2010). For more on Brown, see chapter 1.

14. For more on the black athlete revolt of 1968, see Amy Bass, *Not the Triumph but the Struggle: The 1968 Olympics and the Making of the Black Athlete* (Minneapolis: University of Minnesota Press, 2002); Harry Edwards, *The Revolt of the Black Athlete* (New York: Free

Press, 1969); Douglas Hartmann, *Race, Culture, and the Revolt of the Black Athlete: The 1968 Olympic Protests and Their Aftermath* (Chicago: University of Chicago Press, 2004); Michael Lomax, "Revisiting *The Revolt of the Black Athlete*: Harry Edwards and the Making of the New African-American Sports Studies," *Journal of Sport History* 29, no. 3 (2002): 469–79; and Jack Scott, *The Athletic Revolution* (New York: Free Press, 1971).

15. David K. Wiggins, "'The Year of Awakening,'" in *Glory Bound*, 104–22.

16. For more on the emergence of Black Power, see Peniel Joseph, *Waiting 'Til the Midnight Hour: A Narrative History of Black Power in America* (New York: Henry Holt, 2006); Jeffrey O. G. Ogbar, *Black Power: Radical Politics and African American Identity* (Baltimore: Johns Hopkins University Press, 2004); and William L. Van Deburg, *New Day in Babylon: The Black Power Movement and American Culture, 1965–1975* (Chicago: University of Chicago Press, 1992). For Black Power's wider influences, see Ogbar, *Black Power*, 159–89.

17. See Cahn, *Coming on Strong*; Cahn, "From the 'Muscle Moll' to the 'Butch Ballplayer': Mannishness, Lesbianism, and Homophobia in U.S. Women's Sport," *Feminist Studies* 19 (Summer 1993): 343–68; Pat Griffin, *Strong Women, Deep Closets: Lesbians and Homophobia in Sport* (Amherst: University of Massachusetts Press, 1998); Guttmann, *Women's Sports*; Jennifer H. Lansbury, "Alice Coachman: Quiet Champion of the 1940s," in Wiggins, *Out of the Shadows*, 147–61; and Wilson, "Wilma Rudolph: The Making of an Olympic Icon," 207–221.

18. See, for example, Sara M. Evans, *Born for Liberty* (New York: Free Press, 1997), 243–85; Sara Evans, *Tidal Wave: How Women Changed America at Century's End* (New York: Free Press, 2003); Kirsten Swinth, *Feminism's Forgotten Fight: The Unfinished Struggle for Work and Family* (Boston: Harvard University Press, 2018); and Nancy Woloch, *Women and the American Experience*, 3rd ed. (New York: McGraw-Hill, 2000), 492–549.

19. For a relatively recent survey of 1960s social movements, see Maurice Isserman and Michael Kazin, *America Divided: The Civil War of the 1960s* (New York: Oxford University Press, 2020).

20. See Richard O. Davies, *Sports in American Life: A History*, 3rd ed. (New York: Wiley and Sons, 2016), 265–80; and Travis Vogan, "*Monday Night Football*, *Brian's Song*, and the Roots of the Prime-Time TV Event," in *ABC Sports: The Rise and Fall of Network Sports Television* (Oakland: University of California Press, 2018), 97–125.

21. See Leola Johnson, "'Hertz, Don't It?': White 'Colorblindness' and the Mark(et)ings of O. J. Simpson," in *Colored White: Transcending the Racial Past*, ed. David R. Roediger, 68–94 (Berkeley: University of California Press, 2002) ; James C. Nicholson, *1968: A Pivotal Moment in American Sports* (Knoxville: University of Tennessee Press, 2019), 120; Eunice G. Pollack, "Joe Namath: Player On and Off the Field," in *New York Sports: Glamour and Grit in the Empire City*, ed. Stephen H. Norwood, 107–144 (Fayetteville: University of Arkansas Press, 2018); Emilie Raymond, *Stars for Freedom: Hollywood, Black Celebrities, and the Civil Rights Movement* (Seattle: University of Washington Press, 2015), 208–242; and David Walker, Andrew J. Rausch, and Chris Watson, *Reflections on Blaxploitation: Actors and Directors Speak* (Lanham, MD: Scarecrow Press, 2009), 11–13, 183–85.

22. Susan Ware, *Game, Set, Match: Billie Jean King and the Revolution in Women's Sports* (Chapel Hill: University of North Carolina Press, 2011).

23. See, for example, Sidney Lens, *The Crisis of American Labor* (New York: Sagamore Press, 1959), 12–16; Nelson Lichtenstein, *A Contest of Ideas: Capital, Politics, and Labor* (Urbana: University of Illinois Press, 2013), 95–98; and Kim Moody, *An Injury to All: The Decline of American Unionism* (London: Verso, 1988), xiii-xvi.

24. Stokely Carmichael, "Toward Black Liberation," *Massachusetts Review* 7, no. 4 (1966): 639–51.

25. There is a large amount of literature dedicated to the study of systemic racism and its manifestations in contemporary society. For another important work, see Eduardo Bonilla-Silva, "Rethinking Racism: Toward a Structural Interpretation," *American Sociological Review* 62, no. 3 (1997): 465–80.

26. Gerda Lerner, *The Creation of Patriarchy* (New York: Oxford University Press, 1986), 239.

27. An excellent analysis of patriarchy's ability to limit women's gains is the concept of "patriarchal equilibrium" in Judith M. Bennett, *History Matters: Patriarchy and the Challenge of Feminism* (Philadelphia: University of Pennsylvania Press, 2006), 77.

28. See James Baldwin, *The Fire Next Time* (New York: Dial Press, 1963). See also F. W. Dupee, "James Baldwin and 'the Man,'" *New York Review of Books*, June 1, 1963; Max Hastings, *America 1968: The Fire This Time* (London: Gollancz, 1969); and Jesmyn Ward, *The Fire This Time: A New Generation Speaks about Race* (New York: Scribner, 2016).

Chapter 1. Playing for "Green Power"

1. Hartmann, *Race, Culture, and the Revolt of the Black Athlete*, 9–12.

2. For more on the protest's symbolism, see Hartmann, *Race, Culture, and the Revolt of the Black Athlete*; and Bass, *Not the Triumph but the Struggle*. White Australian sprinter Peter Norman wore an OPHR badge on his tracksuit in support of the gesture as well. See Associated Press (hereafter, AP), "Peter Norman, 64; Shared Podium at '68 Games," *New York Times*, Oct. 4, 2006, A29. For more on the international aspects of the medal stand protest, see Dexter Blackman, "African Americans, Pan-Africanism, and the Anti-Apartheid Campaign to Expel South Africa from the 1968 Olympics," *Journal of Pan African Studies* 5, no. 3 (2012): 1+.

3. As will be discussed later, Brown originally called his organization the Negro Industrial and Economic Union before later changing it to the Black Economic Union. For purposes of consistency, this chapter uses the latter title.

4. See "Lady Netters Face Banning," *Chicago Defender*, Sept. 29, 1970, 26.

5. Michael Ezra, ed., "Introduction: The Economic Dimensions of the Black Freedom Struggle," in *The Economic Civil Rights Movement: African Americans and the Struggle for Economic Power* (New York: Routledge, 2013), 1.

6. "Freedom Bank in Final Formation Drive," *New York Amsterdam News*, March 14, 1964. See also Jackie Robinson with Alfred Duckett, *I Never Had It Made: An Autobiography* (New York: G. P. Putnam's Sons, 1972).

7. Laura Warren Hill and Julia Rabig, *The Business of Black Power: Community Development, Capitalism, and Corporate Responsibility in Postwar America* (Rochester: University of Rochester Press, 2012), 1.

8. Ogbar, *Black Power*, 194–95.

9. Martin Luther King Jr., "Where Do We Go from Here," in *A Call to Conscience: The Landmark Speeches of Dr. Martin Luther King, Jr.*, ed. Clayborne Carson and Kris Shepherd (New York: IPM, 2002), 110.

10. Ibram H. Rogers, "Acquiring 'A Piece of the Action': The Rise and Fall of the Black Capitalism Movement," in *The Economic Civil Rights Movement: African Americans and the Struggle for Economic Power*, ed. Michael Ezra, 172–87 (New York: Routledge, 2013); see especially 173–74.

11. Van Deburg, *New Day in Babylon*, 118.

12. Rogers, "Acquiring 'A Piece of the Action,'" 176; and Van Deburg, *New Day in Babylon*, 134–37.

13. Juliet E. K. Walker, *The History of Black Business in America: Capitalism, Race, Entrepreneurship* (New York: Macmillan Library Reference, 1998), 275.

14. Van Deburg, *New Day in Babylon*, 119.

15. Walker, *History of Black Business in America*, 277.

16. Manning Marable, *How Capitalism Underdeveloped Black America* (Boston: South End Press, 1983), 151. For more on Nixon's plans for black capitalism, see Cecilia A. Conrad, "Black-Owned Businesses: Trends and Prospects," in *African Americans in the U.S. Economy*, ed. Cecilia A. Conrad, John Whitehead, Patrick Mason, and James Stewart (New York: Rowman and Littlefield Publishers, 2005), 237–45; see especially 242.

17. United Press International (hereafter, UPI), "Black Businessmen Assail Nixon 'Game,'" *Chicago Defender*, April 17, 1969, 6.

18. Rogers, "Acquiring 'A Piece of the Action,'" 181.

19. This endorsement did not come without controversy, as many in the black community saw the support of Nixon as a sell-out of the race. See Hill and Rabig, introduction to *Business of Black Power*, 2.

20. For the most substantive autobiographies and biographies of Brown, see Jim Brown, with Myron Cope, *Off My Chest* (New York: Doubleday, 1964); Jim Brown, with Steve Delsohn, *Out of Bounds* (New York: Zebra Books, 1989); Mike Freeman, *Jim Brown: The Fierce Life of an American Hero* (New York: HarperCollins, 2006); J. Thomas Jable, "Jim Brown: Superlative Athlete, Screen Star, Social Activist," in *Out of the Shadows: A Biographical History of Black Athletes*, ed. David K. Wiggins, 241–61 (Fayetteville: University of Arkansas Press, 2006); Roberta J. Newman, "Jim Brown: The Rise and Fall (and Rise) of a Cultural Icon," in *Fame to Infamy: Race, Sport, and the Fall from Grace*, ed. David C. Ogden and Joel Nathan Rosen, 170–90 (Jackson: University Press of Mississippi, 2010); and Dave Zirin, *Jim Brown: Last Man Standing* (New York: Blue Rider Press, 2018).

21. Freeman, *Jim Brown*, 108.

22. Ibid., 120–21, 132–37.

23. See Michael Ezra, "Muhammad Ali's Main Bout: African American Economic Power and the World Heavyweight Title," in *The Economic Civil Rights Movement: African Americans and the Struggle for Economic Power*, ed. Michael Ezra (New York: Routledge, 2013), 104–124; see also Ezra, *Muhammad Ali: The Making of an Icon* (Philadelphia: Temple University Press, 2009), 93, 95, 118.

24. AP, "Wide Business Interests May Lead Brown to Quit," *Los Angeles Sentinel*, Jan. 14, 1966, C3.

25. Dave Brady, "Jim Brown Claims Racial Bias Haunts Fight," *Washington Post*, March 11, 1966, D1.

26. Ezra, "Ali's Main Bout," 104–124.

27. AP, "Brown Focuses on Negro Economics: Jim Brown Drops Curtain on Memorable Career," *Washington Post*, July 15, 1966, D3.

28. See Robert Anthony Bennett III, "You Can't Have Black Power without Green Power: The Black Economic Union" (PhD diss., Ohio State University, 2013), 76–87; and Dave Brady, "Jim Brown Maps Plans for Economic Revolution," *Washington Post*, March 6, 1966, C4.

29. Bill Lane, "The Inside Story," *Los Angeles Sentinel*, Dec. 29, 1966, A3.

30. "Brown Swings in New Acting, Business Jobs," *Chicago Defender*, Aug. 3, 1966, 11.

31. AP, "Brown Focuses on Negro Economics," *Washington Post*, July 15, 1966, D3.

32. Bennett, "You Can't Have Black Power," 89–90.

33. Ibid., 94.

34. Bill Nunn Jr., "Change of Pace," *New Pittsburgh Courier*, Dec. 31, 1966, 10A.

35. Howie Evans, "Sort of Sporty," *New York Amsterdam News*, Sept. 5, 1970, 42.

36. See "Jim Brown's NIEU Opens in Harlem," *New York Amsterdam News*, July 22, 1967, 42; "16-Point Summer Plan Announced," *Los Angeles Sentinel*, May 25, 1967, B10; and "Names in the News," *Black Enterprise* 3 (May 1973): 11.

37. "Jim Brown's NIEU Opens in Harlem," *New York Amsterdam News*, July 22, 1967, 42.

38. See Chuck Porter, "New BEU Campaign Begins," *Los Angeles Sentinel*, Aug. 28, 1969, B7; Howie Evans, "Sort of Sporty," *New York Amsterdam News*, Sept. 5, 1970, 42; and Carol Aldridge, "Jim Brown Opens NIEU Headquarters," *New York Amsterdam News*, Nov. 30, 1968, 7.

39. James Toback, *JIM: The Author's Self-Centered Memoir on the Great Jim Brown* (New York: Doubleday, 1971), 55.

40. "Jim Brown Unit Gets $10,000," *Philadelphia Tribune*, May 14, 1968, 1.

41. "Jim Brown's NIEU Opens in Harlem," *New York Amsterdam News*, July 22, 1967, 42.

42. UPI, "Jim Brown Says Hough Riot Area Is 'Unchanged,'" *Chicago Defender*, April 3, 1967, 4.

43. UPI, "Cleveland Mayor Takes to Streets," *New York Times*, April 12, 1968, 20. For more on the various programs put together by the BEU, see Bennett, "You Can't Have Black Power," 214–67.

44. Toback, *JIM*, 22.

45. UPI, "Jim Brown Lauds Striking Browns," *Washington Post*, July 28, 1967, D2.

46. William N. Wallace, "Sports of the Times: The Group," *New York Times*, Aug. 1, 1967, 36.

47. William N. Wallace, "Jim Brown Carries Ball for Pro Union," *New York Times*, Nov. 10, 1967, S64.

48. Dave Brady, "Jim Brown Seeks 'Justice' for Thomas," *Washington Post*, Nov. 20, 1971, D2.

49. Maggie Hathaway, "Tee Time: A Tour around the Links," *Los Angeles Sentinel*, June 9, 1966, B4; and Lesley Visser, "Blacks in Tennis: Economics—Not Their Talent—Is Served," *Boston Globe*, Sept. 20, 1979, 57.

50. "New Detroit Franchise Unique," *Chicago Defender*, Dec. 26, 1973, 22; and William Oscar Johnson, "The Day the Money Ran Out," *Sports Illustrated*, Dec. 1, 1975.

51. Gregory Kaliss, *Men's College Athletics and the Politics of Racial Equality: Five Pioneer Stories of Black Manliness, White Citizenship, and American Democracy* (Philadelphia: Temple University Press, 2012), 126; see also chapter 3.

52. "The Kansas City Chiefs Gain Offseason Yardage," *Black Enterprise* 1 (Sept. 1970): 16–21.

53. "From Gridiron to Finance," *Baltimore Afro-American*, Jan. 17, 1970, A1.

54. C. B. Downey, "Willie Naulls: Crosstown Fast Break," *Black Enterprise* 5 (Nov. 1975): 57–63.

55. Toback, *JIM*, 87–88.

56. "Steeler Football Stars to Aid Miss. County," *New Pittsburgh Courier*, Feb. 21, 1970, 1; "Officials Greet Jim Brown, Black Union," *Chicago Defender*, Feb. 14, 1970, 2; "Jim Brown Leads Probe," *Baltimore Afro-American*, Feb. 21, 1970, 8; and A. S. "Doc" Young, "Good Morning Sports!" *Chicago Defender*, March 11, 1970, 32.

57. A. S. "Doc" Young, "Good Morning Sports!" *Chicago Defender*, March 11, 1970, 32.

58. "Officials Greet Jim Brown, Black Union," *Chicago Defender*, Feb. 14, 1970, 2.

59. Maggie Hathaway, "Sports Editor Maggie Hathaway's Tee Time," *Los Angeles Sentinel*, March 19, 1970, 17.

60. "Jim Brown's Crusade Lauded in Congress," *Philadelphia Tribune*, June 20, 1970, 23.

61. Ivan C. Brandon, "Anacostia Picked for Project," *Washington Post*, March 31, 1970, C2.

62. "Jim Brown's Union Gets $520,000 Ford Grant," *Chicago Defender*, March 30, 1968, 14.

63. "EDA Funds Help Minority Businesses," *Los Angeles Sentinel*, July 11, 1968, D8.

64. "Nancy Wilson at Apollo Theater," *Los Angeles Sentinel*, April 18, 1968, B9.

65. Maggie Hathaway, "Stars Swing in Brown's Teefest," *Los Angeles Sentinel*, March 26, 1970, B4.

66. Bennett, "You Can't Have Black Power," 233.

67. W. Fitzhugh Brundage, ed., *Up from Slavery by Booker T. Washington with Related Documents* (New York: Bedford/St. Martin's, 2003), 23.

68. [Jim Brown], "Gertrude Gipson: Candid Comments," *Los Angeles Sentinel*, Oct. 20, 1966, B8.

69. Carol Aldridge, "Jim Brown Opens NIEU Headquarters," *New York Amsterdam News*, Nov. 30, 1968, 7.

70. Chuck Porter, "New BEU Campaign Begins," *Los Angeles Sentinel*, Aug. 28, 1969, B7.

71. Hollie I. West, "Jim Brown: Crisp and Direct as a Fullback," *Washington Post*, March 26, 1969, B1. Brown's promise to "manage our own affairs" echoed the words of another prominent black entertainer and supporter of black capitalism: the funk singer James Brown. In his 1968 hit "Say It Loud, I'm Black and I'm Proud," Brown sang that black Americans "demand a chance to do things for ourselves" in the realm of economics. For more on James Brown and the politics of his music, see Brian Ward, *Just My Soul Responding: Rhythm and Blues, Black Consciousness, and Race Relations* (Berkeley: University of California Press, 1998), 388–92.

72. "Drop Assault Charge against Jim Brown," *Chicago Defender*, June 11, 1968, 7.

73. Judy Klemesrud, "Jim Brown: 'I'm No Angel, But . . .'" *New York Times*, April 6, 1969, D13. Later years saw additional domestic violence claims against Brown, and he eventually served jail time in 2002 for an incident with his second wife. See Zirin, chapter 7, "Toxic: Manhood and Violence against Women," in *Jim Brown: Last Man Standing*, 178–205.

74. Steve Estes, *I Am a Man! Race, Manhood, and the Civil Rights Movement* (Chapel Hill: University of North Carolina Press, 2005), 7.

75. A. S. "Doc" Young, "The NEW Negro Athletes," *Los Angeles Sentinel*, Jan. 25, 1968, D3.

76. A. S. "Doc" Young, "Short Items & Comments," *Los Angeles Sentinel*, Jan. 18, 1968, D1.

77. Gene Handsaker, "'Jim Brown Power' Works to Make More for Negroes," *Atlanta Constitution*, Nov. 12, 1967, 12F.

78. Toback, *JIM*, 82–83.

79. Frank Lee, "Ashe Speaks to Ghetto, Says, 'Do It Yourself,'" *Baltimore Afro-American*, March 16, 1968, 26.

80. Eric Allen Hall, *Arthur Ashe: Tennis and Justice in the Civil Rights Era* (Baltimore: Johns Hopkins University Press, 2014), 85–86.

81. "The Kansas City Chiefs Gain Offseason Yardage," *Black Enterprise* 1 (Sept. 1970): 16–21.

82. Toback, *JIM*, 88.

83. Conrad, "Black-Owned Businesses," 242.

84. "Four Organizations Get Minority Business Contracts," *Los Angeles Sentinel*, Aug. 3, 1972, B7.

85. Rogers, "Acquiring 'A Piece of the Action,'" 181.

86. Enrico Beltramini, "Operation Breadbasket in Chicago: Between Civil Rights and Black Capitalism," in Ezra, *Economic Civil Rights Movement*, 125–36; see 134.

87. "Brown Supports Nixon," *Pittsburgh Courier*, Sept. 9, 1972, 17.

88. "The Candidates," *Los Angeles Sentinel*, Nov. 2, 1972, A6.

89. "Scandal Probe Widens," *Chicago Defender*, Nov. 20, 1973, 5.

90. Rogers, "Acquiring 'A Piece of the Action,'" 182. For more on the BEU's funding woes, see Bennett, "You Can't Have Black Power," 303–305.

91. Although the organization continued to exist, media coverage of the BEU declined severely after 1973, and its role as a national organization, for all intents and purposes, ended. For more on later activities of the Cleveland and Kansas City branches, see, for example, Jeanne Allyson Fox, "In Kansas City Missouri," *Black Enterprise* (March 1978): 45–54; and "Parker Hannifin-Backed Rudwick files for Ch. 11," *Crain's Cleveland Business*, Sept. 9, 2002, 6. See also Bennett, "You Can't Have Black Power," 304.

92. There have been a number of biographies and autobiographies by and about King. The most illuminating are the three autobiographies she penned with co-authors. They are Billie Jean King with Kim Chapin, *Billie Jean* (New York: Harper and Row, 1974); Billie Jean King with Frank Deford, *Billie Jean* (New York: Viking, 1982); and Billie Jean King with Cynthia Starr, *We Have Come a Long Way: The Story of Women's Tennis* (New York: McGraw-Hill, 1988). The most complete books about King's work with the Virginia Slims Tour and her role in the Battle of the Sexes match against Bobby Riggs are Selena Roberts, *A Necessary Spectacle: Billie Jean King, Bobby Riggs, and the Tennis Match That Leveled the Game* (New York: Crown, 2005); and Susan Ware, *Game, Set, Match: Billie Jean King and the Revolution in Women's Sports* (Chapel Hill: University of North Carolina Press, 2011).

93. For more on the conservative gender pressures of the 1950s, see Elaine Tyler May, *Homeward Bound: American Families in the Cold War Era*, rev. ed. (New York: Basic Books, 2008).

94. See King with Deford, *Billie Jean*, 42; and David Walsh, "The Big Interview: Billie Jean King," *[London] Sunday Times*, Dec. 9, 2007.

95. For two of the best historical texts that summarize the rise of second-wave feminism, Friedan, and NOW, see Evans, *Born for Liberty*, 243–85; and Woloch, *Women and the American Experience*, 3rd ed., 492–549. To be fair, NOW did pursue social equality for women. The group's statement of purpose, written by Friedan, was "to take action to bring women into full participation in the mainstream of American society **now**, exercising all the privileges and responsibilities thereof in truly equal partnership with men." Nonetheless, most agree that the organization's primary points of focus were on employment and education. The statement of purpose is available at the organization's current website: https://now.org/about/history/statement-of-purpose/.

96. For more on the origins of women's liberation and its broad goals, see Evans, *Tidal Wave*, 18–127.

97. Ware, *Game, Set, Match*, 30. In later years, King, with co-author Cynthia Starr, would write that male players largely drove the movement for professional status because they faced pressure to be the breadwinners in their families. As a result, they were more insistent on making a decent living. See King with Starr, *We Have Come a Long Way*, 98.

98. AP, "Billie Jean King Turns Pro," *Arizona Republic*, April 2, 1968.

99. Ware, *Game, Set, Match*, 31.

100. King with Starr, *We Have Come a Long Way*, 124. See also Christine M. Shelton, "Tennis: Hard Work Pays Off," in *Women in Sport: Issues and Controversies*, ed. Greta L. Cohen (Newbury Park, CA: Sage Publications, 1993), 279.

101. King with Starr, *We Have Come a Long Way*, 121–26. See also Roberts, *Necessary Spectacle*, 77.

102. "Lady Netters Face Banning," *Chicago Defender*, Sept. 29, 1970, 26.

103. "Billie Jean Loses," *Indianapolis Star*, Sept. 25, 1970, 28.

104. Billie Jean King with Christine Brennan, *Pressure Is a Privilege: Lessons I've Learned from Life and the Battle of the Sexes* (New York: LifeTime Media, 2008), 148.

105. Parton Keese, "Women Set Up Tennis Tour," *New York Times*, Oct. 8, 1970, 66.

106. Shelton, "Tennis: Hard Work," 280.

107. King with Starr, *We Have Come a Long Way*, 127.

108. Keese, "Women Set Up Tennis Tour," 66.

109. King with Chapin, *Billie Jean*, 140.

110. King quoted in Curry Kirkpatrick, "The Ball in Two Different Courts," *Sports Illustrated*, Dec. 25, 1972.

111. David Gray, "A Circuit for Leading Ladies," *New York Times*, Oct. 3, 1970, 17.

112. "You've Come a Long Way!" *Austin American Statesman*, Nov. 21, 1974, A53.

113. Neil Admur, "Billie Jean King Talks with Nixon," *New York Times*, Oct. 5, 1971, 53.

114. "World's Top Women Tennis Stars Face Suspension," *South China Morning Post*, Sept. 26, 1970, 2.

115. Roberts, *Necessary Spectacle*, 80.

116. Ibid., 78.

117. Ware, *Game, Set, Match*, 33–34.

118. Mark Asher, "Women's Lob Championed by Top Lady," *Washington Post*, Sept. 5, 1971, M4.

119. King with Chapin, *Billie Jean*, 141.

120. Kirkpatrick, "Ball in Two Different Courts."

121. See Angela Y. Davis, "I Am a Revolutionary Black Woman (1970)," in *Let Nobody Turn Us Around: Voices of Resistance, Reform, and Renewal*, ed. Manning Marable and Leith Mullings, 482–46 (New York: Rowman and Littlefield Publishers, 2003).

122. King with Starr, *We Have Come a Long Way*, 128.

123. For more on this event and its profound legacy, especially in popular media, see Bonnie J. Dow, "Feminism, Miss America, and Media Mythology," *Rhetoric and Public*

Affairs 6 (Spring 2003): 127–49. See also Evans, *Tidal Wave*, 40. Although this event led to the identification of women's liberation members as "bra burners," the items in the Freedom Trash Can (which did include some bras) were not actually burned.

124. Ware, *Game, Set, Match*, 35. Even in 1982, when she penned an updated autobiography with Frank Deford, King saw no problem with selling women athletes' sex appeal. She defended golfer Jan Stephenson, who "posed for a magazine photo lounging on a bed, with a little bit of leg showing." Although some thought it "represented a cheapening—a prostitution if you will—of the game of golf," she thought that was "ridiculous." She supported Stephenson "displaying [her] beauty." She did clarify her position, noting, "I don't mean we should start playing topless." See King with Deford, *Billie Jean*, 147.

125. As will be discussed in the conclusion, these ideas, while always controversial, have come under fire as critics have noted that focusing on sex appeal has done little to build a fan base for women's sports. See, for example, Jennifer Hargreaves, *Sporting Females: Critical Issues in the History and Sociology of Women's Sports*, rprt. ed. (New York: Routledge, 2001), 158–69; and Mary Jo Kane, "Sex Sells Sex, Not Women's Sports," *TheNation.com*, July 27, 2011, https://www.thenation.com/article/archive/sex-sells-sex-not-womens-sports/. Note, too, that the objectification of female athletes was often done to allay suspicions of lesbianism. See Cahn, *Coming on Strong*, 266–67; and Jaime Schultz, *Qualifying Times: Points of Change in U.S. Women's Sport* (Urbana: University of Illinois Press, 2014), 145–46, 159.

126. King with Starr, *We Have Come a Long Way*, 142.

127. Roberts, *Necessary Spectacle*, 81.

128. Ware, *Game, Set, Match*, 33.

129. King with Starr, *We Have Come a Long Way*, 142.

130. Roberts, *Necessary Spectacle*, 1–25.

131. Edward D. Miller, *Tomboys, Pretty Boys, and Outspoken Women: The Media Revolution of 1973* (Ann Arbor: University of Michigan Press, 2001), 54.

132. Charles Maher, "Barnum Would Have Loved It: Riggs Butchered by Mrs. King as Promoters Score a Million," *New York Times*, Sept. 21, 1973, 1. Ironically, Brown believed that Riggs would win the match. Although he and King were united in their quest for economic empowerment, Brown still clung to gender norms that affirmed the dominance of men. See Roberts, *Necessary Spectacle*, 115.

133. King with Starr, *We Have Come a Long Way*, 145.

134. For details on the match, see Roberts, *Necessary Spectacle*, 115–36; and Ware, *Game, Set, Match*, 1–8.

135. Eve Sharbutt, "The Woman in '73: Solid Gains Made," *Austin American Statesman*, Dec. 27, 1973, 48.

136. Judy Klemesrud, "Billie Jean King Scores an Ace at Fund-Raising Rally," *New York Times*, Oct. 21, 1972, 24.

137. See Cahn, *Coming on Strong*, 252.

138. Numerous texts have been written about Title IX (also sometimes referred to as Title IX of the Higher Education Act) and its impacts on sports. For a good quick summary, see Evans, *Tidal Wave*, 134–35, 192–93.

139. Ware, *Game, Set, Match*, 38, 57, 77, 90–99.

140. See Evans, *Tidal Wave*, 192; Jaeah Lee and Maya Dusenberry, "Charts: The State of Women's Athletics, 40 Years after Title IX," *Mother Jones*, https://www.motherjones.com/politics/2012/06/charts-womens-athletics-title-nine-ncaa/; and Amy Wimmer Schwarb, "Number of NCAA College Athletes Climbs Again," NCAA, Oct. 29, 2015, http://www.ncaa.org/about/resources/media-center/news/number-ncaa-college-athletes-climbs-again/.

141. For more on this moment and its impact, see Schultz, *Qualifying Times*.

142. Evans, *Tidal Wave*, 135.

143. Ware, *Game, Set, Match*, 57–67.

144. Christina Cauterucci, "The U.S. Women's Soccer Team Finally Has a Better Contract, but Not Equal Pay," *Slate*, April 5, 2017, https://slate.com/human-interest/2017/04/the-u-s-womens-soccer-team-finally-has-a-better-contract-but-not-equal-pay.html/. For the 2022 agreement, see Steven Goff and Molly Hensley-Clancy, "U.S. Women's and Men's National Soccer Teams Close Pay Gap with 'Game-Changing' Deal," *Washington Post*, May 18, 2022, https://www.washingtonpost.com/sports/2022/05/18/uswnt-equal-pay-deal/.

145. Charlotte Edmond, "How Women Won the Fight for Equal Prize Money at Wimbledon," World Economic Forum, July 7, 2017, https://www.weforum.org/agenda/2017/07/wimbledon-women-equal-prize-money/.

146. There have been a number of works dealing with this subject. See Cahn, *Coming on Strong*, 164–206; Cahn, "From the 'Muscle Moll' to the 'Butch Ballplayer,'" 343–68; and Griffin, *Strong Women, Deep Closets*.

147. Roberts, *Necessary Spectacle*, 142–43.

148. See ibid., 142–48; and Ware, *Game, Set, Match*, 179–83.

149. Elizabeth O'Connell makes the argument that biographers and historians have overemphasized King's quest for pay equity at the expense of her broader connections to women's liberation and to gay rights. However, King's own choices in how she phrased her stands, and the issues she avoided during her career, surely impacted later writers' assessments of her life and career. See Elizabeth O'Connell, "The Woman Who Should Be King: The Simplification of the Life and Career of Billie Jean King," in *A Locker Room of Her Own: Celebrity, Sexuality, and Female Athletes*, ed. David C. Ogden and Joel Nathan Rosen, 43–71 (Jackson: University Press of Mississippi, 2013).

150. King with Deford, *Billie Jean*, 213.

151. William N. Wallace, "Sports of the Times: The Group," *New York Times*, Aug. 1, 1967, 36.

152. William N. Wallace, "Jim Brown Carries Ball for Pro Union," *New York Times*, Nov. 10, 1967, S64.

153. *Ware, Game, Set, Match*, 38.

154. For a brief overview of these developments, see Benjamin G. Rader, *Baseball: A History of America's Game*, 2nd ed. (Urbana: University of Illinois Press, 2002), 204–208. For more on the particulars of Flood's story, see Robert M. Goldman, *One Man Out: Curt Flood versus Baseball* (Lawrence: University Press of Kansas, 2008); and Brad Snyder, *A Well-Paid Slave: Curt Flood's Fight for Free Agency in Professional Sports* (New York: Viking, 2006). See also the conclusion to this book.

155. Republican senator Edward Brooke offered an assessment of this topic in the February 1971 issue of *Black Enterprise*. See Edward W. Brooke, "The Publisher's Page," *Black Enterprise* 1, no. 7 (Feb. 1971): 4.

Chapter 2. Getting into the Race

1. See Andrew Das, "U.S. Wins Record Fourth World Cup Title," *New York Times*, July 7, 2019, https://www.nytimes.com/2019/07/07/sports/soccer/usa-vs-netherlands-score.html/; and Andrew Keh, "U.S. Wins World Cup and Becomes a Champion for Its Time," *New York Times*, July 7, 2019, https://www.nytimes.com/2019/07/07/sports/soccer/world-cup-final-uswnt.html/.

2. "Title IX of the Education Amendments of 1972," Department of Justice, last updated Nov. 13, 2000, https://www.justice.gov/crt/title-ix-education-amendments-1972/.

3. Numerous texts have been written about Title IX and its impacts on sports. For a good quick summary, see Evans, *Tidal Wave*, 134–35, 192–93.

4. For more on King, see chapter 1.

5. Guttmann, *Women's Sports*, 94–95.

6. Cahn, *Coming on Strong*, 8.

7. Guttmann, *Women's Sports*, 96.

8. See Cahn, "From the 'Muscle Moll' to the 'Butch Ballplayer,'" 343–68. See also Cahn, *Coming on Strong*; and Schultz, *Qualifying Times*.

9. See Guttman, *Women's Sports*, 135–39; and Schultz, *Qualifying Times*, 76–78.

10. See Cahn, *Coming on Strong*, 113–14; and Cheryl Cooky, "Women, Sports, and Activism," in *No Slam Dunk: Gender, Sport, and the Unevenness of Social Change*, ed. Cooky and Michael A. Messner, 70–90 (New Brunswick, NJ: Rutgers University Press, 2018); see especially 75–76.

11. Cahn, *Coming on Strong*, 113.

12. See Guttmann, *Women's Sports*, 140–41; and Schultz, *Qualifying Times*, 81–82.

13. Guttmann, *Women's Sports*, 143–45.

14. Schultz, *Qualifying Times*, 106.

15. Guttmann, *Women's Sports*, 146–53.

16. See Oren Renick and Lea Robin Velez, "Racing into the Storm: Roberta Gibb, Kathrine Switzer, and Women's Marathoning," in *A Locker Room of Her Own: Celebrity, Sexuality, and Female Athletes*, ed. David C. Ogden and Joel Nathan Rosen (Oxford:

University Press of Mississippi, 2013), 169; and Kathrine Switzer, *Marathon Woman: Running the Race to Revolutionize Women's Sports* (New York: Carroll and Graf Publishers, 2007), 16.

17. Guttmann, *Women's Sports*, 189–203; and Schultz, *Qualifying Times*, 85–90.

18. Jennifer Lansbury, *A Spectacular Leap: Black Women Athletes in Twentieth-Century America* (Fayetteville: University of Arkansas Press, 2014), 43–74.

19. Rita Liberti and Maureen M. Smith, *Re(Presenting) Wilma Rudolph* (Syracuse, NY: Syracuse University Press, 2015), 73.

20. Wilson, "Wilma Rudolph," 206–221; and Guttmann, *Women's Sports*, 203–204.

21. Cat M. Ariail, *Passing the Baton: Black Women Track Stars and American Identity* (Urbana: University of Illinois Press, 2020), 10, 167–71.

22. Schultz, *Qualifying Times*, 73.

23. On Kennedy and reinvigorated emphasis on physical fitness, see Gloria Averbach, *The Woman Runner: Free to Be the Complete Athlete* (New York: Simon and Schuster, 1984), 4; and Schultz, *Qualifying Times*, 86.

24. For more on second-wave feminism, see chapter 1.

25. See, for example, Nancy Bailey, "Women's Sport and the Feminist Movement: Building Bridges," in *Women in Sport: Issues and Controversies*, ed. Greta L. Cohen (New York: Sage Publications, 1993), 297; Kelly Belanger, *Invisible Seasons: Title IX and the Fight for Equity in College Sports* (Syracuse, NY: Syracuse University Press, 2016), 19; Cooky, "Women, Sports, and Activism"; Pamela J. Creedon, "Women, Media, and Sport: Creating and Reflecting Gender Values," in *Women, Media, and Sport: Challenging Gender Values*, ed. Pamela J. Creedon (Thousand Oaks, CA: Sage Publications, 1994), 7; Guttmann, *Women's Sports*, 209–210; and Michael A. Messner and Donald F. Sabo, eds., *Sport, Men, and the Gender Order: Critical Feminist Perspectives* (Champaign, IL: Human Kinetics Books, 1990), 2.

26. Cooky, "Women, Sports, and Activism," 72.

27. Bailey, "Women's Sport and the Feminist Movement," 297; and Creedon, "Women, Media, and Sport," 7.

28. Cooky, "Women, Sports, and Activism," 72.

29. Bellanger, *Invisible Seasons*, 19.

30. See chapter 1.

31. Guttmann, *Women's Sports*, 209–210; and Cooky, "Women, Sports, and Activism," 83.

32. Renick and Velez, "Racing into the Storm," 164.

33. For a good summary of Gibb's experiences, see Shanti Sosienski, *Women Who Run* (Emeryville, CA: Seal Press, 2006), 4–6; and Renick and Velez, "Racing into the Storm," 165–68.

34. Gwilym Brown, "A Game Girl in a Man's Game," *Sports Illustrated*, May 2, 1966, www.sivault.com/.

35. "Today's Pictures: Resting," *Indianapolis Star*, April 20, 1966, 54.

36. "Queen of the Marathon," *Time*, April 29, 1966, 114.
37. Switzer, *Marathon Woman*, 36–87.
38. Tom C. Brady, "Over the Hills and Far Ahead," *Sports Illustrated*, May 1, 1967, www.sivault.com/.
39. Tom Derderian, *Boston Marathon: A Celebration of the World's Premier Race* (Chicago: Triumph Books, 2014), 34.
40. Renick and Velez, "Racing into the Storm," 168.
41. See Switzer, *Marathon Woman*, 80–111. See also Annemarie Jutel, "'Thou Dost Run as in Flotation': Femininity, Reassurance, and the Emergence of the Women's Marathon," *International Journal of the History of Sport* 20, no. 3 (2003): 17–23. For the famed photo sequence, see Associated Press, "Chivalry's Not Dead," *Louisville Courier-Journal*, April 20, 1967, B10.
42. Brady, "Over the Hills and Far Ahead."
43. Associated Press, "2 Girls and . . . 'Invaders' Enliven Marathon," *Austin American Statesman*, April 20, 1967, A20.
44. "Lady with Desire to Run Crashed Marathon," *New York Times*, April 23, 1967, 199.
45. Bud Collins, "The Gals Bless 'Em; Let 'Em In," *Boston Globe*, April 21, 1967.
46. Switzer, *Marathon Woman*, 94, 102.
47. Renick and Velez, "Racing into the Storm," 167.
48. Associated Press, "2 Girls," A20.
49. "Cheering Kelley Home," *Newsweek*, May 1, 1967, 94.
50. Switzer, *Marathon Woman*, 113.
51. "Male Refuge Shattered," *Atlanta Constitution*, April 20, 1967.
52. Michael Spring, "Praise from Homer," letter to the editor, *Sports Illustrated*, May 23, 1966, 104.
53. Myron Cope, "Angry Overseer of the Marathon: Jock Semple, the Colorful Scot Who Manages Boston's Epic Event, Wages a Passionate Battle for His Race and Against Those Who Mock It," *Sports Illustrated*, April 22, 1968, https://www.si.com/vault/1968/04/22/609806/angry-overseer-of-the-marathon/.
54. Switzer, *Marathon Woman*, 116.
55. Brown, "Game Girl."
56. Jutel, "'Thou Dost Run as in Flotation,'" 23.
57. "2 Girls in Marathon Don't Have Lovely Leg to Stand On," *New York Times*, April 20, 1967, 55.
58. Jutel, "'Thou Dost Run as in Flotation,'" 21.
59. "Lady with Desire to Run," 199.
60. Switzer, *Marathon Woman*, 118.
61. "2 Girls in Marathon," 55.
62. Brown, "Game Girl."
63. Renick and Velez, "Racing into the Storm," 167.
64. "2 Girls in Marathon," 55.

65. Switzer, *Marathon Woman*, 107.

66. "Lady with Desire to Run Crashed Marathon," 199.

67. See Betty Friedan, "Statement of Purpose," NOW.org, October 29, 1966, https://now.org/about/history/statement-of-purpose/.

68. For more on the different mind-sets of Gibb and Switzer, see Renick and Velez, "Racing into the Storm," 170.

69. Brown, "Game Girl."

70. Collins, "The Gals Bless 'Em."

71. Sosienski, *Women Who Run*, 6.

72. Switzer, *Marathon Woman*, 103–104.

73. Sosienski, *Women Who Run*, 11.

74. Messner and Sabo, *Sport, Men, and the Gender Order*, 3–4.

75. Of course, many observers also pointed to sports as a way to showcase the ongoing barriers to an equal opportunity society. Debates about the definitions of terms like "equality" and "equal opportunity" often led to varied readings of sports' meanings. See Kaliss, *Men's College Athletics*, 1–9.

76. See Mary A. Boutilier and Lucinda F. SanGiovanni, *The Sporting Woman* (Champaign, IL: Human Kinetics, 1983), 12–17; and Mary A. Boutilier and Lucinda F. SanGiovanni, "Politics, Public Policy, and Title IX: Some Limitations of Liberal Feminism," in *Women, Sport, and Culture* (Champaign, IL: Human Kinetics, 1994), 97–109.

77. Creedon, "Women, Media, and Sport," 7.

78. Jutel, "'Thou Dost Run as in Flotation,'" 17, 32.

79. Boutilier and SanGiovanni, "Politics, Public Policy, and Title IX," 107.

80. Switzer, *Marathon Woman*, 16.

81. "Lady with Desire to Run," 199.

82. Jutel, "'Thou Dost Run as in Flotation,'" 17.

83. King launched *womenSports* to fill in the gaps in popular magazine coverage of women athletes. Magazines such as *Sports Illustrated* devoted scant attention to women athletes, and *womenSports* devoted focused coverage on women's sports and women's athletic training. Ultimately, the magazine folded in early 1978, unable to turn a profit. See Ware, *Game, Set, Match*, 77–88.

84. Magazines studied are *Better Homes & Gardens, Chatelaine, Cosmopolitan, Essence, Good Housekeeping, Ladies' Home Journal, Parents, Redbook, Seventeen, Town and Country,* and *Woman's Day*. *Ms.* magazine, although geared toward woman, was not included because of its avowedly feminist goals. According to journalist Jane Leavy, *Ms.* did depict women's athletics slightly more often than general-interest women's magazines. See Jane Leavy, "Sports Chic," *womenSports* 4 (March 1977): 53–57.

85. Marjorie Ferguson, *Forever Feminine: Women's Magazines and the Cult of Femininity* (London: Heinemann, 1983), 1.

86. Mary Ellen Zuckerman, *A History of Popular Women's Magazines in the United States, 1792–1995* (Westport, CT: Greenwood Press, 1998), xii.

87. Natalie Fuehrer Taylor, "The Personal Is Political: Women's Magazines for the

'I'm-Not-a-Feminist-But' Generation," in *You've Come a Long Way, Baby: Women, Politics, and Popular Culture*, ed. Lilly J. Goren, 215–32 (Lexington: University of Kentucky Press, 2009); see 217–20.

88. Martha A. Verbrugge, "Gender, Science, and Fitness: Perspectives on Women's Exercise in the United States in the 20th Century," *Health and History* 4, no. 1 (2002): 52–72.

89. For more on the national media attention regarding Didrikson's Olympic performance, see Cahn, *Coming on Strong*, 115–16; and Guttmann, *Women's Sports*, 145–46. See also Susan E. Cayleff, *Babe: The Life and Legend of Babe Didrikson Zaharias* (Urbana: University of Illinois Press, 1995); and Don Van Natta, *Wonder Girl: The Magnificent Sporting Life of Babe Didrikson Zaharias* (New York: Little, Brown, 2011).

90. William Moulton Marston, "How Can a Woman Do It?: Here Is a Real Explanation," *Redbook*, Sept. 1933, 58–60, 63. Marston had a complicated relationship with feminist activism and women's empowerment. For more on Marston and his role in creating the character of Wonder Woman, see Jill Lepore, *The Secret History of Wonder Woman* (New York: Vintage, 2015).

91. Paul Gallico, "Mermaids and Muscle Molls," *Cosmopolitan*, July 1937, 40–41, 151–52.

92. *Ebony* and *Jet*, two publications geared toward the African American community, did cover Rudolph's exploits closely. However, the first national magazine geared toward black women, *Essence*, did not begin publication until 1970 and thus could not report on Rudolph or the marathon pioneers. For an example of the coverage of Rudolph, see "'Winningest' School in Olympics: Tenn. State Takes 7 Gold Medals," *Ebony*, Nov. 1960, 70–76. Neither *Jet* nor *Ebony* reported on the events of the 1967 Boston Marathon.

93. John C. Devlin, "Longer Life for Your Husband," *Woman's Day*, Oct. 1967, 13.

94. "Jogging," *Cosmopolitan*, Aug. 1968, 22.

95. "Beauty Secrets," *Town and Country*, Dec. 1968, 135.

96. "Go Sportin' Lively," *Seventeen*, Feb. 1969, 122.

97. Nancy Spraker, "All That Huffing and Puffing and Perspiring . . . Is Aerobic Exercise Fit for a Lady?" *Woman's Day*, July 1969, 10.

98. See chapter 1. See also Roberts, *Necessary Spectacle*; and Ware, *Game, Set, Match*.

99. Jutel, "'Thou Dost Run as in Flotation,'" 17, 32.

100. Rex Lardner, "Women Athletes: Tell Your Man to Watch Out—The Girls Are Catching Up," *Cosmopolitan*, April 1972, 206.

101. Herbert Stein, "Women's Second Economic Revolution," *Ladies' Home Journal*, Oct. 1972, 28, 34–35, 38, 152.

102. "Hot Lines: Title Wave," *Seventeen*, Sept. 1974, 73–74.

103. Robert Peterson, "The Coming Boom in Girls' Sports: GIRLS AND BOYS TOGETHER?" *Seventeen*, Feb. 1975, 76–77, 146.

104. Joan Nassivera, "Rx for Sexist Education: Title IX," *Seventeen*, Aug. 1975, 58;

and Penny Post and Elizabeth Sheffield, "Sportswomen: They're Off and Running, Riding, Skiing, Dribbling . . ." *Seventeen*, Nov. 1975, 52.

105. Susan Edmiston, "Out from Under! A Major Report on Women Today," *Redbook*, May 1975, 159–68.

106. Alice Lake, "How Much Good Does Exercise Do You?" *Woman's Day*, Oct. 1975, 24.

107. Lenore Hershey, "Editor's Diary," *Ladies' Home Journal*, March 1976, 6.

108. Maureen Lynch and James A. Michener, "LHJ Presents the Women Superstars: What This Sports Competition Can Mean for You," *Ladies' Home Journal*, March 1976, 69–71, 82, 84–85, 72, 74, 76, 78, 80.

109. Leavy, "Sports Chic," 53.

110. Susan Edmiston, "Winners and How They Win," *Woman's Day*, Sept. 1976, 33.

111. Leavy, "Sports Chic," 53.

112. For more on the origins of the AIAW, see Bellanger, *Invisible Seasons*, 28–29; Cahn, *Coming on Strong*, 256; Guttmann, *Women's Sports*, 212–13; Schultz, *Qualifying Times*, 99; and Ying Wushanley, *Playing Nice and Losing: The Struggle for Control of Women's Intercollegiate Athletics, 1960–2000* (Syracuse, NY: Syracuse University Press, 2004), 47–48.

113. Bellanger, *Invisible Seasons*, 27.

114. Wushanley, *Playing Nice and Losing*, 62–70. In the legal case, a group of women affiliated with Marymount College and Broward Community College, including administrators, students, and coaches, sued the AIAW to challenge the organization's ban on athletic scholarships for women athletes. The suit never went to court; in response to the lawsuit, institutions affiliated with the AIAW pressured the group's leaders to permit scholarships.

115. Guttmann, *Women's Sports*, 213.

116. Schultz, *Qualifying Times*, 99.

117. Wushanley, *Playing Nice and Losing*, 72–74.

118. Leavy, "Sports Chic," 53–57.

119. Alison Poe, "Active Women in Ads," *Journal of Communication* 26 (Autumn 1976): 185–92; see 188.

120. Myrna Blyth, "Girl Athletes: What Makes Them Skate, Fence, Swim, Jump, Run?" *Cosmopolitan*, Oct. 1969, 110–12.

121. For the demise of the AIAW, see Wushanley, *Playing Nice and Losing*. See also Cahn, *Coming on Strong*, 256–57; Guttmann, *Women's Sports*, 213; and Schultz, *Qualifying Times*, 134.

122. For the negative effects of the AIAW's demise, see Boutilier and SanGiovanni, "Politics, Public Policy, and Title IX," 103–107; and Schultz, *Qualifying Times*, 99, 134. There had been attempts to merge the NCAA and the AIAW in the 1970s, but the AIAW's insistence on retaining women's administrative leadership for women's sports made the NCAA balk. See Wushanley, *Playing Nice and Losing*, 157.

123. Schultz, *Qualifying Times*, 135.

124. Bellanger, *Invisible Seasons*, 49–50.

125. Brown, "Game Girl."

126. Susan Cheever Cowley, "Women on the Run," *Newsweek*, Nov. 14, 1977, 100.

127. Leavy, "Sports Chic," 57.

128. Runner's World Editors, *The Complete Woman Runner* (Mountain View, CA: World Publications, 1978) and Jutel, "'Thou Dost Run as in Flotation,'" 25–27. Jutel notes that physicians in Europe began to make similar arguments about women's participation in the sport around this same time. See 27–32.

129. Simon Barber, "Let's Get Physical: The New Woman's Niche on the Newsstand," *Washington Journalism Review* (Sept. 1982): 40–43.

130. Ellen McCracken, *Decoding Women's Magazines: From* Mademoiselle *to* Ms. (New York: St. Martin's Press, 1993), 263–65.

131. Barber, "Let's Get Physical," 40–43.

132. "Sportswomanlike Conduct," *Newsweek*, June 3, 1974, 50.

133. Grace Lichtenstein, "Billie Jean, the Brooklyn Dodgers, and Me," *Redbook*, Nov. 1974, 104.

134. Leavy, "Sports Chic," 57.

135. Stories included Alice Lake, "How Much Good Does Exercise Do You?" *Woman's Day*, Oct. 1975, 24; Susan Edmiston, "Winners and How They Win," *Woman's Day*, Sept. 1976, 33; and Janice Kaplan, "Are GIRLS Catching Up to BOYS in Sports?" *Seventeen*, Dec. 1976, 112.

136. Derderian, *Boston Marathon*, 69, 162.

137. Averbach, *Woman Runner*, 5.

138. Switzer, *Marathon Woman*, photo spread 1, 270, 287.

139. See ibid., 328–93. See also Guttmann, *Women's Sports*, 246; and Sosienski, *Women Who Run*, 9.

140. Averbach, *Woman Runner*, 5.

141. Ibid., 6. In some ways these magazines were finally catching up to general interest publications. On July 4, 1977, for example, *People* magazine's cover featured actors Lee Majors and Farrah Fawcett jogging together for a story headlined "Farrah & Lee & Everybody's Doing It: Stars Join the Jogging Craze."

142. Maureen Lynch, "The Beauty of Running," *Ladies' Home Journal*, April 1978, 114.

143. Marty Delman, "A Sporting Chance," *Seventeen*, Nov. 1979, 60. See also James F. Fixx, "Get Happy—Start Running!" *Seventeen*, April 1978, 150; Evalyn Kaufman, "What Makes Women Run," *Redbook*, Nov. 1978, N2; and Susan Edmiston, "The Surprising Rewards of Strenuous Exercise," *Woman's Day*, Nov. 20, 1978, 98.

144. Cooky, "Women, Sports, and Activism," 80–81.

145. Cooky and Messner, *No Slam Dunk*, 3.

146. Timothy J. Curry, Paula A. Arriagada, and Benjamin Cornwell, "Images of Sport in Popular Nonsport Magazines: Power and Performance versus Pleasure and Participation," *Sociological Perspectives* 45, no. 4 (2002): 397–413; see especially 397.

147. See Jay Jennings, "Why Is Running So White?" *Runner's World*, Nov. 15, 2011, https://www.runnersworld.com/runners-stories/a20807821/why-is-running-so-white/; and Melanie Eversley, "Running While Black: Ahmaud Arbery's Killing Reveals Runners' Shared Fears of Profiling," *The Undefeated*, May 8, 2020, https://theundefeated.com/features/running-while-black-ahmaud-arberys-killing-reveals-runners-shared-fears-of-profiling/.

148. See Boutilier and SanGiovanni, "Politics, Public Policy, and Title IX," 107; and Cooky and Messner, *No Slam Dunk*, 1–2.

149. Cooky and Messner, *No Slam Dunk*, 2–3.

150. Cooky, "Women, Sports, and Activism," 81–82.

151. Cowley, "Women on the Run," 100.

152. Ibid.

Chapter 3. College Athletes Flex Their Muscles

1. For more on Scott's career at UNC, see Mark D. Briggs, "A Tale of Two Pioneers: The Integration of College Athletics in the South during the 1960s in the Age of the Civil Rights Movement" (Master's thesis, University of North Carolina at Chapel Hill, 2000); Barry Jacobs, *Across the Line: Profiles in Basketball Courage: Tales of the First Black Players in the ACC and SEC* (Guilford, CT: Lyons Press, 2007), 97–122; and Kaliss, *Men's College Athletics and the Politics of Racial Equality*, chapter 4.

2. Dale Gibson and Ross Scott, "New Demands, Ultimatum Presented by UNC Blacks," *Durham Morning Herald*, Feb. 19, 1969, 1A, 2A, morning edition.

3. Ibid. At that time, freshmen were ineligible to play varsity sports, so Chamberlain was less well-known than Scott.

4. See, for example, Clayborne Carson, *In Struggle: SNCC and the Black Awakening of the 1960s*, rev. ed. (Cambridge, MA: Harvard University Press, 1995); Evans, *Tidal Wave*; and Todd Gitlin, *The Sixties: Years of Hope, Days of Rage*, rev. ed. (New York: Bantam, 1993).

5. Many scholars have written about this shift. For a good summary of these developments, see Kathryn Jay, *More Than Just a Game: Sports in American Life since 1945* (New York: Columbia University Press, 2004), 115–36.

6. Edwards, *Revolt of the Black Athlete*, 17–21. Jack Olson also documented these issues in *The Black Athlete: A Shameful Story: The Myth of Integration in American Sport* (New York: Time-Life Books, 1968).

7. Edwards, *Revolt of the Black Athlete*, 41–44.

8. Ibid., 53, 76–84.

9. For more on the protest, see ibid. See also Bass, *Not the Triumph but the Struggle; Hartmann, Race, Culture, and the Revolt of the Black Athlete*; Lomax, "Revisiting The Revolt of the Black Athlete," 469–79; Scott, *Athletic Revolution*; and David K. Wiggins, "'The Year of Awakening'" and "The Future of College Athletics Is at Stake," in *Glory Bound: Black Athletes in a White America* (Syracuse, NY: Syracuse University Press, 1997),

104–22. See also George Roy, dir., *Fists of Freedom: The Story of the '68 Summer Games* (HBO, 1999); Geoff Small, dir., *Black Power Salute* (TigerLily Films, 2008); and Serena Williams, narrator, *1968: A Mexico City Documentary* (NBC, 2018).

10. See Bass, *Not the Triumph but the Struggle*, 229–30.

11. Rick Maese, "The Forgotten Story of the Harvard Rowers Who Supported Tommie Smith and John Carlos," *Washington Post*, Oct. 9, 2018.

12. See Wyomia Tyus with Elizabeth Terzakis, *Tigerbelle: The Wyomia Tyus Story* (New York: Akashic Books, 2018), 136–40, 154–55.

13. Amira Rose Davis, "Sixty Years Ago She Refused to Stand for the Anthem," Zora.com, Sept. 26, 2019, https://zora.medium.com/sixty-years-ago-she-refused-to-stand-for-the-anthem-cf443b4e75c7/.

14. See Tyus, *Tigerbelle*, 173–74; and Bass, *Not the Triumph but the Struggle*, 279.

15. Dave Zirin, "Uncovering the Hidden Resistance History of Black Women Athletes," *TheNation.com*, May 21, 2018, https://www.thenation.com/article/archive/uncovering-the-hidden-resistance-history-of-black-women-athletes/.

16. See Jay, *More Than Just a Game*, 123–24.

17. Wiggins, "Future of College Athletics," 124.

18. Wiggins, "'Year of Awakening,'" 104–122; see especially 105.

19. Ibid., 110; and Louis Moore, *We Will Win the Day: The Civil Rights Movement, the Black Athlete, and the Quest for Equality* (Santa Barbara, CA: Praeger, 2017), 184–88. Athlete protests were part of a broader pattern of campus activism in which students at colleges and universities across the country challenged institutional norms and practices. The Free Speech movement at Cal-Berkeley in 1964 was an especially important early example of mass student protest. The 1968 protests at Columbia over the school's intentions to build a gymnasium in Morningside Park, in which students occupied campus buildings and disrupted classes and other campus activities for days, garnered considerable attention as well and inspired similar activism at campuses across the country. See Robert Cohen and Reginald Zelnik, eds., *The Free Speech Movement: Reflections on Berkeley in the 1960s* (Berkeley: University of California Press, 2002); and Paul Cronin, ed., *A Time to Stir: Columbia '68* (New York: Columbia University Press, 2018).

20. Taylor Branch, "The Shame of College Sports," *The Atlantic*, Oct. 2011, https://www.theatlantic.com/magazine/archive/2011/10/the-shame-of-college-sports/308643/.

21. Johnny Smith, "The Job Is Football: The Myth of the Student-Athlete," *American Historian*, Aug. 2016, https://www.oah.org/tah/issues/2016/august/the-job-is-football-the-myth-of-the-student-athlete/.

22. See Walter Byers and Charles H. Hammer, *Unsportsmanlike Conduct: Exploiting College Athletes* (Ann Arbor: University of Michigan Press, 1995); Arthur A. Fleisher, Brian L. Goff, and Robert D Tollison, *The National Collegiate Athletic Association: A Study in Cartel Behavior* (Chicago: University of Chicago Press, 1992); John R. Gerdy, *Air Ball: American Education's Failed Experiment with Elite Athletics* (Jackson: University Press of

Mississippi, 2006); Randy R. Grant, John Leadley, and Zenon X. Zygmont, *The Economics of Intercollegiate Sports* (Singapore: World Scientific, 2008); and Ronald A. Smith, *Pay for Play: A History of Big-Time College Athletic Reform* (Urbana: University of Illinois Press, 2011).

23. UPI, "Black Athletes Boycott OU; Charge Racialism, Bias," *Chicago Defender*, May 9, 1968, 38.

24. Ron Teasley, "Sports Spectrum," *Michigan Chronicle*, June 1, 1968, D2.

25. Lee D. Jenkins, "Willie Muldrew Plagued after Militant Stand," *Chicago Defender*, May 29, 1969, 29.

26. Wiggins, "Future of College Athletics," 125.

27. Edwards, *Revolt of the Black Athlete*, 22.

28. "Nevada Southern Black Gridders in Bias Protest," *Chicago Defender*, Nov. 30, 1968, 16.

29. "Black Athletes 'Get Involved' in 1969," *Chicago Defender*, Dec. 23, 1969, 26. The story also appeared in the *Afro-American*, with a byline of Stu Camen. See Stu Camen, "More Athletes Stand Up for Fair Play," *Afro-American*, Dec. 27, 1969, 8.

30. UPI, "8 UTEP Athletes Boycott Triangular Meet at BYU," *Chicago Defender*, Apr. 20, 1968, 18. See also Wiggins, "Future of College Athletics," 125.

31. "New Threat Cripples San Jose Sports Card," *Afro-American*, Nov. 30, 1968, 17.

32. See "Black Cagers Strike Out against Bias," *Michigan Chronicle*, Jan. 31, 1970, A4; "N. Mexico Warns Black Athletes," *Chicago Defender*, March 26, 1969, 35; UPI, "Blacks Plan Game Boycott," *Chicago Defender*, Oct. 2, 1969, 46; and Wiggins, "Future of College Athletics," 125.

33. "Black Student Rebellion within WAC Conference," *Chicago Defender*, Oct. 23, 1969, 40. In addition to BYU, the other schools in the conference included the University of Arizona, Arizona State University, Colorado State University, the University of New Mexico, the University of Texas at El Paso, the University of Utah, and the University of Wyoming.

34. "Stanford Drops Brigham Young," *Chicago Defender*, Nov. 13, 1969, 41.

35. Simon Henderson, "Beyond Mexico City: Sport, Race, Culture, and Politics," in *Sidelined: How American Sports Challenged the Black Freedom Struggle* (Lexington: University Press of Kentucky, 2013), 121–48.

36. Wiggins, "Future of College Athletics," 134–38.

37. See, for example, A. S. Young, "Rebellion at Cal," *Chicago Defender*, Feb. 1, 1968, 32; and Sheep Jackson, "From the Sheep," *Call and Post*, Oct. 17, 1970, 13B.

38. Henderson, "Beyond Mexico City," 126–27.

39. Olson's articles formed the basis of his book *The Black Athlete: A Shameful Story: The Myth of Integration in American Sport* (New York: Time-Life Books, 1968).

40. Jack Olson, "In an Alien World," July 15, 1968, *SportsIllustrated.com*, https://vault.si.com/vault/1968/07/15/in-an-alien-world/.

41. "Black Athletes 'Get Involved' in 1969," *Chicago Defender*, Dec. 23, 1969, 26.

42. "Black Players Stage Boycott of Practice," *Michigan Chronicle*, May 1, 1971, A4.

43. See, for example, Ron Teasley, "Sports Spectrum," *Michigan Chronicle*, June 1, 1968, D2. For a good summary, see also Jay, *More Than Just a Game*, 129.

44. Dave Zirin, "The Athlete-Activists of the '60s," SocialistWorker.org, Nov. 16, 2015, https://socialistworker.org/2015/11/16/athlete-activists-of-the-1960s/. See also Wiggins, "Future of College Athletics," 133–34.

45. See, for example, A. S. "Doc" Young, "Good Morning Sports!" *Chicago Defender*, Sept. 23, 1969, 24; Claude Harrison Jr., "Sports Roundup," *Philadelphia Tribune*, Jan. 13, 1970, 14; and John Henry Johnson, "Off-Guard," *New Pittsburgh Courier*, April 28, 1973, 27.

46. Wiggins, "Future of College Athletics," 150.

47. Edwards, *Revolt of the Black Athlete*, 21.

48. Sheep Jackson, "From the Sheep," *Call and Post*, Oct. 17, 1970, 13B.

49. UPI, "Marquette U. Protest Ends Peacefully," *Chicago Defender*, May 21, 1968, 19.

50. Ron Teasley, "Sports Spectrum," *Michigan Chronicle*, June 1, 1968, D2.

51. Wiggins, "Future of College Athletics," 123.

52. See Fabio Rojas, *From Black Power to Black Studies: How a Radical Social Movement Became an Academic Discipline* (Baltimore: Johns Hopkins University Press, 2007), 45–92.

53. Jacobs, *Across the Line*, 116.

54. Briggs, "Tale of Two Pioneers, 96–97. Scott was not alone in rejecting the boycott. For an interesting discussion of athletes' responses to Edwards's plan, see "Should Negroes Boycott the Olympics? Ebony Poll of Athletes Indicates Majority Prefer to Participate in This Year's Mexico City Sports Spectacular," *Ebony*, March 1968, 110–16.

55. "Games of the XIXth Olympiad—1968," *USA Basketball*, June 10, 2010, https://www.usab.com/history/national-team-mens/games-of-the-xixth-olympiad-1968.aspx/.

56. Briggs, "Tale of Two Pioneers," 98.

57. Todd Cohen, "UNC Black Movement Will Seek Mainstream Awareness," *Daily Tar Heel*, Sept. 17, 1968, 1.

58. "Black Students' Demands Deserve Action, Study," editorial, *Daily Tar Heel*, Dec. 12 1968, 2.

59. "Sitterson Replies to BSM Demands: 'Cannot Provide Unique Treatment for Any Race,'" *Daily Tar Heel*, Feb. 4, 1969, 3.

60. Briggs, "Tale of Two Pioneers," 100–103.

61. Kaliss, *Men's College Athletics and the Politics of Racial Equality*, 134–35.

62. Dale Gibson and Ross Scott, "New Demands, Ultimatum Presented by UNC Blacks," *Durham Morning Herald*, Feb. 19, 1969, 1A, 2A, morning edition.

63. Jacobs, *Across the Line*, 119. Scott did not begrudge Smith his hesitance, arguing that the idea of a boycott was more of "a power move by the black students" than a genuine good cause.

64. Briggs, "Tale of Two Pioneers," 102–103.

65. See "Threat in Black Student Demands," editorial, *Durham Morning Herald*, Feb. 21, 1969, 4A; and "Not 'Revolution,'" editorial, *Raleigh News and Observer*, Feb. 20, 1969, 4.

66. "Boycott Food Services until Workers Get Action on Grievances," *Daily Tar Heel*, Feb. 25, 1969, 2; and Bryan Cumming, "Boycott Closes Chase, Monogram," *Daily Tar Heel*, Feb. 26, 1969, 1.

67. Kaliss, *Men's College Athletics and the Politics of Racial Equality*, 124–33.

68. Art Chansky, *The Dean's List: A Celebration of Tar Heel Basketball and Dean Smith* (New York: Warner Books, 1996), 48.

69. Briggs, "Tale of Two Pioneers," 83.

70. See "Scott Sore at ACC Coach, Player Picks," *Morning Herald*, March 16, 1969, 2C.

71. Briggs, "Tale of Two Pioneers," 81–82.

72. F. Wilton Avery, "The Greatest Scott of All," letter to the editor, *Chapel Hill Weekly*, March 23, 1969, B2.

73. Bill Ballenger, "Scott Hints He May Quit; Miffed by All-ACC Voting," *Charlotte News*, March 14, 1969, 16A.

74. "Scott Sore at ACC Coach," *Morning Herald*, March 16, 1969, 2C.

75. Briggs, "Tale of Two Pioneers," 102–103. Scott's dilemma in this regard was certainly not unique; as Wiggins has argued, black athletes across the nation in the late 1960s had "to come to grips with their conflicting roles and demands as athletes and black Americans" and determine their level of participation in the civil rights movement. Jay, too, notes that the changing tenor of activism and the rise of Black Power "placed difficult demands on black players." On many campuses, "black radicals" sought to make use of the public visibility of black athletes to bring about "social change." However, athletes had to balance a sense of "loyalty to a team" with "their desire to be a part of the black community on campus." See Wiggins, "'Year of Awakening,'" 105, 110; and Jay, *More Than Just a Game*, 127.

76. James T. Wooten, "Negro Basketball Star a Hero to Many North Carolina Whites," *New York Times*, March 22, 1969, 20.

77. "Scott, Chamberlain Right in Supporting Demands," editorial, *Daily Tar Heel*, Feb. 19, 1969, 2. The *Daily Tar Heel* was also the lone area newspaper to support the demands brought forth by the BSM. When Sitterson initially balked at the BSM's grievances, the *Daily Tar Heel* editorial board called his response "an unfortunate failure." On that same page the newspaper printed editorials from the *Greensboro Daily News*, the *Durham Herald*, and the *Charlotte Observer*—praising Sitterson for his response to the demands. See "University Has No Case for Racial Complacency," editorial, *Daily Tar Heel*, Feb. 5, 1969, 2. Even the local *Chapel Hill News*, which often employed a progressive perspective, expressed bemusement at on-campus black activism. An editorial commented ironically that in contrast to the aims of the civil rights movements of the 1950s and early 1960s, the current conflicts were marked by "black students demanding all-black dormitories, black curricula, black deans for black students, black student government

for blacks in brief, a black microcosm within predominantly white institutions." These new aims seemed to the editors to be "flatly opposed to those in the forefront of the civil rights movement" of the recent past. See "A Most Confusing Situation," editorial, *Chapel Hill News*, Feb. 19, 1969, II-2.

78. Owen Davis, "Heel Prints," *Daily Tar Heel*, Feb. 21, 1969, 5.

79. Kaliss, *Men's College Athletics and the Politics of Racial Equality*, 134–35.

80. Briggs, "Tale of Two Pioneers," 91.

81. For two complete accounts of the Wyoming 14, see Lane Demas, "'Beat the Devil Out of BYU': Football and Black Power in the Mountain West, 1968–1970," in *Integrating the Gridiron: Black Civil Rights and American College Football* (New Brunswick, NJ: Rutgers University Press, 2010), 102–133; and Phil White, "The Black 14: Race, Politics, Religion, and Wyoming Football," Nov. 8, 2014, WyoHistory.org, https://www.wyohistory.org/encyclopedia/black-14-race-politics-religion-and-wyoming-football/.

82. Pat Putnam, "No Defeats, Loads of Trouble," *Sports Illustrated*, Nov. 3, 1969, https://vault.si.com/vault/1969/11/03/no-defeats-loads-of-trouble/.

83. Demas, "'Beat the Devil Out of BYU,'" 115.

84. White, "The Black 14."

85. Demas, "'Beat the Devil Out of BYU,'" 120.

86. John Underwood, "The Desperate Coach," Aug. 25, 1969, *Sports Illustrated*, https://vault.si.com/vault/1969/08/25/the-desperate-coach/.

87. Anthony Ripley, "Negro Athletes Spark Uproar at U. of Wyoming," *New York Times*, Nov. 1, 1969, 15.

88. Anthony Ripley, "Irate Black Athletes Stir Campus Tension," *New York Times*, Nov. 16, 1969.

89. Neil Admur, "Campus Crossfire: Coaches Trapped between Dissenting Athletes and Rigid Policies," *New York Times*, Dec. 13, 1970.

90. Ripley, "Irate Black Athletes."

91. Demas, "'Beat the Devil Out of BYU,'" 122–23.

92. Robert Lipsyte, "Sports of The Times: Revolting Developments," *New York Times*, Nov. 6, 1969, 60.

93. "School Faculty Senate Backs Black Athletes," *Chicago Defender*, Oct. 21, 1969, 26.

94. Demas, "'Beat the Devil Out of BYU,'" 124–25.

95. Lipsyte, "Sports of The Times: Revolting Developments," 60.

96. Robert Lipsyte, "Sports of The Times: Looking West," *New York Times*, Nov. 8, 1969, 40.

97. See, for example, "Among 14 University . . .," photograph, *Philadelphia Tribune*, Oct. 21, 1969, 19; "Race Issue Ousts 14 at Wyoming," *Afro-American*, Oct. 25, 1969, 8; "Wyoming Axed Blacks," photograph, Oct. 25, 1969, 14; and "Wyoming Fires 14 Black Gridders," *Call and Post*, Oct. 25, 1969, 11B. See also "Dismissal of Black Wyoming Gridders Stirs League," *Jet*, Nov. 6, 1969, 65.

98. A. S. "Doc" Young, "Good Morning Sports!: The Wyoming Mess," *Chicago Defender*, Oct. 30, 1969, 40.

99. Sheep Jackson, "Wyoming U. Off Base," *Call and Post*, Nov. 1, 1969, 13B.

100. Sam Lacy, "'Owe My Soul to the Company Store,'" *Afro-American*, Nov. 8, 1969, 8.

101. William Ashworth, "Inside Story of Fired Black Athletes: Mormon Church's Race Policy," *Jet*, Nov. 13, 1969, 62–69.

102. Ibid., 64–65.

103. Sam Lacy, "What He Thinks and What I Think," *Afro-American*, Dec. 6, 1969, 7. Stanton's piece was reprinted in the *Laramie Daily Boomerang*. See "Blacks Ill-Advised, Says Football Writer," Nov. 22, 1969, 9. See also Demas, *Integrating the Gridiron*, 164n82.

104. Lacy, "What He Thinks and What I Think," 7.

105. Jim Ingram, "Like It Really Is," *Michigan Chronicle*, Dec. 13, 1969, A14.

106. Ashworth, "Inside Story," 66.

107. Sheep Jackson, "Wyoming U. Off Base," *Call and Post*, Nov. 1, 1969, 13B.

108. A. S. "Doc" Young, "Good Morning Sports!: The Wyoming Mess," *Chicago Defender*, Oct. 30, 1969, 40.

109. Ingram, "Like It Really Is."

110. Black football coaches also faced unrest in this era, although not to the extent that white coaches did. Howard University saw a wave of protests in 1968, for example, although many of them had to do with perceived inadequacies of funding for sports teams and athletes. See Cal Jacox, "From the Press Box," *New Journal and Guide*, June 22, 1968, 13.

111. A. S. "Doc" Young, "Good Morning Sports!: More on Wyoming Mess," *Chicago Defender*, Oct. 27, 1969, 24.

112. Lacy, "'Owe My Soul to the Company Store,'" 8.

113. Cal Jacox, "From the Press Box: This Corner Doubts That," *New Journal and Guide*, Nov. 15, 1969, 13.

114. Lacy, "What He Thinks and What I Think," 7.

115. *Black Journal*, episode 18, November 24, 1969, Library of Congress, American Archive of Public Broadcasting, http://americanarchive.org/catalog/cpb-aacip-512-nsoks6k508/, accessed Dec. 21, 2020.

116. Ibid.

117. Lacy, "'Owe My Soul to the Company Store,'" 8.

118. Demas, *Integrating the Gridiron*, 120.

119. See "Athletes Reinstatement Sought; Suit Is Filed," *Chicago Defender*, Oct. 29, 1969, 28; Demas, *Integrating the Gridiron*, 125, 131; "Judge Kerr Rules against Black-14," *Chicago Defender*, Oct. 19, 1971, 28; and White, "The Black 14." Kerr was not an unbiased arbitrator of the situation; according to a local newspaper account, he had been present for an event honoring the team and Coach Eaton on November 25, 1969, when he was still considering the players' first case. See White, "The Black 14."

120. White, "The Black 14."

121. Wesley Lowery and Jacob Bogage, "Fifty Years after the 'Black 14' Were Banished, Wyoming Football Reckons with the Past," Nov. 30, 2019, *Washington Post* online, https://www.washingtonpost.com/national/fifty-years-after-the-black-14-were-banished-wyoming-football-reckons-with-the-past/2019/11/30/fb7e9286-e93d-11e9-9c6d-436a0df4f31d_story.html/.

122. Demas, "'Beat the Devil Out of BYU,'" 129.

123. Alf Van Hoose, "The '71 Tide: Larger, with Longer Hair," *Birmingham News*, Aug. 17, 1971, 15; and John David Briley, *Career in Crisis: Paul "Bear" Bryant and the 1971 Season of Change* (Macon, GA: Mercer University Press, 2006), 110.

124. See Kaliss, *Men's College Athletics and the Politics of Racial Equality*, 142–50.

125. Marion Jackson, "World Sports," *Atlanta Daily World*, Jan. 4, 1972, 3.

126. Hartmann, *Race, Culture, and the Revolt of the Black Athlete*, 242–46.

127. Wiggins, "Vince Matthews, Wayne Collett, and the Forgotten Disruption in Munich," 278–303.

128. Michael Oriard, *Bowled Over: Big-Time College Football from the Sixties to the BCS Era* (Chapel Hill: University of North Carolina Press, 2009), 139.

129. Jim McGregor, "Alabama College Basketers Unanimous on 1972 Captain," *Afro-American*, June 12, 1971, 7.

130. John C. Mitcham, "Troy University Football," *Encyclopedia of Alabama*, April 25, 2019, http://www.encyclopediaofalabama.org/article/h-2406/.

131. Jimmy Bryan, "Walkout Terminated Blacks' Football," *Birmingham News*, Oct. 4, 1972, 29, 30; quotation from p. 29.

132. UPI, "TSU Athletes Quit," *The Tropolitan*, Oct. 6, 1972.

133. AP, "Just Walked Out, Didn't Quit the Team," *Birmingham News*, Oct. 5, 1972, 30.

134. AP, "More Black Wave Athletes Protest Unjust Treatment," *Montgomery Advertiser*, Oct. 5, 1972, 49.

135. Alf Van Hoose, "Applause Rings from Afar for Troy's Coach Jones," *Birmingham News*, Oct. 6, 1972, 11.

136. Jimmy Bryan, "Support from All Over for Jones' Stand," *Birmingham News*, Oct. 11, 1972, 36.

137. Van Hoose, "Applause Rings," 11.

138. Branch, "Shame of College Sports."

139. Oriard, *Bowled Over*, 128.

140. See "OK Grants to Protesting Black Athletes," *Chicago Defender*, April 1, 1974, 22; "N.M. Blacks Deny 'Militant Stand,'" *Chicago Defender*, April 2, 1974, 23; "Blacks Hold Out as Boycott Ends," *Chicago Defender*, April 4, 1974, 34; and "Black Footballers End New Mexico U. Boycott," *Los Angeles Sentinel*, April 11, 1974, B3. See also "End Boycott of N. Mexico U.," *New Pittsburgh Courier*, April 20, 1974, 3.

141. Jenkins, "Willie Muldrew Plagued after Militant Stand," 29.

Chapter 4. Black Men / Black Gladiators

1. Michael Arkush, *The Fight of the Century: Ali vs. Frazier March 8, 1971* (New York: Wiley, 2007), 196–97.

2. For the two most definitive biographies of Ali, see Muhammad Ali, with Richard Durham, *The Greatest: My Own Story* (New York: Random House, 1975); and Thomas Hauser, *Muhammad Ali: His Life and Times* (New York: Simon and Schuster, 1991).

3. See Frazier's autobiography, Joe Frazier with Phil Berger, *Smokin' Joe* (New York: Macmillan, 1996).

4. Dave Anderson, "Ali and Frazier Make It Official: They Sign for the Title Fight Here March 8," *New York Times*, Dec. 31, 1970, 31; and "Sport: Free at Last?" *Time*, March 2, 1970. Retrieved from online archive on August 30, 2010, at http://www.time.com/time/magazine/article/0,9171,904227-1,00.html/.

5. Bederman, *Manliness and Civilization*, 4.

6. For more on Johnson, see Gilmore, *Bad Nigger!*; Hietala, *The Fight of the Century*; Roberts, *Papa Jack*; and G. Ward, *Unforgivable Blackness*. See also the discussion of Johnson in the introduction.

7. G. Ward, *Unforgivable Blackness*, 216; originally in "A Word to the Black Man," *Los Angeles Times*, July 6, 1910.

8. Grundy, *Learning to Win*, 282.

9. For more on Pollard, Robeson, and Washington, see Kaliss, *Men's College Athletics and the Politics of Racial Equality*, chapters 1 and 2. The material on Jackie Robinson is extensive. See, especially, Alfred Duckett and Jackie Robinson, *I Never Had It Made: An Autobiography* (New York: G. P. Putnam's Sons, 1972); and Jules Tygiel, *Baseball's Great Experiment: Jackie Robinson and His Legacy* (New York: Oxford University Press, 1983).

10. Anthony O. Edmonds, "Joe Louis, Boxing, and American Culture," in *Out of the Shadows*, 138. For more on Louis, see Theresa E. Runstedtler, "In Sports the Best Man Wins: How Joe Louis Whupped Jim Crow," in *In the Game: Race, Identity, and Sports in the Twentieth Century*, ed. Amy Bass, 47–92 (New York: Palgrave Macmillan, 2005).

11. The literature on blackface minstrelsy is extensive. See, especially, W. T. Lhamon, *Raising Cane: Blackface Performance from Jim Crow to Hip Hop* (Cambridge: Harvard University Press, 1998); Eric Lott, *Love and Theft: Blackface Minstrelsy and the American Working Class* (New York: Oxford University Press, 1993); and Robert C. Toll, *Blacking Up: The Minstrel Show in Nineteenth-Century America* (New York: Oxford University Press, 1974).

12. See David Wondrich, *Stomp and Swerve: American Music Gets Hot, 1843–1924* (Chicago: Chicago Review Press, 2003).

13. Donald Bogle, *Toms, Coons, Mulattoes, Mammies, and Bucks: An Interpretive History of Blacks in American Films* (New York: Continuum, 1989).

14. Darlene Clark Hine and Earnestine Jenkins, introduction to *A Question of Manhood: A Reader in U.S. Black Men's History and Masculinity*, vol. 1 (Bloomington: Indiana University Press, 1999), 2.

15. Michele Wallace, *Black Macho and the Myth of the Superwoman* (New York: Dial Press, 1978), 37.

16. Estes, *I Am a Man!* 7.

17. Ibid., 132.

18. Michael Kimmel, *Manhood in America: A Cultural History* (New York: Free Press, 1996), 271.

19. See Estes, *I Am a Man!* 133–46.

20. Kimmel, *Manhood in America*, 271.

21. bell hooks, *We Real Cool: Black Men and Masculinity* (New York: Routledge, 2004), 16.

22. Estes, *I Am a Man!* 7.

23. hooks, *We Real Cool*, 12.

24. Estes, *I Am a Man!* 7. See also Robert Staples, *Black Masculinity: The Black Male's Role in American Society* (San Francisco: Black Scholar Press, 1982), 1.

25. Wallace, *Black Macho*, 14.

26. Lacy J. Banks, "The Biggest Fight in History," *Ebony*, March, 1971, 134–35.

27. Mark Kram, "At the Bell . . .," *Sports Illustrated*, March 8, 1971, http://sportsillustrated.cnn.com/vault/article/magazine/MAG1135508/index.htm/.

28. Arkush, *Fight of the Century*, 152.

29. Sam Lacy, "What Does A to Z Have against Ali," *Baltimore Afro-American*, Jan. 2, 1971, 7.

30. Dick Edwards, "The 'Oracle' Picks Muhammad in Six," *New York Amsterdam News*, March 6, 1971, 33.

31. Hauser, *Muhammad Ali: His Life and Times*, 224.

32. Jeffrey Sammons, "Rebel with a Cause: Muhammad Ali as Sixties Protest Symbol," in *Muhammad Ali: The People's Champ*, ed. Eliot J. Gorn (Urbana: University of Illinois Press, 1995), 157. For more on Ali's larger meaning as an anti-establishment figure, see Gerald Early, "Muhammad Ali: Flawed Rebel with a Cause," in *Out of the Shadows*, 263–78; Eliot J. Gorn, introduction to *Muhammad Ali: The People's Champ*; Mike Marqusee, *Redemption Song: Muhammad Ali and the Spirit of the Sixties* (New York: Verso, 1999); Sammons, *Beyond the Ring*, 191–99; and William L. Van Deburg, *Black Camelot: African-American Culture Heroes in Their Times, 1960–1980* (Chicago: University of Chicago Press, 1997), 121–25.

33. Banks, "Biggest Fight," 135.

34. Arkush, *Fight of the Century*, 153.

35. Lacy J. Banks, "Can Anybody Beat This Man," *Jet*, Feb. 18, 1971, 52–56; quotation on 56.

36. Budd Schulberg, *Loser and Still Champion: Muhammad Ali* (Garden City, NY: Doubleday, 1972), 139.

37. Thomas Thompson, "The Battle of the Undefeated Giants," *Life*, March 5, 1971, 40–48; quotation on 44–45.

38. Robert W. Kelley, "The Fight," letter to the editor, *Life*, April 9, 1971, 18A.

39. Ruth M. Langstaff, letter to the editor, *Time*, March 29, 1971.

40. Hauser, *Muhammad Ali: His Life and Times*, 219.

41. Marqusee, *Redemption Song*, 259.

42. A. S. Young, "The Greedy Ones," *Chicago Defender*, Jan. 18, 1971, 24.

43. Hauser, *Muhammad Ali: His Life and Times*, 224.

44. Ali, *The Greatest*, 259.

45. See James Baldwin, "Everybody's Protest Novel," in *Notes of a Native Son* (Boston: Beacon Press, 1955), 13–23; Bogle, *Toms, Coons, Mulattoes, Mammies, and Bucks*, 3–7; Joel Dinerstein, "'Uncle Tom Is Dead!': Wright, Himes, and Ellison Lay a Mask to Rest," *African American Review* 43, no. 1 (2009): 83–98; and Jason Richards, *Imitation Nation: Red, White, and Blackface in Early and Antebellum US Literature* (Charlottesville: University of Virginia Press, 2017), 115–33.

46. Pete McCormack, dir., *Facing Ali* (Network Entertainment, 2009).

47. Frazier, *Smokin' Joe*, 97.

48. Ibid.

49. Arkush, *Fight of the Century*, 153, 165.

50. Frazier, *Smokin' Joe*, 98.

51. "Sport: Free at Last?" *Time*, March 2, 1970, http://www.time.com/time/magazine/article/0,9171,904227-1,00.html/.

52. "Take the Money and Run," *Newsweek*, March 8, 1971, 94–95; quotation on 94.

53. See Ross Newhan, "Staggering Profit Margin Assured as Cooke Markets Ali-Frazier Bout," *Washington Times*, Jan. 17, 1971, 39; and "The Purse Snatchers," *Time*, Jan. 25, 1971, http://www.time.com/time/magazine/article/0,9171,904682,00.html/.

54. Dave Anderson, "Ali and Frazier Make It Official: They Sign for the Title Fight Here March 8," *New York Times*, Dec. 31, 1970, 31.

55. A. S. "Doc" Young, "The Greedy Ones," *Chicago Daily Defender*, Jan. 19, 1971, 24.

56. Harrison was probably right. According to inflation calculators based on the Consumer Price Index, ten dollars in 1971 would be worth about sixty-three dollars in today's money. Although comparable to what one might pay today for a pay-per-view fight, these patrons did not get to watch the bout in the comfort of their own home, and the projection technology was often rather inferior.

57. Claude Harrison, "The Price Is Right at $10," *Philadelphia Tribune*, Jan. 9, 1971, 20.

58. "Core Gets Bout on Closed Circuit," *New York Times*, Jan. 19, 1971, 43.

59. "CORE Gets Right to Show Frazier-Ali Bout," *Jet*, Feb. 25, 1971, 51.

60. The fight netted CORE approximately twenty thousand dollars in the Washington, D.C., area and nearly seventy-five thousand dollars in Harlem. See Dave Brady, "Fight TV Nets Core $20,000," *Washington Times*, March 30, 1971, D4; "CORE Scheduled to Sign TV Pact for Fight Today," *New York Times*, Jan. 28, 1971, 30; and William Wallace, "Fight Telecast Reported a Financial and Artistic Success," *New York Times*, March 10, 1971, 50.

61. Claude Harrison Jr., "SCLC's Joe Peters Says Yank Durham Will Regret His 'Drop Dead' Remarks," *Philadelphia Tribune*, Feb. 2, 1971, 15.

62. "Ali-Frazier TV Tickets Prices Arouse Pickets," *Philadelphia Tribune*, Feb. 16, 1971, 1, 3.

63. Ibid., 3.

64. Schulberg, *Loser and Still Champion*, 105.

65. Claude Harrison, "Shadow of Doubt," *Philadelphia Tribune*, March 2, 1971, 14.

66. Claude Harrison, "Yank Durham Talks," *Philadelphia Tribune*, Feb. 20, 1971, 22.

67. Hauser, *Muhammad Ali: His Life and Times*, 222.

68. Maurice R. Berube, "The Defeat of the Great Black Hope," *Commonweal*, March 26, 1971, 54–55.

69. See, for example, Joe Frazier, "Cassius WHO?" *Ebony*, May 1972, 68–76.

70. Claude Harrison Jr., "SCLC's Joe Peters Says Yank Durham Will Regret His 'Drop Dead' Remarks," *Philadelphia Tribune*, Feb. 2, 1971, 15.

71. Claude Harrison, "Piece of the Action," *Philadelphia Tribune*, Feb. 6, 1971, 20.

72. Harrison, "Price Is Right," 20.

73. Harrison, "SCLC's Joe Peters," 15.

74. AP, "Fight Boycott Threat Eases, Meeting Is Set," *Washington Times*, Jan. 17, 1971, 39.

75. Ali, *The Greatest*, 348. Not only did Ali not make an effort to have the fight's promotion benefit black Americans generally, but he also did not even insist that the fight be handled by Top Rank Inc., despite the fact that Ali's attorney in his antiwar case, Chauncey Eskridge, also worked with Top Rank. See Shirley Povich, "This Morning . . .," *Washington Times*, Dec. 31, 1970, D1.

76. Edward W. Brooke, "The Publisher's Page," *Black Enterprise* 1, no. 7 (1971), 4.

77. Marqusee, *Redemption Song*, 265–66.

78. Les Gapay, "Frazier-Ali Fight Promoters Claim a Profit Victory," *Wall Street Journal*, March 10, 1971, 18.

79. Robert E. Johnson, "World's Biggest Event Brings Mixed Reactions," *Jet*, March 25, 1971, 12–17; quotation on 12.

80. Ibid., 12.

81. "Blacks Fail to Get All Money Expected from Frazier-Ali Bout," *Jet*, June 3, 1971, 52.

82. Michael Stewart, "Bread and Circuses: The Big Fight Rip-Off," *Workers' Power*, March 12, 1971, 14.

83. Carmichael, "Toward Black Liberation," 643.

84. Stewart, "Big Fight Rip-Off," 14.

85. "Ali vs Frazier: Promoters Win," *Wildcat*, April 1971, 15.

86. See note 23 in the introduction.

87. Ferdie Pacheco, *Muhammad Ali: A View from the Corner* (New York: Birch Lane Press, 1992), 99.

88. "Ali vs Frazier: Promoters Win," 15. Certainly, many black radical groups, such as the Black Panthers, also criticized capitalism as an institution and saw it as the root of many evils facing the black community. However, though Panther leader Huey

Newton did praise Ali in the wake of the fight, he did not comment specifically on the fight's promotion and financing. See "Ali Still Champ of Black Manhood: Newton," *Jet*, May 6, 1971, 53; and Huey Newton, "Black Capitalism Re-Analyzed I: June 5, 1971," in *The Huey Newton Reader*, ed. David Hilliard and Donald Weise, 227–33 (New York: Seven Stories Press, 2002).

89. See "Ali, Frazier Could Each Make $167,000 a Minute," *Baltimore Afro-American*, Jan. 9, 1971, 1; Sam Lacy, "Sam Lacy Picks Frazier over Ali," *Baltimore Afro-American*, March 6, 1971, 1; Leslie Matthews, "The Sports Whirl," *New York Amsterdam News*, Jan. 23, 1971, 34; and Tex Maule and Morton Sharnik, "It's Gonna Be the Champ and the Tramp," *Sports Illustrated*, Feb. 1, 1971.

90. "Questions & Answers," *Chicago Daily Defender*, Feb 1, 1971, 13.

91. Schulberg, *Loser and Still Champion*, 28.

92. See, for example, Lacy, "What Does A to Z Have against Ali," 7; and Young, "Greedy Ones," 24.

93. Art Fisher and Neal Marshall, *Garden of Innocents* (New York: E. P. Dutton, 1972), 160–61.

94. Hauser, *Muhammad Ali: His Life and Times*, 221–22.

95. See, for example, Lacy Banks, "The Winner, the Loser, the Crowd: Championship Fight Is Replete with Psychological Overtones," *Ebony*, May 1971, 132–34+.

96. "Reader Poll Favors Muhammad to Win," *Chicago Defender*, March 8, 1971, 1.

97. Johnson, "World's Biggest Event," 12.

98. Moneta Sleet Jr., photograph, *Jet*, March 25, 1971, 1.

99. Thomas Mitchell Jr., letter to the editor, "And in This Corner," *Jet*, March 25, 1971, 4.

100. Pleasant Williams, letter to the editor, "Says Ali Is Still Champion," *Jet*, March 25, 1971, 4.

101. Johnson, "World's Biggest Event," 15.

102. "Ali Still Champ of Black Manhood: Newton," 53.

103. Deborah Altman, "Ali-Frazier Fight," letter to the editor, *Ebony*, May 1971, 16; emphasis mine.

104. Quoted in Marqusee, *Redemption Song*, 260.

105. Ritzy Gail Wright, "Ali No Longer 'Super Bad,'" letter to the editor, *Jet*, April 8, 1971, 4.

106. Barbara A. Gray, "Wrap to *Jet*'s Knuckles," letter to the editor, *Jet*, April 15, 1971, 4.

107. Da Gretta N. Johnson, "In Defense of Frazier," letter to the editor, *Jet*, April 22, 1971, 4.

108. A. S. Young, "Joe Wins Big One," *Chicago Defender*, March 16, 1971, 24.

109. Doris Bradley, "The Fight," letter to the editor, *Philadelphia Tribune*, March 20, 1971, 8.

110. Frazier, *Smokin' Joe*, 121–22.

111. Hauser, *Muhammad Ali: His Life and Times*, 234.

112. "'Success' Can't Hide American Nightmare," *SOBU* newsletter, April 17, 1971, 4.

113. Michael Guarino, "Ali vs. Frazier: Cheering the Death of a Hero," *Soul*, May 24, 1971, 6.

114. Eloise Valentine, "You Know Who She's For," letter to the editor, *New York Amsterdam News*, March 20, 1971, 6.

115. Dave Brady, "Frazier-Ali Listed for Forum in 1972: Core Wants Partnership," *Washington Times*, April 4, 1971, 161.

116. Johnson, "World's Biggest Event," 16.

117. Marable, *How Capitalism Underdeveloped Black America*, 139.

118. Isaac Sutton, "The Quiet Family Life of Muhammad Ali," *Ebony*, Jan. 1971, 118–22.

119. Hans J. Massaquoi, "The Private World of Muhammad Ali," *Ebony*, Sept. 1972, 144–52.

120. Grace Piro, "Muhammad Ali," letter to the editor, *Ebony*, March 1971, 12.

121. Gwendolyn Brooks, "Black Steel," *Fight of the Champions* official program, March 8, 1971. See also George Palmer, "Tavern Topics," *New York Amsterdam News*, March 6, 1971, 16.

122. Rutha Frazier, "Quit Kicking Joe Frazier," letter to the editor, *Jet*, May 13, 1971, 4.

123. UPI, "Frazier-Ali Match Like Society," *Chicago Defender*, March 11, 1971, 5.

124. "Now There Is One Champion," *Newsweek*, March 22, 1971, 75.

Chapter 5. The ABA and the Origins of Hip-Hop America

1. For more on the slam dunk contest, see Terry Pluto, *Loose Balls: The Short, Wild Life of the American Basketball Association*, rev. ed. (1990; New York: Simon and Schuster, 2007), 25–29.

2. For more on the early years of urban basketball, especially with regard to Jewish immigrants and African Americans, see Lars Anderson and Chad Millman, *Pickup Artists: Street Basketball in America* (New York: Verso, 1998); Nelson George, *Elevating the Game: Black Men and Basketball* (Lincoln: University of Nebraska Press, 1992), 1–56; Bob Kuska, *Hot Potato: How Washington and New York Gave Birth to Black Basketball and Changed America's Game Forever* (Charlottesville: University of Virginia Press, 2004); Robert Peterson, *Cages to Jump Shots: Pro Basketball's Early Years* (Lincoln: University of Nebraska Press, 1990); Charley Rosen, *The Chosen Game: A Jewish Basketball History* (Lincoln: University of Nebraska Press, 2017); Doug Stark, *The SPHAs: The Life and Times of Basketball's Greatest Jewish Team* (Philadelphia: Temple University Press, 2011); and Doug Stark, *When Basketball Was Jewish: Voices of Those Who Played the Game* (Lincoln: University of Nebraska Press, 2017).

3. Gena Dagel Caponi, introduction to *Signifyin(g), Sanctifyin', and Slam Dunking: A Reader in African American Expressive Culture*, ed. Gena Dagel Caponi (Amherst: Univer-

sity of Massachusetts Press, 1990), 7. Gena Dagel Caponi changed her name to Gena Caponi-Tabery at a later date. Because I refer to works created under both names, I have used the more recent name throughout the text of this chapter for consistency but have cited the works according to the name under which they were written.

4. Ibid., 10.

5. Shane White and Graham White, *Stylin': African American Expressive Culture from Its Beginnings to the Zoot Suit* (Ithaca, NY: Cornell University Press, 1998), 23–24.

6. For a collection of essays on this subject, see Caponi, ed., *Signifyin(g), Sanctifyin', and Slam Dunking*.

7. George, *Elevating the Game*, xiv-xv.

8. Ralph Ellison, "What America Would Be Like without Blacks"; originally published in *Time*, April 6, 1970. Available online at Teaching American History.org, http://teachingamericanhistory.org/library/document/what-america-would-be-like-without-blacks/, accessed Jan. 11, 2018.

9. See Jules Tygiel, *Extra Bases: Reflections on Jackie Robinson, Race, and Baseball History* (Lincoln: University of Nebraska Press, 2002), 64–65; and "Inning 5: Shadow Ball (1930–1940)" and "Inning 6: The National Pastime (1940–1950)," in Ken Burns, dir., *Baseball* (Florentine Films, 1994).

10. Caponi-Tabery, *Jump for Joy*, xi.

11. Ibid., 86–87; George, *Elevating the Game*, 86–91.

12. See George, *Elevating the Game*, 86–91; and Milton S. Katz, *Breaking Through: John B. McLendon, Basketball Legend and Civil Rights Pioneer* (Fayetteville: University of Arkansas Press, 2007).

13. Caponi-Tabery, *Jump for Joy*, 87, 89.

14. Ibid., 89.

15. Pamela Grundy, "A Special Type of Discipline: Manhood and Community in African-American Institutions, 1923–1957," in *Sport and the Color Line: Black Athletes and Race Relations in Twentieth-Century America*, ed. Patrick B. Miller and David K. Wiggins (New York: Routledge, 2004), 109, 115.

16. For more on the Rens, see George, *Elevating the Game*, 34–40; Kuska, *Hot Potato*; Peterson, *Cages to Jump Shots*, 95–101; and R. Thomas, *They Cleared the Lane*, 7–10.

17. Green, *Spinning the Globe*, 55. For more on the history of the team, see Green, *Spinning the Globe*; and George, *Elevating the Game*, 41–51.

18. See Kuska, *Hot Potato*, 181; and Peterson, *Cages to Jumpshots*, 100.

19. Green, *Spinning the Globe*, 54–55.

20. George, *Elevating the Game*, 55. The Globetrotters, of course, faced considerable backlash because of their clowning routines. While the games offered an opportunity to show off virtuosity and skill, they also played into long-standing stereotypes of blacks as clowns eager to please whites in power. For more on these controversies, see George, *Elevating the Game*, 42; Green, *Spinning the Globe*, 58, 90–93, 101–102, 163, 293–94, 349–52, 373; and D. Thomas, *Globetrotting*, 53–60.

21. For more on the merger of the BAA and the NBL, see David George Surdam, *The Rise of the National Basketball Association* (Urbana: University of Illinois Press, 2012), 20–86.

22. The most thorough account of the NBA's integration is in R. Thomas, *They Cleared the Lane*.

23. All-Star game rosters are available at the NBA's official website. By the 1964 game, the majority of the participants were black players, a sign of their growing prominence in the sport. See NBA.com Staff, "1964 NBA All-Star Recap," NBA.com, August 24, 2017, http://www.nba.com/history/all-star/1964/.

24. For more on the ABA's origins, see Pluto, *Loose Balls*, 39–90.

25. Ibid., 40–42.

26. "Only in the ABA," *Remember the ABA*, http://www.remembertheaba.com/index.html/, accessed January 22, 2019.

27. Josh Ozersky, "The Rogue League," *American Legacy*, Jan. 2007, 28, 31.

28. Franz Lidz, "The ABA Was Short-Lived, but Its Impact on Basketball Is Eternal," *Smithsonian*, Oct. 2017, online edition: https://www.smithsonianmag.com/arts-culture/aba-short-lived-impact-on-court-eternal-180964775/#r23LmPotlZjoRbRi.99/.

29. See, for example, Hartmann, *Race, Culture, and the Revolt of the Black Athlete*, 241–44; and William C. Rhoden, *Forty Million Dollar Slaves: The Rise, Fall, and Redemption of the Black Athlete* (New York: Crown, 2006).

30. See Arkush, *Fight of the Century*, 152; Gregory Kaliss, "Ali-Frazier 1: Black Gladiators, White Promoters, and the Economics of Big-Time Boxing," *International Journal of the History of Sport* 34, no. 11 (2017): 1003–1019, and chapter 4.

31. Van Deburg, *New Day in Babylon*, 27.

32. James Smethurst, "Black Arts Movement," in *Black Power 50*, ed. Sylviane A. Diouf and Komozi Woodard, 88–101 (New York: New Press, 2016); quotation on 98.

33. See Van Deburg, *New Day in Babylon*.

34. The most complete history of the ABA is Pluto, *Loose Balls*. See also Ross Greenburg, dir., *Longshots: The Life and Times of the American Basketball Association* (Home Box Office, 1997).

35. Pluto, *Loose Balls*, 77.

36. Greenburg, *Longshots*.

37. Pluto, *Loose Balls*, 30.

38. Greenburg, *Longshots*.

39. Pluto, *Loose Balls*, 30.

40. Brett Ballantini, interview with Van Vance, Apr. 20, 1999, available at *Remember the ABA*, http://www.remembertheaba.com/ABAArticles/BallantiniInterviewVance.html/, accessed Jan. 8, 2018.

41. Gary Hoenig, "Doctor J's Toughest Case," *New York Times*, Feb. 13, 1977, SM15.

42. Pluto, *Loose Balls*, 318.

43. Ibid., 229.

44. Seymour S. Smith, "Erving Says NBA Needs ABA, Too," *Baltimore Sun*, June 1, 1976, C6.

45. Pluto, *Loose Balls*, 322.

46. Jeff Greenfield, "The Black and White Truth about Basketball," in Caponi, *Signifyin(g), Sanctifyin', and Slam Dunking*, 373–78; see especially 376.

47. John Henry Johnson, "Off-Guard: Why Blacks Dig Basketball," *New Pittsburgh Courier*, March 10, 1973, 28.

48. Ibid.

49. Jeffrey O. G. Ogbar, "Black Power: The Looks," in *Black Power 50*, ed. Sylviane A. Diouf and Komozi Woodard (New York: New Press, 2016), 125–36; quotation on 125.

50. Ibid., 126.

51. Tanisha C. Ford, *Liberated Threads: Black Women, Style, and the Global Politics of Soul* (Chapel Hill: University of North Carolina Press, 2015), 4, 7.

52. Ibid., 4.

53. Greenburg, *Longshots*.

54. Daniel H. Forer, dir., *Free Spirits* (ESPN Films, 2013).

55. Pluto, *Loose Balls*, 30.

56. Peter Bailey, "From Jets to Mets to Knicks?" *Ebony*, March 1970, 124.

57. This embrace of a nontraditional life was not exclusive to basketball. As Joel Dinerstein notes, this was the same era that quarterback Joe Namath shook up the world of professional football with "his long hair, late-night partying, and straight talk." See Dinerstein, "Backfield in Motion: The Transformation of the NFL by Black Culture," in *In the Game: Race, Identity, and Sports in the Twentieth Century*, ed. Amy Bass, 169–89 (New York: Palgrave Macmillan, 2005); quotation on 174.

58. "ABA Fashion Guide," *Remember the ABA*, http://www.remembertheaba.com/index.html/, accessed Jan. 22, 2019.

59. Ogbar, "Black Power: The Looks," 126, 128.

60. Ward, *Just My Soul Responding*, 395.

61. "Negro Youth in Sports," *Ebony*, Dec. 1967, 132.

62. George, *Elevating the Game*, 138, 149.

63. Ibid., 138.

64. Greenburg, *Longshots*. See also Pluto, *Loose Balls*, photo number 40.

65. Martin Fennelly, "Dr. J, Ice Recall ABA's Fun Times," *Social Hoops*, http://www.socalhoops.com/nba/DrJIce.htm/, accessed Jan. 8, 2018; originally published in *Tampa Tribune*, Oct. 15, 1997.

66. Pluto, *Loose Balls*, 30.

67. Hartmann, *Race, Culture, and the Revolt of the Black Athlete*, 177.

68. Pluto, *Loose Balls*, 26.

69. Bill Rhoden, "The Incredible 'Dr. J,'" *Ebony*, March 1975, 44–52; see especially 50.

70. "'Dr. J' Leads New York Nets to ABA Championship," *Jet*, June 3, 1976, 48.

71. George, *Elevating the Game*, xvii.

72. Donald Roe, "Basketball," in *Encyclopedia of African American History 1896 to the Present*, vol. 1, ed. Paul Finkelman, 149–54 (New York: Oxford University Press, 2009); see especially 152.

73. Rhoden, *Forty Million Dollar Slaves*, 143.

74. George, *Elevating the Game*, 72.

75. Pete Axthelm, "Sky King," *Newsweek*, May 24, 1976, 55.

76. George, *Elevating the Game*, xvii, 12.

77. For more on the origins of the Rucker Tournament, see Anderson and Millman, *Pickup Artists*, 65–68; and Vincent M. Mallozzi, *Asphalt Gods: An Oral History of the Rucker Tournament* (New York: Doubleday, 2003), 10–80.

78. Mallozzi, *Asphalt Gods*, 13.

79. Axthelm, "Sky King," 55.

80. Mallozzi, *Asphalt Gods*, 20, 68, 79.

81. George, *Elevating the Game*, 76.

82. Jeffrey M. Landaw, "The Glory That Was Team Basketball," *Baltimore Sun*, Aug. 26, 1979, D5.

83. Anderson and Millman, *Pickup Artists*, 68.

84. John Schulian and David DuPree, "The Black Tide," *Atlanta Constitution*, Feb. 8, 1976, 2D.

85. Greenfield, "Black and White Truth," 375.

86. Forer, *Free Spirits*.

87. For more on white flight and urban blight, see, for example, Eric Avila, *Popular Culture in the Age of White Flight: Fear and Fantasy in Suburban Los Angeles* (Berkeley: University of California Press, 2006); and Thomas J. Sugrue, *The Origins of the Urban Crisis: Race and Inequality in Postwar Detroit* (Princeton, NJ: Princeton University Press, 1997). For more on the connection of these developments with hip-hop's emergence, see Adam Bradley and Andrew DuBois, introduction to *The Anthology of Rap*, ed. Adam Bradley and Andrew DuBois (New Haven, CT: Yale University Press, 2010), xxxix; Jeff Chang, *Can't Stop, Won't Stop: A History of the Hip-Hop Generation* (New York: St. Martin's, 2005), 11–12; Michael Eric Dyson, "Gangsta Rap and American Culture," in *Between God and Gangsta Rap: Bearing Witness to Black Culture* (New York: Oxford University Press, 1996), 177; Nelson George, *Hip Hop America* (New York: Viking, 1998), viii-xiv; Marcus Reeves, *Somebody Scream! Rap Music's Rise to Prominence in the Aftershock of Black Power* (New York: Faber and Faber, 2008), x-xii; and Tricia Rose, *Black Noise: Rap Music and Black Culture in Contemporary America* (Hanover, CT: Wesleyan University Press, 1994), 27–61.

88. For more on the four elements of hip-hop culture, see Chang, *Can't Stop, Won't Stop*; Paul Edwards, *The Concise Guide to Hip-Hop Music: A Fresh Look at the Art of Hip-Hop, from Old-School Beats to Freestyle Rap* (New York: St. Martin's Griffin, 2015), 11; and George, *Hip Hop America*, 11–19.

89. Dyson, "Gangsta Rap and American Culture," 177.

90. For more on the importance of "Rapper's Delight," see Chang, *Can't Stop, Won't Stop*, 129–32; and Reeves, *Somebody Scream!* 22.

91. Rose, *Black Noise*, 21.

92. Greenfield, "Black and White Truth," 377.

93. George, *Hip Hop America*, xii.

94. Chang, *Can't Stop, Won't Stop*, 74.

95. Quoted in Hoyt W. Fuller, "Towards a Black Aesthetic," in *The Black Aesthetic*, ed. Addison Gayle Jr. (1971; New York: Doubleday, paperback ed., 1972), 10.

96. George, *Elevating the Game*, 181.

97. Sam Goldaper, "Nets Put on Show in Routing Squires for 2–0 Playoff Lead," *New York Times*, April 2, 1974, 49.

98. Axthelm, "Sky King," 55.

99. Rhoden, "Incredible 'Dr. J,'" 46–48; and Hoenig, "Doctor J's Toughest Case," SM15.

100. Brett Ballantini, interview with Bob Costas, April 20, 1999; available at *Remember the ABA*, http://www.remembertheaba.com/ABAArticles/BallantiniInterview Costas.html/, accessed Jan. 8, 2018.

101. George, *Elevating the Game*, 199.

102. Pluto, *Loose Balls*, 425–36.

103. Michael Eric Dyson, "Crossing Jordan," in *Between God and Gangsta Rap* (New York: Oxford University Press, 1996), 56–59; quotation on 58.

104. Adam J. Criblez, "White Men Playing a Black Man's Game: Basketball's 'Great White Hopes' of the 1970s," *Journal of Sport History* 42 (Fall 2015): 371–81; see especially 373.

105. Pluto, *Loose Balls*, 241.

106. Johnson, "Why Blacks Dig Basketball," 28.

107. Ulish Carter, "Jabali Is Looking for a Job—Why?" *New Pittsburgh Courier*, March 16, 1974, 24.

108. Alan Goldstein, "Pro Basketball: ABA All-Star Is Out in Cold," *Baltimore Sun*, Feb. 22, 1974, C1.

109. Carter, "Jabali Is Looking for a Job," 24.

110. Because the records of the ABA were poorly maintained, determining the racial identity of owners and executives is difficult. However, evidence suggests that the only owner of color was Art Kim, a Chinese American from Hawaii, who founded the Anaheim Amigos in 1967. After only one season rife with financial struggles, Kim sold the team to a white construction executive who moved the team to Los Angeles, where they became the Stars. By the time of the ABA-NBA merger in 1976, all six of the surviving ABA teams were owned by white men. See "Anaheim Amigos," *Remember the ABA*, http://www.remembertheaba.com/Anaheim-Amigos.html/, accessed May 17, 2021; and Pluto, *Loose Balls*, 427–34.

111. Criblez, "White Men Playing," 374.

112. A significant amount of literature is available on this subject. One of the most important stories about the topic to appear in the mainstream press came in 1987 in a *New York Times* story about the values assigned to Larry Bird as a white star basketball player: Ira Berkow, "The Coloring of Bird," *New York Times*, June 2, 1987, D27. For examples from academic literature, see Erica Childs, "Images of the Black Athlete: Intersection of Race, Sexuality, and Sports," *Journal of African American Men* 4, no. 2

(1999): 19–38; Patrick Miller, "The Anatomy of Scientific Racism: Racialist Responses to Black Athletic Achievement," *Journal of Sport History* 25, no. 1 (1998): 119–51; and David K. Wiggins, "'Great Speed But Little Stamina': The Historical Debate over Black Athletic Superiority," *Journal of Sport History* 16, no. 2 (1989): 158–85.

113. Criblez, "White Men Playing," 374–79; and Caponi-Tabery, *Jump for Joy*, 105.

114. John Edgar Wideman, "Michael Jordan Leaps the Great Divide," in Caponi, *Signifyin(g), Sanctifyin', and Slam Dunking*, 388–406; quotation from 396.

115. Bill Simmons, *The Book of Basketball* (New York: Ballantine, 2009), 129.

116. Alan Goldstein, "Pro Basketball: ABA May Run-and-Gun but in the NBA It's Dee-fense," *Baltimore Sun*, March 2, 1975, 37.

117. George, *Elevating the Game*, 190–91.

118. Dinerstein, "Backfield in Motion," 182. This observation fits well with Caponi-Tabery's argument that the black aesthetic engaged "the whole person and the whole community."

119. Wideman, "Michael Jordan Leaps the Great Divide," 395.

120. Hoenig, "Doctor J's Toughest Case," SM15.

121. Caponi-Tabery, *Jump for Joy*, 109, 111.

122. Leviatin, "Evolution and Commodification of Black Basketball Style," 162.

123. See, for example, Todd Boyd, "The Day the Niggaz Took Over: Basketball, Commodity Culture, and Black Masculinity," in *Out of Bounds: Sports, Media, and the Politics of Identity*, ed. Aaron Baker and Todd Boyd, 123–42 (Bloomington: Indiana University Press, 1997); and Todd Boyd, *Young, Black, Rich, and Famous: The Rise of the NBA, the Hip Hop Invasion, and the Transformation of American Culture*, rev. ed. (Lincoln: University of Nebraska Press, 2008). See also Jeffrey Lane, *Under the Boards: The Cultural Revolution in Basketball* (Lincoln: University of Nebraska Press, 2007), 37–66.

124. For more on Jordan and his global market success, see David L. Andrews, ed., *Michael Jordan, Inc.: Corporate Sport, Media Culture, Late Modern America* (Albany: State University of New York Press, 2001); Douglas Kellner, "The Sports Spectacle, Michael Jordan, and Nike," in *Sport and the Color Line*, 305–326; Walter LaFeber, *Michael Jordan and the New Global Capitalism* (New York: Norton, 1999); and Rhoden, *Forty Million Dollar Slaves*, 201–215.

125. Wideman, "Michael Jordan Leaps the Great Divide," 398.

126. Roe, "Basketball," 152.

127. Rhoden, *Forty Million Dollar Slaves*, 167.

128. For more on Iverson and other black athletes who embraced a black hip-hop identity, see Thabiti Lewis, *Ballers of the New School: Race and Sports in America* (Chicago: Third World Press, 2010), 23–98.

129. See, for example, Dave Zirin, "6 Times Athletes Spoke Out in Support of #BlackLivesMatter This Week," *The Nation*, July 8, 2016, https://www.thenation.com/article/6-times-athletes-spoke-out-in-support-of-blacklivesmatter-this-week/. Jordan, so often criticized for his refusal to wade in to political issues, broke his si-

lence with a heartfelt statement in the summer of 2016 about the death of unarmed black men at the hands of police and the targeting of police officers in retaliation. See Michael Jordan, "I Can No Longer Stay Silent," *The Undefeated*, July 25, 2016, https://theundefeated.com/features/michael-jordan-i-can-no-longer-stay-silent/. However, even in 2016, market pressures still impacted athletes' willingness to engage with controversial topics. See Danielle Sarver Coombs and David Cassilo, "Athletes and/or Activists: LeBron James and Black Lives Matter," *Journal of Sport and Social Issues* 41 (Oct. 2017): 425–44. See also the conclusion to this book.

130. Ellison, "What America Would Be Like without Blacks."

Conclusion

1. For a brief overview of these developments, see Rader, *Baseball*, 204–208. For more on the particulars of Flood's story, see Goldman, *One Man Out*; and Snyder, *Well-Paid Slave*.

2. See Charles P. Korr, *The End of Baseball as We Knew It: The Players Union, 1960–1981* (Urbana: University of Illinois Press, 2002), 96–97; and Snyder, *Well-Paid Slave*, 103–104.

3. Andrew O'Toole, *The Best Man Plays: Major League Baseball and the Black Athlete, 1901–2002* (Jefferson, NC: McFarland, 2003), 85.

4. Abraham Iqbal Khan, *Curt Flood in the Media: Baseball, Race, and the Demise of the Activist Athlete* (Oxford: University Press of Mississippi, 2011), 38–40.

5. See Gerald Early, "Curt Flood, Gratitude, and the Image of Baseball," in *A Level Playing Field: African American Athletes and the Republic of Sports* (Cambridge: Harvard University Press, 2011), 86–87; and Snyder, *Well-Paid Slave*, 120.

6. See Rader, *Baseball*, 208.

7. See Edwards, *Revolt of the Black Athlete*, 51, 53, 76–81; Grant Jarvie and Irene Reid, "Sport in South Africa," in *The International Politics of Sport in the Twentieth Century*, ed. James Riordan and Arnd Krüger, 234–45 (New York: Routledge, 1999); and Robert Skinner, "Antidiscrimination: Racism and the Case of South Africa," in *The Ideals of Global Sport: From Peace to Human Rights*, ed. Barbara J. Keys, 47–67 (Philadelphia: University of Pennsylvania Press, 2019).

8. See Hall, *Arthur Ashe*, especially 110–16, 261–63; and Eric J. Morgan, "Black and White at Center Court: Arthur Ashe and the Confrontation of Apartheid in South Africa," *Diplomatic History* 36, no. 5 (2012): 815–41.

9. See, for example, Peter Harris, "South Africa Sports Boycott Is Timely," *Baltimore Afro-American*, April, 11, 1981, 9; Louis Martin, "We Have Come a Long Way in a Circle," *Michigan Chronicle*, Sept. 23, 1972, 8; "Stars, Athletes Gather to Aid Apartheid Fight," *Los Angeles Sentinel*, March 28, 1985, A3; UPI, "U.S. Blacks, Africans Unite," *Chicago Defender*, Aug. 22, 1972, 28; and "U.S. Athletes, Coaches Urged to Nix S.A. Games," *Baltimore Afro-American*, March 17, 1973, 8.

10. For the best summary and analysis of these issues, see Adrian Burgos Jr., *Playing America's Game: Baseball, Latinos, and the Color Line* (Berkeley: University of California Press, 2007).

11. For more on Clemente, see David Maraniss, *Clemente: The Passion and Grace of Baseball's Last Hero* (New York: Simon and Schuster, 2006); and David C. Ogden, "Roberto Clemente: From Ignominy to Icon," in *Reconstructing Fame: Sport, Race, and Evolving Reputations*, ed. David C. Ogden and Joel Nathan Rosen (Jackson: University Press of Mississippi, 2008).

12. See Burgos, *Playing America's Game*, 230–42; and Arturo J. Marcano Guevara and David P. Fidler, *Stealing Lives: The Globalization of Baseball and the Tragic Story of Alexis Quiroz* (Bloomington: Indiana University Press, 2002).

13. See, for example, Mark Heisler, "Let's Face It: Racism Is Alive and Well in Major League Basebrawl," CityWatch, May 19, 2016, https://www.citywatchla.com/index.php/cw/important-reads/11136-let-s-face-it-racism-is-alive-and-well-in-major-league-basebrawl/; and Chris Lamb, "When Latino Sluggers Flip Their Bats, It's Called Disrespectful," *Washington Post*, Oct. 20, 2015, https://www.washingtonpost.com/posteverything/wp/2015/10/20/when-it-comes-to-baseballs-ethnic-tensions-problems-run-deeper-than-bat-flips/.

14. See, for example, Sheldon Anderson, *The Politics and Culture of Modern Sports* (Lanham, MD: Lexington Books, 2015), 267–308; and Jay, *More Than Just a Game*, 226–30.

15. See, for example, Ohm Youngmisuk, "Yao Ming Sprung a Generation of Asian NBA Fans around the World," ESPN.com, April 4, 2016, https://www.espn.com/nba/story/_/id/15131532/nba-yao-ming-impact-asian-american-basketball-fans-was-long-reach/.

16. See David Leonard, "Lin, Te'o, and Asian American Masculinities in Sporting Flux," and Oliver Wang, "Everybody Loves an Underdog: Learning from Linsanity," both in *Asian American Sporting Cultures*, ed. Stanley I. Thangaraj, Constancio Arnaldo, and Christina B. Chin, 75–101 and 221–46 (New York: NYU Press, 2016).

17. For more on the difficulties faced by Gibson and Rudolph, see Rex Miller, dir., *Althea* (Rexpix Media, 2014), Mary Jo Festle, "'Jackie Robinson without the Charm': The Challenges of Being Althea Gibson," in *Out of the Shadows*, 203–204; and Wilson, "Wilma Rudolph," 216–21.

18. The first black owner in the NBA was Black Entertainment Television (BET) founder Robert Johnson, who purchased the expansion Charlotte (NC) Bobcats franchise in December 2002. See Richard Sandomir, "Founder of TV Network Becomes First Black Owner in Major Sports," *New York Times*, Dec. 19, 2002.

19. Ali, *The Greatest*, 369.

20. Sammons, *Beyond the Ring*, 220.

21. Diane Weathers, "The Promoters," *Black Enterprise* 7, no. 12 (July 1976): 22–25; quotation on 22.

22. Marable, *How Capitalism Underdeveloped Black America*, 147.

23. See Jack Newfield, *The Life and Crimes of Don King: The Shame of Boxing in America* (1995; New York: Harbor Electronic Publishing, 2003), 147; and Lewis A. Erenberg, "'Rumble in the Jungle': Muhammad Ali vs. George Foreman in the Age of Global Spectacle," *Journal of Sport History* 39 (Spring 2012): 81–97.

24. Hauser, *Muhammad Ali: His Life and Times*, 428.

25. Sammons discusses the controversial rise of Don King but sees white resentment of King and the persistence of stereotypes as the primary reasons for his controversial status. See Sammons, *Beyond the Ring*, 219–25.

26. Adam Howard, "Analysis: Why Donald Trump and Don King Make Sense Together," NBCNews.com, Sept. 22, 2016, https://www.nbcnews.com/politics/2016-election/analysis-why-donald-trump-don-king-make-sense-together-n652531/.

27. Neil Bhutta, Andrew C. Chang, Lisa J. Dettling, and Joanne W. Hsu, with assistance from Julia Hewitt, "Disparities in Wealth by Race and Ethnicity in the 2019 Survey of Consumer Finances," FederalReserve.gov, Sept. 28, 2020, https://www.federalreserve.gov/econres/notes/feds-notes/disparities-in-wealth-by-race-and-ethnicity-in-the-2019-survey-of-consumer-finances-20200928.htm/.

28. Dionissi Aliprantis and Daniel R. Carroll, "What Is Behind the Persistence of the Racial Wealth Gap?" Federal Reserve Bank of Cleveland, Feb. 28, 2019, https://www.clevelandfed.org/newsroom-and-events/publications/economic-commentary/2019-economic-commentaries/ec-201903-what-is-behind-the-persistence-of-the-racial-wealth-gap.aspx/.

29. Ahiza Garcia, "These Are the Only Two Owners of Color in the NFL," Money.CNN.com, May 18, 2018, https://money.cnn.com/2018/05/18/news/nfl-nba-mlb-owners-diversity/index.html/. Of the six people of color who are majority owners of pro sports teams, only one, Michael Jordan, is African American.

30. See Richard Lapchick and Nicole Cabral, *2019 Racial and Gender Report Card* (Orlando: University of Central Florida, 2019), 29.

31. Robinson, *I Never Had It Made*, 258–59. For more on Robinson's frustrations regarding the lack of black managers in baseball, see Arnold Rampersad, *Jackie Robinson: A Biography* (New York: Alfred A. Knopf, 1997), 458–59.

32. See, for example, David Harvey, *A Brief History of Neoliberalism* (New York: Oxford University Press, 2007); and Michael L. Silk and David L. Andrews, eds., *Sport and Neoliberalism: Politics, Consumption, and Culture* (Philadelphia: Temple University Press, 2012), 1–11.

33. For more on the persistence of racially-segregated ghettos, see Greg Rosalsky, "What a 1968 Report Tells Us about the Persistence of Racial Inequality," NPR.org, June 9, 2020, https://www.npr.org/sections/money/2020/06/09/872402262/what-a-1968-report-tells-us-about-the-persistence-of-racial-inequality/.

34. See, for example, Ronald A. Smith, *The Myth of the Amateur: A History of College Athletic Scholarships* (Austin: University of Texas Press, 2021), 143–46. See also George, *Elevating the Game*, 238.

35. For Thompson's account of these events, see John Thompson with Jesse Washington, *I Came as a Shadow: An Autobiography* (New York: Henry Holt, 2020), 221–30. See also R. Smith, *Pay for Play*, 154–58.

36. See Lynn Zinser, "Florida St. Penalized for Fraud," *New York Times*, March 7, 2009; Sara Ganim and Devon Sayers, "UNC Report Finds 18 Years of Academic Fraud to Keep Athletes Playing," CNN.com, Oct. 23, 2014, https://www.cnn.com/2014/10/22/us/unc-report-academic-fraud/index.html/; and Doug Lederman, "NCAA Punishes Missouri in Blatant Academic Fraud Case," InsideHigherEd.com, Feb. 1, 2019, https://www.insidehighered.com/news/2019/02/01/ncaa-punishes-missouri-blatant-case-academic-fraud/.

37. See, for example, Shaun Harper, *Black Male Student-Athletes and Racial Inequities in NCAA Division 1 College Sports* (Los Angeles: University of Southern California Race and Equity Center, 2018).

38. Kurt Streeter, "NCAA Is Sued by Former Athletes," *Los Angeles Times*, July 22, 2009, https://www.latimes.com/archives/la-xpm-2009-jul-22-sp-videogames-lawsuit22-story.html/.

39. See Branch, "Shame of College Sports."

40. See Johnny Smith, "The Job Is Football; The Myth of the Student-Athlete," *American Historian*, https://www.oah.org/tah/issues/2016/august/the-job-is-football-the-myth-of-the-student-athlete/.

41. For the report, see Commission on College Basketball, "Report and Recommendations to Address the Issues Facing Collegiate Basketball," NCAA.org, April 2018, https://www.ncaa.org/sites/default/files/2018CCBReportFinal_web_20180501.pdf/.

42. See, for example, Seth Berkman, "National Women's Team Prevails in Its Face-Off against U.S.A. Hockey," *New York Times*, March 29, 2017, B11; Courtney Connley, "Closing the Gap: The US Open Awards Men and Women Equal Prize Money—but Tennis Still Has a Pay Gap," CNBC.com, Sept. 11, 2019, https://www.cnbc.com/2019/09/11/despite-equal-grand-slam-tournement-prizes-tennis-still-has-a-pay-gap.html/; Cooky and Messner, *No Slam Dunk*, 2; Vanessa Romo, "U.S. Women's Soccer Team Settles Part of Gender Discrimination Suit," NPR.org, Dec. 1, 2020, https://www.npr.org/2020/12/01/940965382/u-s-womens-soccer-team-settles-part-of-gender-discrimination-suit/; Tom Spiggle, "U.S. Women's Soccer Suffers Setback in Fight for Equal Pay," Forbes.com, May 12, 2020, https://www.forbes.com/sites/tomspiggle/2020/05/12/us-womens-soccer-suffers-setback-in-fight-for-equal-pay/?sh=213dd8f56107/; Steven Goff and Molly Hensley-Clancy, "U.S. Women's and Men's National Soccer Teams Close Pay Gap with 'Game-Changing' Deal," WashingtonPost.com, May 18, 2022, https://www.washingtonpost.com/sports/2022/05/18/uswnt-equal-pay-deal/; and Jabari Young, "WNBA Agrees to 53% Pay Raise, Maternity Benefits for Players in New Collective Bargaining Agreement," CNBC.com, Jan. 14, 2020, https://www.cnbc.com/2020/01/14/wnba-agrees-to-53percent-pay-raise-maternity-benefits-for-players-in-new-collective-bargaining-agreement.html/.

43. Cahn, *Coming on Strong*, 287; and Schultz, *Qualifying Times*, 189.

44. Cooky and Messner, *No Slam Dunk*, 3; Cheryl Cooky, Michael Messner, and Michela Musto, "'It's Dude Time!': A Quarter Century of Excluding Women's Sports in Televised News and Highlight Shows," in Cooky, *No Slam Dunk*, 209–234.

45. Michael A. Messner, *Taking the Field: Women, Men, and Sports* (Minneapolis: University of Minnesota Press, 2002), xviii.

46. Cahn, *Coming on Strong*, 298–301; and Schultz, *Qualifying Times*, 193–95.

47. Jaime Schultz, "Reading the Catsuit: Serena Williams and the Production of Blackness at the 2002 U.S. Open," *Journal of Sport and Social Issues* 29, no. 3 (2005): 338–57.

48. See, for example, David Carr, "Networks Condemn Remarks by Imus," *New York Times*, April 7, 2007, B7; Jemele Hill, "Gabby Douglas' Hair Draws Criticism," ESPN.com, Aug. 3, 2012, https://www.espn.com/olympics/summer/2012/espnw/story/_/id/8232063/espnw-gabby-douglas-hair-criticized-social-media-sites/; Nick Zaccardi, "Italian Gymnast Apologizes for Comment about U.S.' Simone Biles," NBCSports.com, Oct. 9, 2013, https://olympics.nbcsports.com/2013/10/09/italian-gymnast-carlotta-ferlito-racist-comment-simone-biles/. See also Schultz, *Qualifying Times*, 6–7.

49. Cahn, *Coming on Strong*, 279.

50. Catalina Vechiu, "The Role of Hypermasculinity as a Risk Factor in Sexual Assault Perpetration," *in Handbook of Sexual Assault and Sexual Assault Prevention*, ed. W. O'Donohue and P. Schewe (New York: Springer, 2019): 257–73.

51. See Michael Messner, *Power at Play: Sports and the Problem of Masculinity* (Boston: Beacon Press, 1992), 95–102.

52. See Brad Reagan, "Baylor Regents Found Alleged Sexual Assaults by Football Players 'Horrifying,'" *Wall Street Journal*, Oct. 28, 2016, https://www.wsj.com/articles/baylor-details-horrifying-alleged-sexual-assaults-by-football-players-1477681988/; and Mark Tracy and Dan Barry, "Baylor's Pride Turns to Shame in Rape Scandal," *New York Times*, March 10, 2017, A1.

53. Brandon Sternod, "Come Out and Play: Confronting Homophobia in Sports," in *Learning Culture through Sports: Perspectives on Society and Organized Sports*, 2nd ed., ed. Sandra Spickard Prettyman and Brian Lampman, 92–106 (Lanham, MD: Rowman and Littlefield Publishers, 2011).

54. See Barbara Ravel and Geneviève Rail, "Strong Women, Fragile Closets: The Queering of Women's Sport," in *Learning Culture through Sports*, 251–59; and Liz Robbins, "Swoopes Says She Is Gay, and Exhales," *New York Times*, Oct. 27, 2005, D1.

55. See, for example, Eric Anderson, "Masculinities and Sexualities in Sport and Physical Cultures: Three Decades of Evolving Research," *Journal of Homosexuality* 58, no. 5 (2011): 565–78; Michael A. Messner, *Out of Play: Critical Essays on Gender and Sport* (Albany: SUNY Press, 2007), 109–112; and Messner, *Power at Play*, 34–37.

56. See David Kopay and Perry Deane Young, *The David Kopay Story* (New York: Arbor House, 1977); and Selena Roberts, "Homophobia Is Alive in Men's Locker Rooms," *New York Times*, Oct. 28, 2005, D1.

57. See Howard Beck and John Branch, "With the Words 'I'm Gay,' an N.B.A. Center Breaks a Barrier," *New York Times*, Apr. 30, 2013; and Billy Witz, "Rogers Says He's Ready for a Role as a Pioneer," *New York Times*, May 26, 2013.

58. Ken Belson, "Raiders' Carl Nassib Announces He's Gay, an N.F.L. First," *New York Times*, June 14, 2021, https://www.nytimes.com/2021/06/21/sports/football/carl-nassib-gay-nfl.html/.

59. Manny Millan, "She's a Transgender Pioneer, but Renée Richards Prefers to Stay Out of the Spotlight," SportsIllustrated.com, June 28, 2019, https://www.si.com/tennis/2019/06/28/renee-richards-gender-identity-politics-transgender-where-are-they-now/. See also Renée Richards and John Michael Ames, *Second Serve: The Renée Richards Story* (New York: Stein and Day, 1983); and Renée Richards and John Michael Ames, *No Way Renée: The Second Half of My Notorious Life* (New York: Simon and Schuster, 2007).

60. Ware, *Game, Set, Match*, 196.

61. Millan, "She's a Transgender Pioneer."

62. The year 2021 saw a marked increase in debates about transgender athletes in the United States. See, for example, "As States Consider Restrictions on Trans Athletes, What Does the Science Say?" NPR.org, March 14, 2021, https://www.npr.org/2021/03/14/977215399/as-states-consider-restrictions-on-trans-athletes-what-does-the-science-say/; and Laine Higgins, "Debate over Transgender Athletes Sweeps through U.S. Statehouses," WSJ.com, April 30, 2021, https://www.wsj.com/articles/debate-over-transgender-athletes-sweeps-through-u-s-statehouses-11619762614/.

63. bell hooks, "Eating the Other: Desire and Resistance," in *Black Looks: Race and Representation* (Boston: South End Press, 1992), 21–39.

64. See Patricia Hill Collins, "New Commodities, New Consumers: Selling Blackness in a Global Marketplace," *Ethnicities* 6, no. 30 (2006): 297–317; Abby Ferber, "The Construction of Black Masculinity: White Supremacy Now and Then," *Journal of Sport and Social Issues* 31, no. 1 (2007): 11–24; David J. Leonard and C. Richard King, eds., *Commodified and Criminalized: New Racism and African Americans in Contemporary Sports* (Lanham, MD: Rowman and Littlefield Publishers, 2011); and Nyambura Njee, "Share Cropping Blackness: White Supremacy and the Hyper-Consumption of Black Popular Culture," *McNair Scholars Research Journal* 9, no. 1 (2016): article 10.

65. Boyd, *Young, Black, Rich, and Famous*, 1–7.

66. Arthur R. Ashe Jr., *A Hard Road to Glory: A History of the African-American Athlete since 1946* (New York: Warner Books, 1988), 139; Johnson and Roediger, "'Hertz, Don't It?'" 40–73; and Rhoden, *Forty Million Dollar Slaves*, 203–204.

67. For more on Simpson's muted political voice, see Johnson and Roediger, "'Hertz, Don't It?'" 40–73. For more on the connections between Simpson and Jordan, see Rhoden, *Forty Million Dollar Slaves*, 201–215. To be fair to Jordan, he eventually used his wealth to purchase a majority share in the NBA's Charlotte Bobcats (now Hornets) from black television media entrepreneur Robert L. Johnson in 2010, giving him more

power than any black athlete had ever had in the sport. See Richard Sandomir, "N.B.A. Board Approves Jordan's Purchase of the Bobcats," *New York Times*, March 18, 2010.

68. Jason Hehir, dir., *The Last Dance*, "Episode V," aired May 3, 2020, on ESPN.

69. William C. Rhoden, "Hodges Criticizes Jordan for His Silence on Issues," *New York Times*, June 5, 1992.

70. Craig Hodges with Rory Fanning, *Long Shot: The Triumphs and Struggles of an NBA Freedom Fighter* (Chicago: Haymarket Books, 2017), 163–74. Howard Bryant also talks about Hodges's role as an activist in contrast to Jordan in *The Heritage: Black Athletes, A Divided America, and the Politics of Patriotism* (Boston: Beacon Press, 2018), 129–32.

71. See the introduction to this book.

72. For more on Brown's critiques of Jordan and Woods, see David Scott, prod., "Legends," season 15, episode 6, *Real Sports with Bryant Gumbel*, HBO, June 23, 2009.

73. Rhoden, *Forty Million Dollar Slaves*, 2, 7.

74. See, especially, Michelle Alexander, *The New Jim Crow: Mass Incarceration in the Age of Colorblindness* (New York: New Press, 2020), 125; and Eduardo Bonilla-Silva, *Racism without Racists: Color-Blind Racism and the Persistence of Racial Inequality in the United States* (Durham, NC: Duke University Press, 2006).

75. Jacquelyn Dowd Hall, "The Long Civil Rights Movement and the Political Uses of the Past," *Journal of American History* 91, no. 4 (2005): 1233–63.

76. See, for example, Emma Peaslee, "Atlanta Dream, Co-Owned by Former Sen. Kelly Loeffler, Is Close to Being Sold," NPR.org, Jan. 21, 2021, https://www.npr.org/2021/01/21/959247641/atlanta-dream-co-owned-by-former-sen-kelly-loeffler-is-close-to-being-sold/. For more on Osaka, see Sanya Mansoor, "Naomi Osaka Says She Wore 7 Masks about Black Lives during This Year's U.S. Open to 'Make People Start Talking,'" Time.com, Sept. 13, 2020, https://time.com/5888583/naomi-osaka-masks-black-lives-matter-us-open/.

77. Laurel Wamsley, "Before March Madness, College Athletes Declare They Are #NotNCAAProperty," NPR.org, March 18, 2021, https://www.npr.org/2021/03/18/978829815/before-march-madness-college-athletes-declare-they-are-not ncaaproperty/.

78. Zac Cornell, "WNBA Gets Support from NBA Players and Other Celebs #OrangeHoodie," InsideSportsJournal.com, Oct. 25, 2020, https://insidesportsjournal.com/2020/10/25/wnba-gets-support-from-nba-players-and-other-celebs-orange hoodie/.

79. *The Combahee River Collective Statement*, 1977, available online at https://www.loc.gov/item/lcwaN0028151/; and Kimberlé Crenshaw, "Demarginalizing the Intersection of Race and Sex: A Black Feminist Critique of Antidiscrimination Doctrine, Feminist Theory, and Antiracist Politics," *University of Chicago Legal Forum*, vol. 1989, no. 1, article 8.

80. Dylan Mickanen, "Sedona Prince's Viral TikTok Shows the NCAA Had Enough Space for an Equal Weight Room," NBCSports.com, March 19, 2021, https://www

.nbcsports.com/northwest/oregon-ducks/sedona-princes-viral-tiktok-shows-ncaa-had-enough-space-equal-weight-room/.

81. Isaac Chotiner, "LeBron James's Agent Is Transforming the Business of Basketball," *New Yorker*, June 7, 2021, https://www.newyorker.com/magazine/2021/06/07/lebron-james-agent-is-transforming-the-business-of-basketball/.

82. For more on *The Shop: Uninterrupted*, see Julian Kimble, "Inside the Making of LeBron James's HBO Talk Show *The Shop: Uninterrupted*," GQ.com, July 30, 2021, https://www.gq.com/story/lebron-james-the-shop-hbo-rob-alexander-director-interview/; and Ian Ward and Calder McHugh, "What Democrats Learned from LeBron James," Politico.com, May 21, 2021, https://www.politico.com/news/magazine/2021/05/21/democrats-activist-athletes-politics-489670/. For the specific episode mentioned, see the episode guide by HBO at https://www.hbo.com/the-shop-uninterrupted/season-2/6-the-shop-uninterrupted/.

BIBLIOGRAPHY

Newspapers, Magazines, Television Programs, and Select Websites

American Legacy
Arizona Republic
Atlanta Constitution
The Atlantic
Austin American Statesman
Baltimore Afro-American
Baltimore Sun
Better Homes & Gardens
Birmingham News
Black Enterprise
Black Journal
Boston Globe
CBS Sports.com
Chapel Hill News
Chapel Hill Weekly
Charlotte News
Chatelaine
Chicago Defender
Cleveland Call and Post
Commonweal
Cosmopolitan
Crain's Cleveland Business
Daily Tar Heel
Durham Morning Herald
Ebony
ESPN.com
Essence
Good Housekeeping
GQ
Indianapolis Star
Jet
Ladies' Home Journal
Life
London Sunday Times
Los Angeles Sentinel
Los Angeles Times
Louisville Courier-Journal
Michigan Chronicle
Montgomery Advertiser
Mother Jones
The Nation
NBC Sports.com

NCAA.org
Newsweek
New York Amsterdam News
The New Yorker
New York Review of Books
New York Times
Norfolk New Journal and Guide
NPR.org
Parents
People
Philadelphia Tribune
Pittsburgh Courier
Raleigh News and Observer
Redbook
Remember the ABA.com
Runner's World
Seventeen
Slate.com
Smithsonian
South China Morning Post
Sports Illustrated
Time
Town and Country
The Undefeated.com
Wall Street Journal
Washington Post
Washington Times
Wildcat
Woman's Day
Workers' Power
WyoHistory.org
Zora.com

Books, Theses, Films, and Journal Articles

Adams, David Wallace. "More Than a Game: The Carlisle Indians Take to the Gridiron, 1893–1917." *Western Historical Quarterly* 32, no. 1 (2001): 25–53.

Alexander, Michelle. *The New Jim Crow: Mass Incarceration in the Age of Colorblindness*. New York: New Press, 2020.

Ali, Muhammad, with Richard Durham. *The Greatest: My Own Story*. New York: Random House, 1975.

Anderson, Eric. "Masculinities and Sexualities in Sport and Physical Cultures: Three Decades of Evolving Research." *Journal of Homosexuality* 58, no. 5 (2011): 565–78.

Anderson, Lars, and Chad Millman. *Pickup Artists: Street Basketball in America*. New York: Verso, 1998.

Anderson, Sheldon. *The Politics and Culture of Modern Sports*. Lanham, MD: Lexington Books, 2015.

Andrews, David L., ed. *Michael Jordan, Inc.: Corporate Sport, Media Culture, Late Modern America*. Albany: State University of New York Press, 2001.

Ariail, Cat. *Passing the Baton: Black Women Track Stars and American Identity*. Urbana: University of Illinois Press, 2020.

Arkush, Michael. *The Fight of the Century: Ali vs. Frazier March 8, 1971*. New York: Wiley, 2007.

Ashe, Arthur, Jr. *A Hard Road to Glory: A History of the African-American Athlete since 1946*. New York: Warner Books, 1988.

Averbach, Gloria. *The Woman Runner: Free to Be the Complete Athlete*. New York: Simon and Schuster, 1984.

Avila, Eric. *Popular Culture in the Age of White Flight: Fear and Fantasy in Suburban Los Angeles*. Berkeley: University of California Press, 2006.

Bailey, Nancy. "Women's Sport and the Feminist Movement: Building Bridges." In *Women in Sport: Issues and Controversies*, edited by Greta L. Cohen, 297–304. New York: Sage Publications, 1993.

Baldwin, James. *The Fire Next Time*. New York: Dial Press, 1963.

——. *Notes of a Native Son*. Boston: Beacon Press, 1955.

Barber, Simon. "Let's Get Physical: The New Woman's Niche on the Newsstand." *Washington Journalism Review* (September 1982): 40–43.

Bass, Amy. *Not the Triumph but the Struggle: The 1968 Olympics and the Making of the Black Athlete*. Minneapolis: University of Minnesota Press, 2002.

Bederman, Gail. *Manliness and Civilization: A Cultural History of Gender and Race in the United States, 1880–1917*. Chicago: University of Chicago Press, 1995.

Belanger, Kelly. *Invisible Seasons: Title IX and the Fight for Equity in College Sports*. Syracuse, NY: Syracuse University Press, 2016.

Bennett, Judith. *History Matters: Patriarchy and the Challenge of Feminism*. Philadelphia: University of Pennsylvania Press, 2006.

Bennett, Robert Anthony, III. "You Can't Have Black Power without Green Power: The Black Economic Union." PhD diss., Ohio State University, 2013.

Blackman, Dexter. "African Americans, Pan-Africanism, and the Anti-Apartheid Campaign to Expel South Africa from the 1968 Olympics." *Journal of Pan African Studies* 5, no. 3 (2012): 1+.

Bloom, John. *To Show What an Indian Can Do: Sports at Native American Boarding Schools*. Minneapolis: University of Minnesota Press, 2005.

Bloom, John, and Michael Nevin Willard, eds. *Sports Matters: Race, Recreation, and Culture*. New York: New York University Press, 2002.

Bogle, Donald. *Toms, Coons, Mulattoes, Mammies, and Bucks: An Interpretive History of Blacks in American Films*. New York: Continuum International, 2002.

Bond, Gregory. "The Strange Career of William Henry Lewis." In Wiggins, *Out of the Shadows*, 38–57.

Bonilla-Silva, Eduardo. *Racism without Racists: Color-Blind Racism and the Persistence of Racial Inequality in the United States*. Durham, NC: Duke University Press, 2006.

——. "Rethinking Racism: Toward a Structural Interpretation." *American Sociological Review* 62, no. 3 (1997): 465–80.

Boutilier, Mary A., and Lucinda F. SanGiovanni. "Politics, Public Policy, and Title IX: Some Limitations of Liberal Feminism." In *Women, Sport, and Culture*. Champaign, IL: Human Kinetics, 1994.

——. *The Sporting Woman*. Champaign, IL: Human Kinetics, 1983.

Bowen, William G., and Sarah A. Levin. *Reclaiming the Game: College Sports and Educational Values*. Princeton, NJ: Princeton University Press, 2003.

Boyd, Todd. "The Day the Niggaz Took Over: Basketball, Commodity Culture, and Black Masculinity." In *Out of Bounds: Sports, Media, and the Politics of Identity*, edited by Aaron Baker and Todd Boyd, 123–42. Bloomington: Indiana University Press, 1997.

——. *Young, Black, Rich, and Famous: The Rise of the NBA, the Hip Hop Invasion, and the Transformation of American Culture*, rev. ed. Lincoln: University of Nebraska Press, 2008.

Bradley, Adam, and Andrew DuBois, eds. *The Anthology of Rap*. New Haven, CT: Yale University Press, 2010.

Branch, Taylor. *Parting the Waters: America in the King Years, 1954–63*. New York: Simon and Schuster, 1988.

Briggs, Mark D. "A Tale of Two Pioneers: The Integration of College Athletics in the South during the 1960s in the Age of the Civil Rights Movement." Master's thesis, University of North Carolina, Chapel Hill, 2000.

Briley, John David. *Career in Crisis: Paul "Bear" Bryant and the 1971 Season of Change*. Macon, GA: Mercer University Press, 2006.

Brown, Jim, with Myron Cope. *Off My Chest*. New York: Doubleday, 1964.

Brown, Jim, with Steve Delsohn. *Out of Bounds*. New York: Zebra Books, 1989.

Brundage, W. Fitzhugh, ed. *Up from Slavery by Booker T. Washington with Related Documents*. New York: Bedford/St. Martin's, 2003.

Bryant, Howard. *The Heritage: Black Athletes, A Divided America, and the Politics of Patriotism*. Boston: Beacon Press, 2018.

Burgos, Adrian, Jr. *Playing America's Game: Baseball, Latinos, and the Color Line*. Berkeley: University of California Press, 2007.

Burns, Ken, dir. *Baseball*. Florentine Films, 1994.

Byers, Walter, and Charles H. Hammer. *Unsportsmanlike Conduct: Exploiting College Athletes*. Ann Arbor: University of Michigan Press, 1995.

Cahn, Susan. *Coming on Strong: Gender and Sexuality in Women's Sport*, 2nd ed. Urbana: University of Illinois Press, 2015.

——. "From the 'Muscle Moll' to the 'Butch Ballplayer': Mannishness, Lesbianism, and Homophobia in U.S. Women's Sport." *Feminist Studies* 19 (Summer 1993): 343–68.

Caponi, Gena Dagel. Introduction to *Signifyin(g), Sanctifyin', and Slam Dunking: A Reader in African American Expressive Culture*, edited by Gena Dagel Caponi. Amherst: University of Massachusetts Press, 1990.

Caponi-Tabery, Gena. *Jump for Joy: Jazz, Basketball, and Black Culture in 1930s America*. Amherst: University of Massachusetts Press, 2008.

Carmichael, Stokely. "Toward Black Liberation." *Massachusetts Review* 7, no. 4 (1966): 639–51.

Carroll, John M. *Fritz Pollard: Pioneer in Racial Advancement*. Urbana: University of Illinois Press, 1992.

Carson, Clayborne. *In Struggle: SNCC and the Black Awakening of the 1960s*, rev. ed. Cambridge, MA: Harvard University Press, 1995.

Carson, Clayborne, and Kris Shepherd, eds. *A Call to Conscience: The Landmark Speeches of Dr. Martin Luther King, Jr.* New York: IPM, 2002.

Cayleff, Susan E. *Babe: The Life and Legend of Babe Didrikson Zaharias*. Urbana: University of Illinois Press, 1995.

Chang, Jeff. *Can't Stop, Won't Stop: A History of the Hip-Hop Generation*. New York: St. Martin's, 2005.

Chansky, Art. *The Dean's List: A Celebration of Tar Heel Basketball and Dean Smith*. New York: Warner Books, 1996.

Childs, Erica. "Images of the Black Athlete: Intersection of Race, Sexuality, and Sports." *Journal of African American Men* 4, no. 2 (1999): 19–38.

Cohen, Robert, and Reginald Zelnik, eds. *The Free Speech Movement: Reflections on Berkeley in the 1960s*. Berkeley: University of California Press, 2002.

Collins, Patricia Hill. "New Commodities, New Consumers: Selling Blackness in a Global Marketplace." *Ethnicities* 6, no. 30 (2006): 297–317.

Conrad, Cecilia A. "Black-Owned Businesses: Trends and Prospects." In *African Americans in the U.S. Economy*, edited by Cecilia A. Conrad, John Whitehead, Patrick Mason, and James Stewart, 237–45. New York: Rowman and Littlefield Publishers, 2005.

Cooky, Cheryl. "Women, Sports, and Activism." In *No Slam Dunk: Gender, Sport, and the Unevenness of Social Change*, edited by Cheryl Cooky and Michael A. Messner, 70–90. New Brunswick, NJ: Rutgers University Press, 2018.

Coombs, Danielle Sarver, and David Cassilo. "Athletes and/or Activists: LeBron James and Black Lives Matter." *Journal of Sport and Social Issues* 41 (Oct. 2017): 425–44.

Creedon, Pamela J. "Women, Media, and Sport: Creating and Reflecting Gender Values." In *Women, Media, and Sport: Challenging Gender Values*, edited by Pamela J. Creedon, 3–27. Thousand Oaks, CA: Sage Publications, 1994.

Crenshaw, Kimberlé. "Demarginalizing the Intersection of Race and Sex: A Black Feminist Critique of Antidiscrimination Doctrine, Feminist Theory, and Antiracist Politics." *University of Chicago Legal Forum*. Vol. 1989, no. 1 (1989): article 8.

Criblez, Adam J. "White Men Playing a Black Man's Game: Basketball's 'Great White Hopes' of the 1970s." *Journal of Sport History* 42 (Fall 2015): 371–81.

Cronin, Paul, ed. *A Time to Stir: Columbia '68*. New York: Columbia University Press, 2018.

Curry, Timothy J., Paula A. Arriagada, and Benjamin Cornwell. "Images of Sport in Popular Nonsport Magazines: Power and Performance versus Pleasure and Participation." *Sociological Perspectives* 45, no. 4 (2002): 397–413.

Davies, Richard O. *Sports in American Life: A History*, 3rd ed. New York: Wiley and Sons, 2016.

Davis, Angela Y. "I Am a Revolutionary Black Woman (1970)." In *Let Nobody Turn Us Around: Voices of Resistance, Reform, and Renewal*, edited by Manning Marable and Leith Mullings, 482–46. New York: Rowman and Littlefield Publishers, 2003.

Demas, Lane. *Integrating the Gridiron: Black Civil Rights and American College Football*. New Brunswick, NJ: Rutgers University Press, 2010.

Derderian, Tom. *Boston Marathon: A Celebration of the World's Premier Race*. Chicago: Triumph Books, 2014.

Dinerstein, Joel. "Backfield in Motion: The Transformation of the NFL by Black Culture." In *In the Game: Race, Identity, and Sports in the Twentieth Century*, edited by Amy Bass, 169–89. New York: Palgrave Macmillan, 2005.

———. "'Uncle Tom Is Dead!': Wright, Himes, and Ellison Lay a Mask to Rest." *African American Review* 43, no. 1 (2009): 83–98.

Dow, Bonnie J. "Feminism, Miss America, and Media Mythology." *Rhetoric and Public Affairs* 6 (Spring 2003): 127–49.

Duckett, Alfred, and Jackie Robinson. *I Never Had It Made: An Autobiography*. New York: G. P. Putnam's Sons, 1972.

Dyson, Michael Eric. *Between God and Gangsta Rap: Bearing Witness to Black Culture*. New York: Oxford University Press, 1996.

Early, Gerald Lyn. *A Level Playing Field: African American Athletes and the Republic of Sports*. Cambridge, MA: Harvard University Press, 2011.

———. "Muhammad Ali: Flawed Rebel with a Cause." In Wiggins, *Out of the Shadows*, edited, 263–78.

———. *The Muhammad Ali Reader*. Hopewell, NJ: Ecco Press, 1998.

Edmonds, Anthony O. "Joe Louis, Boxing, and American Culture." In Wiggins, *Out of the Shadows*, 133–45.

———. *Muhammad Ali: A Biography*. Westport, CT: Greenwood Press, 2006.

Edwards, Harry. *The Revolt of the Black Athlete*. New York: Free Press, 1969.

Edwards, Paul. *The Concise Guide to Hip-Hop Music: A Fresh Look at the Art of Hip-Hop, from Old-School Beats to Freestyle Rap*. New York: St. Martin's Griffin, 2015.

Erenberg, Lewis A. "'Rumble in the Jungle': Muhammad Ali vs. George Foreman in the Age of Global Spectacle." *Journal of Sport History* 39 (Spring 2012): 81–97.

Estes, Steve. *I Am a Man! Race, Manhood, and the Civil Rights Movement*. Chapel Hill: University of North Carolina Press, 2005.

Evans, Sara. *Born for Liberty*. New York: Free Press, 1997.

———. *Tidal Wave: How Women Changed America at Century's End*. New York: Free Press, 2003.

Ezra, Michael, ed. *The Economic Civil Rights Movement: African Americans and the Struggle for Economic Power*. New York: Routledge, 2013.

———. *Muhammad Ali: The Making of an Icon*. Philadelphia: Temple University Press, 2009.

———. "Muhammad Ali's Main Bout: African American Economic Power and the World Heavyweight Title." In Ezra, *Economic Civil Rights Movement*, 104–124.

Ferber, Abby. "The Construction of Black Masculinity: White Supremacy Now and Then." *Journal of Sport and Social Issues* 31, no. 1 (2007): 11–24.

Ferguson, Marjorie. *Forever Feminine: Women's Magazines and the Cult of Femininity*. London: Heinemann, 1983.

Festle, Mary Jo. "'Jackie Robinson without the Charm': The Challenges of Being Althea Gibson." In Wiggins, *Out of the Shadows*, 203–204.

Fleisher, Arthur A., Brian L. Goff, and Robert D Tollison. *The National Collegiate Athletic Association: A Study in Cartel Behavior*. Chicago: University of Chicago Press, 1992.

Ford, Tanisha. *Liberated Threads: Black Women, Style, and the Global Politics of Soul*. Chapel Hill: University of North Carolina Press, 2015.

Forer, Daniel H., dir. *Free Spirits*. ESPN Films, 2013.

Frazier, Joe, with Phil Berger. *Smokin' Joe*. New York: Macmillan, 1996.

Freeman, Mike. *Jim Brown: The Fierce Life of an American Hero*. New York: HarperCollins, 2006.

Fuller, Hoyt W. "Towards a Black Aesthetic." In *The Black Aesthetic*, edited by Addison Gayle Jr. 1971; New York: Doubleday, paperback ed., 1972.

George, Nelson. *Elevating the Game: Black Men and Basketball*. Lincoln: University of Nebraska Press, 1992.

———. *Hip Hop America*. New York: Viking, 1998.

Gerdy, John R. *Air Ball: American Education's Failed Experiment with Elite Athletics*. Jackson: University Press of Mississippi, 2006.

Gilmore, Al-Tony. *Bad Nigger! The National Impact of Jack Johnson*. Port Washington, NY: Kennikat Press, 1975.

Gitlin, Todd. *The Sixties: Years of Hope, Days of Rage*, rev. ed. New York: Bantam, 1993.

Goldman, Robert M. *One Man Out: Curt Flood versus Baseball*. Lawrence: University Press of Kansas, 2008.

Gorn, Elliott J. *The Manly Art: Bare-Knuckle Prize Fighting in America*. Ithaca, NY: Cornell University Press, 1986.

———, ed. *Muhammad Ali: The People's Champ*. Urbana: University of Illinois Press, 1995.

Goudsouzian, Aram. *King of the Court: Bill Russell and the Basketball Revolution*. Berkeley: University of California Press, 2010.

Grant, Randy R., John Leadley, and Zenon X. Zygmont. *The Economics of Intercollegiate Sports*. Singapore: World Scientific, 2008.

Green, Ben. *Spinning the Globe: The Rise, Fall, and Return to Greatness of the Harlem Globetrotters*. New York: Amistad, 2005.

Greenburg, Ross, dir. *Longshots: The Life and Times of the American Basketball Association*. Home Box Office, 1997.

Greenfield, Jeff. "The Black and White Truth about Basketball." In Caponi, *Signifyin(g), Sanctifyin', and Slam Dunking*, 373–78.

Griffin, Pat. *Strong Women, Deep Closets: Lesbians and Homophobia in Sport*. Amherst: University of Massachusetts Press, 1998.

Grundy, Pamela. *Learning to Win: Sports, Education, and Social Change in Twentieth-Century North Carolina*. Chapel Hill: University of North Carolina Press, 2001.

———. "A Special Type of Discipline: Manhood and Community in African-American Institutions, 1923–1957." In Miller and Wiggins, *Sport and the Color Line*, 101–22.

Guevara, Arturo J. Marcano, and David P. Fidler. *Stealing Lives: The Globalization of Baseball and the Tragic Story of Alexis Quiroz*. Bloomington: Indiana University Press, 2002.

Guttmann, Allen. *The Olympics: A History of the Modern Games*, 2nd ed. Urbana: University of Illinois Press, 2002.

———. *Women's Sports: A History*. New York: Columbia University Press, 1991.

Hall, Eric Allen. *Arthur Ashe: Tennis and Justice in the Civil Rights Era*. Baltimore: Johns Hopkins University Press, 2014.

Hall, Jacquelyn Dowd. "The Long Civil Rights Movement and the Political Uses of the Past." *Journal of American History* 91, no. 4 (2005): 1233–63.

Hargreaves, Jennifer. *Sporting Females: Critical Issues in the History and Sociology of Women's Sports*, rprt. ed. New York: Routledge, 2001.

Harper, Shaun. *Black Male Student-Athletes and Racial Inequities in NCAA Division 1 College Sports*. Los Angeles: University of Southern California Race and Equity Center, 2018.

Hartmann, Douglas. *Race, Culture, and the Revolt of the Black Athlete: The 1968 Olympic Protests and Their Aftermath*. Chicago: University of Chicago Press, 2003.

Harvey, David. *A Brief History of Neoliberalism*. New York: Oxford University Press, 2007.

Hastings, James. *America 1968: The Fire This Time*. London: Gollancz, 1969.

Hauser, Thomas. *Muhammad Ali: His Life and Times*. New York: Simon and Schuster, 1991.

Heaphy, Leslie. *The Negro Leagues, 1869–1960*. Jefferson, NC: McFarland, 2003.

Hehir, Jason, dir. *The Last Dance*. ESPN Films, 2020.

Henderson, Simon. *Sidelined: How American Sports Challenged the Black Freedom Struggle*. Lexington: University Press of Kentucky, 2013.

Hietala, Thomas R. *The Fight of the Century: Jack Johnson, Joe Louis, and the Struggle for Racial Equality*. Armonk, NY: M. E. Sharpe, 2002.

Hill, Laura Warren, and Julia Rabig. *The Business of Black Power: Community Development, Capitalism, and Corporate Responsibility in Postwar America*. Rochester: University of Rochester Press, 2012.

Hine, Darlene Clark, and Earnestine Jenkins. *A Question of Manhood: A Reader in U.S. Black Men's History and Masculinity*. Vol. 1. Indianapolis: Indiana University Press, 1999.

Hoberman, John. *Darwin's Athletes: How Sports Has Damaged Black America and Preserved the Myth of Race*. New York: Houghton Mifflin, 1997.

Hodges, Craig, with Rory Fanning. *Long Shot: The Triumphs and Struggles of an NBA Freedom Fighter*. Chicago: Haymarket Books, 2017.

hooks, bell. *Black Looks: Race and Representation*. Boston: South End Press, 1992.

——. *We Real Cool: Black Men and Masculinity*. New York: Routledge, 2004.

Isserman, Maurice, and Michael Kazin. *America Divided: The Civil War of the 1960s*. New York: Oxford University Press, 2020.

Jable, J. Thomas. "Jim Brown: Superlative Athlete, Screen Star, Social Activist." In Wiggins, *Out of the Shadows*, 241–61.

Jacobs, Barry. *Across the Line: Profiles in Courage; Tales of the First Black Players in the ACC and SEC*. Guilford, CT: Lyons Press, 2008.

Jarvie, Grant, and Irene Reid. "Sport in South Africa." In *The International Politics of Sport in the Twentieth Century*, edited by James Riordan and Arnd Krüger, 234–45. New York: Routledge, 1999.

Jay, Kathryn. *More Than Just a Game: Sports in American Life since 1945*. New York: Columbia University Press, 2004.

Jenkins, Earnestine, and Darlene Clark Hine, eds. *A Question of Manhood: A Reader in U.S. Black Men's History and Masculinity*. Vol. 2, *The 19th Century: From Emancipation to Jim Crow*. Bloomington: Indiana University Press, 2001.

Johnson, Leola. "'Hertz, Don't It?': White 'Colorblindness' and the Mark(et)ings of O. J. Simpson." In *Colored White: Transcending the Racial Past*, edited by David R. Roediger, 68–94. Berkeley: University of California Press, 2002.

Joseph, Peniel E. *Waiting 'Til the Midnight Hour: A Narrative History of Black Power in America*. New York: Henry Holt, 2006.

Jutel, Annemarie. "'Thou Dost Run as in Flotation': Femininity, Reassurance, and the Emergence of the Women's Marathon." *International Journal of the History of Sport* 20, no. 3 (2003): 17–23.

Kaliss, Gregory. "Ali-Frazier 1: Black Gladiators, White Promoters, and the Economics of Big-Time Boxing." *International Journal of the History of Sport* 34, no. 11 (2017): 1003–1019.

———. *Men's College Athletics and the Politics of Racial Equality: Five Pioneer Stories of Black Manliness, White Citizenship, and American Democracy*. Philadelphia: Temple University Press, 2012.

Katz, Milton S. *Breaking Through: John B. McLendon, Basketball Legend and Civil Rights Pioneer*. Fayetteville: University of Arkansas Press, 2007.

Kellner, Douglas. "The Sports Spectacle, Michael Jordan, and Nike." In Miller and Wiggins, *Sport and the Color Line*, 305–326.

Kemper, Kurt Edward. *College Football and American Culture in the Cold War Era*. Urbana: University of Illinois Press, 2009.

Khan, Abraham Iqbal. *Curt Flood in the Media: Baseball, Race, and the Demise of the Activist Athlete*. Oxford: University Press of Mississippi, 2011.

Kimmel, Michael. *Manhood in America: A Cultural History*. New York: Free Press, 1996.

King, Billie Jean, with Christine Brennan. *Pressure Is a Privilege: Lessons I've Learned from Life and the Battle of the Sexes*. New York: LifeTime Media, 2008.

King, Billie Jean, with Kim Chapin. *Billie Jean*. New York: Harper and Row, 1974.

King, Billie Jean, with Frank Deford. *Billie Jean*. New York: Viking, 1982.

King, Billie Jean, with Cynthia Starr. *We Have Come a Long Way: The Story of Women's Tennis*. New York: McGraw-Hill, 1988.

Kopay, David, and Perry Deane Young. *The David Kopay Story*. New York: Arbor House, 1977.

Korr, Charles P. *The End of Baseball as We Knew It: The Players Union, 1960–1981*. Urbana: University of Illinois Press, 2002.

Kuska, Bob. *Hot Potato: How Washington and New York Gave Birth to Black Basketball and Changed America's Game Forever*. Charlottesville: University of Virginia Press, 2004.

LaFeber, Walter. *Michael Jordan and the New Global Capitalism*. New York: Norton, 1999.

Lane, Jeffrey. *Under the Boards: The Cultural Revolution in Basketball*. Lincoln: University of Nebraska Press, 2007.

Lansbury, Jennifer H. "Alice Coachman: Quiet Champion of the 1940s." In Wiggins, *Out of the Shadows*, 147–61.

———. *A Spectacular Leap: Black Women Athletes in Twentieth-Century America*. Fayetteville: University of Arkansas Press, 2014.

Lapchick, Richard, and Nicole Cabral. *2019 Racial and Gender Report Card*. Orlando: University of Central Florida, 2019.

Leavy, Jane. "Sports Chic." *womenSports* 4 (March 1977): 53–57.

Lens, Sydney. *The Crisis of American Labor*. New York: Sagamore Press, 1959.

Leonard, David. "Lin, Te'o, and Asian American Masculinities in Sporting Flux." In *Asian American Sporting Cultures*, edited by Stanley I. Thangaraj, Constancio Arnaldo, and Christina B. Chin, 75–101. New York: NYU Press, 2016.

Leonard, David J., and C. Richard King, eds. *Commodified and Criminalized: New Racism and African Americans in Contemporary Sports*. Lanham, MD: Rowman and Littlefield Publishers, 2011.

Lepore, Jill. *The Secret History of Wonder Woman*. New York: Vintage, 2015.

Lerner, Gerda. *The Creation of Patriarchy*. New York: Oxford University Press, 1986.

Lewis, Thabiti. *Ballers of the New School: Race and Sports in America*. Chicago: Third World Press, 2010.

Lhamon, W. T. *Raising Cane: Blackface Performance from Jim Crow to Hip Hop*. Cambridge, MA: Harvard University Press, 1998.

Liberti, Rita. "'We Were Ladies, We Just Played Like Boys': African American Women and Competitive Basketball at Bennett College, 1928–42." In *Sporting World of the Modern South*, edited by Patrick B. Miller, 153–74. Urbana: University of Illinois Press, 2002.

Liberti, Rita, and Maureen M. Smith. *Re(Presenting) Wilma Rudolph*. Syracuse, NY: Syracuse University Press, 2015.

Lichtenstein, Nelson. *A Contest of Ideas: Capital, Politics, and Labor*. Urbana: University of Illinois Press, 2013.

Lomax, Michael. "Revisiting *The Revolt of the Black Athlete*: Harry Edwards and the Making of the New African-American Sports Studies." *Journal of Sport History* 29, no. 3 (2002): 469–79.

Lott, Eric. *Love and Theft: Blackface Minstrelsy and the American Working Class*. New York: Oxford University Press, 1993.

Mallozzi, Vincent M. *Asphalt Gods: An Oral History of the Rucker Tournament*. New York: Doubleday, 2003.

Marable, Manning. *How Capitalism Underdeveloped Black America*. Boston: South End Press, 1983.

Maraniss, David. *Clemente: The Passion and Grace of Baseball's Last Hero*. New York: Simon and Schuster, 2006.

Marqusee, Mike. *Redemption Song: Muhammad Ali and the Spirit of the Sixties*. New York: Verso, 2000.

May, Elaine Tyler. *Homeward Bound: American Families in the Cold War Era*, rev. ed. New York: Basic Books, 2008.

McCormack, Pete, dir. *Facing Ali*. Network Entertainment, 2009.

McCracken, Ellen. *Decoding Women's Magazines: From* Mademoiselle *to* Ms. New York: St. Martin's Press, 1993.

Messner, Michael. *Out of Play: Critical Essays on Gender and Sport*. Albany: State University of New York Press, 2007.

——. *Power at Play: Sports and the Problem of Masculinity*. Boston: Beacon Press, 1992.

——. *Taking the Field: Women, Men, and Sports*. Minneapolis: University of Minnesota Press, 2002.

Messner, Michael A., and Donald F. Sabo, eds. *Sport, Men, and the Gender Order: Critical Feminist Perspectives*. Champaign, IL: Human Kinetics Books, 1990.

Miller, Edward D. *Tomboys, Pretty Boys, and Outspoken Women: The Media Revolution of 1973*. Ann Arbor: University of Michigan Press, 2001.

Miller, Patrick B. "To 'Bring the Race along Rapidly': Sport, Student Culture, and Educational Mission at Historically Black Colleges during the Interwar Years." In *Sporting World of the Modern South*, edited by Patrick B. Miller, 129–52. Urbana: University of Illinois Press, 2002.

——. "The Anatomy of Scientific Racism: Racialist Responses to Black Athletic Achievement." *Journal of Sport History* 25, no. 1 (1998): 119–51.

Miller, Patrick B., and David K. Wiggins, eds. *Sport and the Color Line: Black Athletes and Race Relations in Twentieth-Century America*. New York: Routledge, 2004.

Miller, Rex, dir. *Althea*. Rexpix Media, 2014.

Moody, Kim. *An Injury to All: The Decline of American Unionism*. London: Verso, 1988.

Moore, Louis. *We Will Win the Day: The Civil Rights Movement, the Black Athlete, and the Quest for Equality*. Santa Barbara, CA: Praeger, 2017.

Morgan, Eric J. "Black and White at Center Court: Arthur Ashe and the Confrontation of Apartheid in South Africa." *Diplomatic History* 36, no. 5 (2012): 815–41.

Nelson, Kadir. *We Are the Ship: The Story of Negro League Baseball*. New York: Little, Brown, 2008.

Newfield, Jack. *The Life and Crimes of Don King: The Shame of Boxing in America*. 1995; New York: Harbor Electronic Publishing, 2003.

Newman, Roberta J. "Jim Brown: The Rise and Fall (and Rise) of a Cultural Icon." In *Fame to Infamy: Race, Sport, and the Fall from Grace*, edited by David C. Ogden and Joel Nathan Rosen, 170–90. Jackson: University Press of Mississippi, 2010.

Newton, Huey. "Black Capitalism Re-Analyzed I: June 5, 1971." In *The Huey Newton Reader*, edited by David Hilliard and Donald Weise, 227–33. New York: Seven Stories Press, 2002.

Nicholson, James. *1968: A Pivotal Moment in American Sports*. Knoxville: University of Tennessee Press, 2019.

Njee, Nyambura. "Share Cropping Blackness: White Supremacy and the Hyper-Consumption of Black Popular Culture." *McNair Scholars Research Journal* 9, no. 1 (2016): article 10.

O'Connell, Elizabeth. "The Woman Who Should Be King: The Simplification of the Life and Career of Billie Jean King." In *A Locker Room of Her Own: Celebrity, Sexuality, and Female Athletes*, edited by David C. Ogden and Joel Nathan Rosen, 43–71. Jackson: University Press of Mississippi, 2013.

Ogbar, Jeffrey O. G. "Black Power: The Looks." In *Black Power 50*, edited by Sylviane A. Diouf and Komozi Woodard, 125–36. New York: New Press, 2016.

——. *Black Power: Radical Politics and African American Identity*. Baltimore: Johns Hopkins University Press, 2004.

Ogden, David C. "Roberto Clemente: From Ignominy to Icon." In *Reconstructing Fame: Sport, Race, and Evolving Reputations*, edited by David C. Ogden and Joel Nathan Rosen, 16–28. Jackson: University Press of Mississippi, 2008.

Olson, Jack. *The Black Athlete: A Shameful Story; The Myth of Integration in American Sport*. New York: Time-Life Books, 1968.

Oriard, Michael. *Bowled Over: Big-Time College Football from the Sixties to the BCS Era*. Chapel Hill: University of North Carolina Press, 2009.

O'Toole, Andrew. *The Best Man Plays: Major League Baseball and the Black Athlete, 1901–2002*. Jefferson, NC: McFarland, 2003.

Pacheco, Ferdie. *Muhammad Ali: A View from the Corner*. New York: Birch Lane Press, 1992.

Peterson, Robert. *Cages to Jump Shots: Pro Basketball's Early Years*. Lincoln: University of Nebraska, 1990.

——. *Only the Ball Was White: A History of Legendary Black Players and All-Black Professional Teams*, rprt. ed. New York: Oxford University Press, 1992.

Pluto, Terry. *Loose Balls: The Short, Wild Life of the American Basketball Association*, rev. ed. 1990; New York: Simon and Schuster, 2007.

Poe, Alison. "Active Women in Ads." *Journal of Communication* 26 (Autumn 1976): 185–92.

Pollack, Eunice G. "Joe Namath: Player On and Off the Field." In *New York Sports: Glamour and Grit in the Empire City*, edited by Stephen H. Norwood, 107–144. Fayetteville: University of Arkansas Press, 2018.

Rader, Benjamin G. *Baseball: A History of America's Game*, 2nd ed. Urbana: University of Illinois Press: 2002.

Rampersad, Arnold. *Jackie Robinson: A Biography*. New York: Knopf, 1997.

Ravel, Barbara, and Geneviève Rail. "Strong Women, Fragile Closets: The Queering of Women's Sport." In *Learning Culture through Sports: Perspectives on Society and Organized Sports*, 2nd ed., edited by Sandra Spickard Prettyman and Brian Lampman, 251–59. Lanham, MD: Rowman and Littlefield Publishers, 2011.

Raymond, Emilie. *Stars for Freedom: Hollywood, Black Celebrities, and the Civil Rights Movement*. Seattle: University of Washington Press, 2015.

Reeves, Marcus. *Somebody Scream! Rap Music's Rise to Prominence in the Aftershock of Black Power*. New York: Faber and Faber, 2008.

Remnick, David. *King of the World: Muhammad Ali and the Rise of an American Hero*. New York: Random House, 1998.

Renick, Oren, and Lea Robin Velez. "Racing into the Storm: Roberta Gibb, Kathrine Switzer, and Women's Marathoning." In *A Locker Room of Her Own: Celebrity, Sexual-*

ity, and Female Athletes, edited by David C. Ogden and Joel Nathan Rosen, 162–74. Oxford: University Press of Mississippi, 2013.

Rhoden, William C. *Forty Million Dollar Slaves: The Rise, Fall, and Redemption of the Black Athlete*. New York: Crown, 2006.

Richards, Jason. *Imitation Nation: Red, White, and Blackface in Early and Antebellum US Literature*. Charlottesville: University of Virginia Press, 2017.

Richards, Renée, and John Michael Ames. *No Way Renée: The Second Half of My Notorious Life*. New York: Simon and Schuster, 2007.

———. *Second Serve: The Renée Richards Story*. New York: Stein and Day, 1983.

Roberts, Randy. *Papa Jack: Jack Johnson and the Era of White Hopes*. New York: Free Press, 1983.

Roberts, Selena. *A Necessary Spectacle: Billie Jean King, Bobby Riggs, and the Tennis Match That Leveled the Game*. New York: Crown, 2005.

Robinson, Jackie, and Alfred Duckett. *I Never Had It Made: An Autobiography*. New York: G. P. Putnam, 1972.

Roe, Donald. "Basketball." In *Encyclopedia of African American History 1896 to the Present*. Vol. 1, edited by Paul Finkelman, 149–54. New York: Oxford University Press, 2009.

Rogers, Ibram H. "Acquiring 'A Piece of the Action': The Rise and Fall of the Black Capitalism Movement." In Ezra, *Economic Civil Rights Movement*, 172–87.

Rojas, Fabio. *From Black Power to Black Studies: How a Radical Social Movement Became an Academic Discipline*. Baltimore: Johns Hopkins University Press, 2007.

Rose, Tricia. *Black Noise: Rap Music and Black Culture in Contemporary America*. Hanover, CT: Wesleyan University Press, 1994.

Rosen, Charley. *The Chosen Game: A Jewish Basketball History*. Lincoln: University of Nebraska Press, 2017.

Roy, George, dir. *Fists of Freedom: The Story of the '68 Summer Games*. HBO, 1999.

Runner's World Editors. *The Complete Woman Runner*. Mountain View, CA: World Publications, 1978.

Runstedtler, Theresa E. "In Sports the Best Man Wins: How Joe Louis Whupped Jim Crow." In *In the Game: Race, Identity, and Sports in the Twentieth Century*, edited by Amy Bass, 47–92. New York: Palgrave Macmillan, 2005.

Sammons, Jeffrey. *Beyond the Ring: The Role of Boxing in American Society*. Urbana: University of Illinois Press, 1990.

———. "Rebel with a Cause: Muhammad Ali as Sixties Protest Symbol." In Gorn, *Muhammad Ali: The People's Champ*, 160–64.

Schulberg, Budd. *Loser and Still Champion: Muhammad Ali*. Garden City, NY: Doubleday, 1972.

Schultz, Jaime. *Qualifying Times: Points of Change in U.S. Women's Sport*. Urbana: University of Illinois Press, 2014.

———. "Reading the Catsuit: Serena Williams and the Production of Blackness at the 2002 U.S. Open." *Journal of Sport and Social Issues* 29, no. 3 (2005): 338–57.

Scott, David, prod. "Legends," season 15, episode 6. *Real Sports with Bryant Gumbel*. HBO, 2009.

Scott, Jack. *The Athletic Revolution*. New York: Free Press, 1971.

Shelton, Christine M. "Tennis: Hard Work Pays Off." In *Women in Sport: Issues and Controversies*, edited by Greta L. Cohen. Newbury Park, CA: Sage Publications, 1993.

Silk, Michael L., and David L. Andrews, eds. *Sport and Neoliberalism: Politics, Consumption, and Culture*. Philadelphia: Temple University Press, 2012.

Simmons, Bill. *The Book of Basketball*. New York: Ballantine, 2009.

Skinner, Robert. "Antidiscrimination: Racism and the Case of South Africa." In *The Ideals of Global Sport: From Peace to Human Rights*, edited by Barbara J. Keys, 47–67. Philadelphia: University of Pennsylvania Press, 2019.

Small, Geoff, dir. *Black Power Salute*. TigerLily Films, 2008.

Smethurst, James. "Black Arts Movement." In *Black Power 50*, edited by Sylviane A. Diouf and Komozi Woodard, 88–101. New York: New Press, 2016.

Smith, Johnny, and Randy Roberts. *Blood Brothers: The Fatal Friendship between Muhammad Ali and Malcolm X*. New York: Basic Books, 2016.

Smith, Ronald A. *The Myth of the Amateur: A History of College Athletic Scholarships*. Austin: University of Texas, 2021.

———. *Pay for Play: A History of Big-Time College Athletic Reform*. Urbana: University of Illinois Press, 2011.

Snyder, Bradley. *A Well-Paid Slave: Curt Flood's Fight for Free Agency in Professional Sports*. New York: Viking, 2006.

Sosienski, Shanti. *Women Who Run*. Emeryville, CA: Seal Press, 2006.

Staples, Robert. *Black Masculinity: The Black Male's Role in American Society*. San Francisco: Black Scholar Press, 1982.

Stark, Doug. *The SPHAs: The Life and Times of Basketball's Greatest Jewish Team*. Philadelphia: Temple University Press, 2011.

———. *When Basketball Was Jewish: Voices of Those Who Played the Game*. Lincoln: University of Nebraska Press, 2017.

Sterngass, John. "Cheating, Gender Roles, and the Nineteenth-Century Croquet Craze." *Journal of Sport History* 25 (1998): 398–418.

Sternod, Brandon. "Come Out and Play: Confronting Homophobia in Sports." In *Learning Culture through Sports: Perspectives on Society and Organized Sports*, 2nd ed., edited by Sandra Spickard Prettyman and Brian Lampman, 92–106. Lanham, MD: Rowman and Littlefield Publishers, 2011.

Sugrue, Thomas J. *The Origins of the Urban Crisis: Race and Inequality in Postwar Detroit*. Princeton, NJ: Princeton University Press, 1997.

Surdam, David George. *The Rise of the National Basketball Association*. Urbana: University of Illinois, 2012.

Swinth, Kirsten. *Feminism's Forgotten Fight: The Unfinished Struggle for Work and Family*. Boston: Harvard University Press, 2018.

Switzer, Kathrine. *Marathon Woman: Running the Race to Revolutionize Women's Sports*. New York: Carroll and Graf Publishers, 2007.

Taylor, Natalie Fuehrer. "The Personal Is Political: Women's Magazines for the 'I'm-Not-a-Feminist-But' Generation." In *You've Come a Long Way, Baby: Women, Politics, and Popular Culture*, edited by Lilly J. Goren, 215–32. Lexington: University of Kentucky Press, 2009.

Thomas, Damion. *Globetrotting: African American Athletes and Cold War Politics*. Urbana: University of Illinois Press, 2012.

Thomas, Ron. *They Cleared the Lane: The NBA's Black Pioneers*. Lincoln: University of Nebraska Press, 2002.

Thompson, John, with Jesse Washington. *I Came as a Shadow: An Autobiography*. New York: Henry Holt, 2020.

Toback, James. *JIM: The Author's Self-Centered Memoir on the Great Jim Brown*. New York: Doubleday, 1971.

Toll, Robert C. *Blacking Up: The Minstrel Show in Nineteenth-Century America*. New York: Oxford University Press, 1974.

Tygiel, Jules. *Baseball's Great Experiment: Jackie Robinson and His Legacy*, 25th Anniversary Edition. New York: Oxford University Press, 2008.

———. *Extra Bases: Reflections on Jackie Robinson, Race, and Baseball History*. Lincoln: University of Nebraska Press, 2002.

———. "The Negro Leagues." *OAH Magazine of History* 7, no. 1 (1992): 24–27.

Tyus, Wyomia, with Elizabeth Terzakis. *Tigerbelle: The Wyomia Tyus Story*. New York: Akashic Books, 2018.

Van Deburg, William. *Black Camelot: African-American Culture Heroes in Their Times, 1960–1980*. Chicago: University of Chicago Press, 1997.

———. *New Day in Babylon: The Black Power Movement and American Culture, 1965–1975*. Chicago: University of Chicago Press, 1992.

Van Natta, Dan. *Wonder Girl: The Magnificent Sporting Life of Babe Didrikson Zaharias*. New York: Little, Brown, 2011.

Vechiu, Catalina. "The Role of Hypermasculinity as a Risk Factor in Sexual Assault Perpetration." In *Handbook of Sexual Assault and Sexual Assault Prevention*, edited by W. O'Donohue and P. Schewe, 257–73. New York: Springer, 2019.

Verbrugge, Martha A. "Gender, Science, and Fitness: Perspectives on Women's Exercise in the United States in the 20th Century." *Health and History* 4, no. 1 (2002): 52–72.

Vogan, Travis. *ABC Sports: The Rise and Fall of Network Sports Television*. Oakland: University of California Press, 2018.

Walker, David, Andrew J. Rausch, and Chris Watson. *Reflections on Blaxploitation: Actors and Directors Speak*. Lanham, MD: Scarecrow Press, 2009.

Walker, Juliet E. K. *The History of Black Business in America: Capitalism, Race, Entrepreneurship*. New York: Macmillan Library Reference, 1998.

Wallace, Michele. *Black Macho and the Myth of the Superwoman*. New York: Dial Press, 1978.

Wang, Oliver. "Everybody Loves an Underdog: Learning from Linsanity." In *Asian American Sporting Cultures*, edited by Stanley I. Thangaraj, Constancio Arnaldo, and Christina B. Chin, 221–46. New York: New York University Press, 2016.

Ward, Brian. *Just My Soul Responding: Rhythm and Blues, Black Consciousness, and Race Relations*. Berkeley: University of California Press, 1998.

Ward, Geoffrey C. *Unforgivable Blackness: The Rise and Fall of Jack Johnson*. New York: Knopf, 2004.

Ward, Jesmyn. *The Fire This Time: A New Generation Speaks about Race*. New York: Scribner, 2016.

Ware, Susan. *Game, Set, Match: Billie Jean King and the Revolution in Women's Sports*. Chapel Hill: University of North Carolina Press, 2011.

Washington, Booker T. *Up from Slavery*, with related documents, edited by W. Fitzhugh Brundage. New York: Bedford/St. Martin's, 2003.

White, Shane, and Graham White. *Stylin': African American Expressive Culture from Its Beginnings to the Zoo Suit*. Ithaca, NY: Cornell University Press, 1998.

Wideman, "Michael Jordan Leaps the Great Divide." In Caponi, *Signifyin(g), Sanctifyin', and Slam Dunking*, 388–406.

Wiggins, David K. *Glory Bound: Black Athletes in a White America*. Syracuse, NY: Syracuse University Press, 1997.

———. "'Great Speed but Little Stamina': The Historical Debate over Black Athletic Superiority." *Journal of Sport History* 16, no. 2 (1989): 158–85.

———. "Vince Matthews, Wayne Collett, and the Forgotten Disruption in Munich." *Journal of African American History* 106, no. 2 (2021): 278–303.

Wiggins, David K., ed. *Out of the Shadows: A Biographical History of African American Athletes*. Fayetteville: University of Arkansas Press, 2008.

Williams, Serena, narrator. *1968: A Mexico City Documentary*. NBC, 2018.

Wilson, Wayne. "Wilma Rudolph: The Making of an Olympic Icon." In Wiggins, *Out of the Shadows*, 207–221.

Woloch, Nancy. *Women and the American Experience*, 3rd ed. New York: McGraw-Hill, 2000.

Wondrich, David. *Stomp and Swerve: American Music Gets Hot, 1843–1924*. Chicago: Chicago Review Press, 2003.

Wushanley, Ying. *Playing Nice and Losing: The Struggle for Control of Women's Intercollegiate Athletics, 1960–2000*. Syracuse, NY: Syracuse University Press, 2004.

Zirin, Dave. *Jim Brown: Last Man Standing*. New York: Blue Rider Press, 2018.

Zuckerman, Mary Ellen. *A History of Popular Women's Magazines in the United States, 1792–1995*. Westport, CT: Greenwood Press, 1998.

INDEX

GREGORY J. KALISS is an assistant professor of history at York College of Pennsylvania and author of *Men's College Athletics and the Politics of Racial Equality: Five Pioneer Stories of Black Manliness, White Citizenship and American Democracy*.

SPORT AND SOCIETY

A Sporting Time: New York City and the Rise of Modern Athletics, 1820–70 *Melvin L. Adelman*
Sandlot Seasons: Sport in Black Pittsburgh *Rob Ruck*
West Ham United: The Making of a Football Club *Charles Korr*
Beyond the Ring: The Role of Boxing in American Society *Jeffrey T. Sammons*
John L. Sullivan and His America *Michael T. Isenberg*
Television and National Sport: The United States and Britain *Joan M. Chandler*
The Creation of American Team Sports: Baseball and Cricket, 1838–72 *George B. Kirsch*
City Games: The Evolution of American Urban Society and the Rise of Sports *Steven A. Riess*
The Brawn Drain: Foreign Student-Athletes in American Universities *John Bale*
The Business of Professional Sports *Edited by Paul D. Staudohar and James A. Mangan*
Fritz Pollard: Pioneer in Racial Advancement *John M. Carroll*
A View from the Bench: The Story of an Ordinary Player on a Big-Time Football Team (formerly Go Big Red! The Story of a Nebraska Football Player) *George Mills*
Sport and Exercise Science: Essays in the History of Sports Medicine *Edited by Jack W. Berryman and Roberta J. Park*
Minor League Baseball and Local Economic Development *Arthur T. Johnson*
Harry Hooper: An American Baseball Life *Paul J. Zingg*
Cowgirls of the Rodeo: Pioneer Professional Athletes *Mary Lou LeCompte*
Sandow the Magnificent: Eugen Sandow and the Beginnings of Bodybuilding *David Chapman*
Big-Time Football at Harvard, 1905: The Diary of Coach Bill Reid *Edited by Ronald A. Smith*
Leftist Theories of Sport: A Critique and Reconstruction *William J. Morgan*
Babe: The Life and Legend of Babe Didrikson Zaharias *Susan E. Cayleff*
Stagg's University: The Rise, Decline, and Fall of Big-Time Football at Chicago *Robin Lester*
Muhammad Ali, the People's Champ *Edited by Elliott J. Gorn*
People of Prowess: Sport, Leisure, and Labor in Early Anglo-America *Nancy L. Struna*
The New American Sport History: Recent Approaches and Perspectives *Edited by S. W. Pope*
Making the Team: The Cultural Work of Baseball Fiction *Timothy Morris*
Making the American Team: Sport, Culture, and the Olympic Experience *Mark Dyreson*
Viva Baseball! Latin Major Leaguers and Their Special Hunger *Samuel O. Regalado*
Touching Base: Professional Baseball and American Culture in the Progressive Era (rev. ed.) *Steven A. Riess*
Red Grange and the Rise of Modern Football *John M. Carroll*
Golf and the American Country Club *Richard J. Moss*
Extra Innings: Writing on Baseball *Richard Peterson*
Global Games *Maarten Van Bottenburg*

The Sporting World of the Modern South *Edited by Patrick B. Miller*
Female Gladiators: Gender, Law, and Contact Sport in America *Sarah K. Fields*
The End of Baseball As We Knew It: The Players Union, 1960–81 *Charles P. Korr*
Rocky Marciano: The Rock of His Times *Russell Sullivan*
Saying It's So: A Cultural History of the Black Sox Scandal *Daniel A. Nathan*
The Nazi Olympics: Sport, Politics, and Appeasement in the 1930s *Edited by Arnd Krüger and William Murray*
The Unlevel Playing Field: A Documentary History of the African American Experience in Sport *David K. Wiggins and Patrick B. Miller*
Sports in Zion: Mormon Recreation, 1890–1940 *Richard Ian Kimball*
Sweet William: The Life of Billy Conn *Andrew O'Toole*
Sports in Chicago *Edited by Elliot J. Gorn*
The Chicago Sports Reader *Edited by Steven A. Riess and Gerald R. Gems*
College Football and American Culture in the Cold War Era *Kurt Edward Kemper*
The End of Amateurism in American Track and Field *Joseph M. Turrini*
Benching Jim Crow: The Rise and Fall of the Color Line in Southern College Sports, 1890–1980 *Charles H. Martin*
Pay for Play: A History of Big-Time College Athletic Reform *Ronald A. Smith*
Globetrotting: African American Athletes and Cold War Politics *Damion L. Thomas*
Cheating the Spread: Gamblers, Point Shavers, and Game Fixers in College Football and Basketball *Albert J. Figone*
The Sons of Westwood: John Wooden, UCLA, and the Dynasty That Changed College Basketball *John Matthew Smith*
Qualifying Times: Points of Change in U.S. Women's Sport *Jaime Schultz*
NFL Football: A History of America's New National Pastime *Richard C. Crepeau*
Marvin Miller, Baseball Revolutionary *Robert F. Burk*
I Wore Babe Ruth's Hat: Field Notes from a Life in Sports *David W. Zang*
Changing the Playbook: How Power, Profit, and Politics Transformed College Sports *Howard P. Chudacoff*
Team Chemistry: The History of Drugs and Alcohol in Major League Baseball *Nathan Michael Corzine*
Wounded Lions: Joe Paterno, Jerry Sandusky, and the Crises in Penn State Athletics *Ronald A. Smith*
Sex Testing: Gender Policing in Women's Sports *Lindsay Parks Pieper*
Cold War Games: Propaganda, the Olympics, and U.S. Foreign Policy *Toby C. Rider*
Game Faces: Sport Celebrity and the Laws of Reputation *Sarah K. Fields*
The Rise and Fall of Olympic Amateurism *Matthew P. Llewellyn and John Gleaves*
Bloomer Girls: Women Baseball Pioneers *Debra A. Shattuck*
I Fight for a Living: Boxing and the Battle for Black Manhood, 1880–1915 *Louis Moore*
The Revolt of the Black Athlete: 50th Anniversary Edition *Harry Edwards*
Pigskin Nation: How the NFL Remade American Politics *Jesse Berrett*
Hockey: A Global History *Stephen Hardy and Andrew C. Holman*
Baseball: A History of America's Game *Benjamin G. Rader*

Kansas City vs. Oakland: The Bitter Sports Rivalry That Defined an Era
Matthew C. Ehrlich
The Gold in the Rings: The People and Events That Transformed the Olympic Games
Stephen R. Wenn and Robert K. Barney
Before March Madness: The Wars for the Soul of College Basketball
Kurt Edward Kemper
The Sport Marriage: Women Who Make It Work *Steven M. Ortiz*
NFL Football: A History of America's New National Pastime, NFL Centennial Edition
Richard C. Crepeau
Passing the Baton: Black Women Track Stars and American Identity *Cat M. Ariail*
Degrees of Difficulty: How Women's Gymnastics Rose to Prominence and Fell from Grace *Georgia Cervin*
From Football to Soccer: The Early History of the Beautiful Game in the United States *Brian D. Bunk*
Tennis: A History from American Amateurs to Global Professionals *Greg Ruth*
Surf and Rescue: George Freeth and the Birth of California Beach Culture *Patrick Moser*
Dyed in Crimson: Football, Faith, and Remaking Harvard's America *Zev Eleff*
Beyond the Black Power Salute: Athlete Activism in an Era of Change *Gregory J. Kaliss*

REPRINT EDITIONS
The Nazi Olympics *Richard D. Mandell*
Sports in the Western World (2nd ed.) *William J. Baker*
Jesse Owens: An American Life *William J. Baker*

The University of Illinois Press
is a founding member of the
Association of University Presses.

Composed in 10.25/13 Marat Pro
with Trade Gothic LT Std display
by Lisa Connery
at the University of Illinois Press
Manufactured by Sheridan Books, Inc.

University of Illinois Press
1325 South Oak Street
Champaign, IL 61820-6903
www.press.uillinois.edu